Praise for *Hidden Cities*

"*Hidden Cities* offers a thrilling glimpse into the secret worlds that surround us. Moses Gates has crafted an endlessly absorbing book that succeeds on many levels—as a compelling travelogue, a nuts-and-bolts how-to manual, and a deep-feeling and highly relatable personal memoir. Anybody who reads it will emerge invigorated by possibility."

—Davy Rothbart, creator of *Found Magazine*, author of *My Heart Is an Idiot*, and frequent contributor to NPR's *This American Life*

"*Hidden Cities* is long anticipated by those of us who have spent the last five years enjoying Moses Gates's wild dispatches—posts from below, above, and inside quarters of cities that we never would have dreamed of visiting and probably did not know were even there. This book is a measured and heartfelt look at some wild times in some crazy places, but it is most of all a paean to curiosity and where it takes you."

—Robert Sullivan, author of *Rats* and *My American Revolution*

"An intrepid urban sherpa's impassioned salute to the 'joy of trespassing.' Part guidebook, part social history, part coming-of-age story. Dig in: you'll never look at cities the same way again."

—Robert Neuwirth, author of *Stealth of Nations* and *Shadow Cities*

"I am a yellow-livered coward. I have also never been in shape: I have never seen my abs—I don't believe I have any. That's why when it comes to true urban exploration, you need intrepid individuals such as Moses Gates and Steve Duncan, who have the intestinal fortitude to invade places like the catacombs of Paris, the tops of New York City's great bridges, the sewers of Rome, and the underground rivers of Moscow—and the savoir faire and aplomb to talk their way out of prosecution from the local authorities. Follow Moses, Steve, and others as they truly experience the world's great cities in ways far removed from how Frommer's, Fodor's, or any Michelin guide would encourage you to do. *Hidden Cities* is a rollicking travelogue packed with secrets of the world's metropoli that the local constabulary would rather you not discover."

—Kevin Walsh, author of *Forgotten New York*

"The strongest human desires, we might agree, are for love, food, a warm place to stay, sex, and the like. These obvious requirements for living a good life are joined, in the case of serious urban explorers, with the NEED to explore. A great city at night is a massive playground, a wonderland imprinted by the dreams, desires, and accomplishments of those millions who have lived and do yet live there. Moses Gates knows this and has beautifully described that yearning some humans have to explore the built environment. Whether you are an armchair adventurer or the most accomplished climber/explorer in the world, you will find the stories in this book charming, inspirational, and filled with examples of that most human of needs: the need to see and know."

—John Law, coauthor of *Tales of the San Francisco Cacophony Society*, Suicide Club member emeritus, and cofounder of the Burning Man Festival

MARCH, 2013

DEAR JEFF –

    THOUGHT IMMEDIATELY OF YOU
WHEN I HEARD AN INTERVIEW
WITH THE AUTHOR OF THIS BOOK.
REMEMBER... ADVENTURE IS

[**HIDDEN CITIES**]

WHEREVER YOU FIND IT!

      ENJOY!

        LOVE,
          DAD

HIDDEN CITIES

*Travels to the Secret Corners
of the World's Great Metropolises—
A Memoir of Urban Exploration*

MOSES GATES

JEREMY P. TARCHER/PENGUIN
a member of Penguin Group (USA) Inc.
New York

JEREMY P. TARCHER/PENGUIN
Published by the Penguin Group
Penguin Group (USA) Inc., 375 Hudson Street,
New York, New York 10014, USA

USA · Canada · UK · Ireland · Australia
New Zealand · India · South Africa · China

Penguin Books Ltd, Registered Offices:
80 Strand, London WC2R 0RL, England
For more information about the Penguin Group visit penguin.com

Most Tarcher/Penguin books are available at special quantity discounts for bulk purchase
for sales promotions, premiums, fund-raising, and educational needs. Special books
or book excerpts also can be created to fit specific needs. For details, write
Penguin Group (USA) Inc. Special Markets, 375 Hudson Street, New York, NY 10014.

Library of Congress Cataloging-in-Publication Data

Gates, Moses.
Hidden cities : travels to the secret corners of the world's great metropolises—
a memoir of urban exploration / Moses Gates.
            p.   cm.
Includes bibliographical references.
ISBN 978-1-58542-934-9
1. Voyages and travels.   2. Gates, Moses—Travel.   3. Cities and towns.
4. City and town life.   5. Adventure and adventurers.   I. Title.
G465.G38   2013   2012039954
         910.9173'2—dc23

Printed in the United States of America
1   3   5   7   9   10   8   6   4   2

BOOK DESIGN BY AMANDA DEWEY

For my Grandmother Ethel,
who is the coolest person I know

PROLOGUE

Paris, December 2007

I have just rung the bell of Notre Dame. It's the dumbest thing I've ever done.

It's the dumbest thing I've ever done, because I haven't paid an admission fee and queued up to get to the bell. You can't— this isn't the part of the building they let tourists into. I'm not a historian, or preservationist, or bell tuner invited up by the cathedral. I'm not a priest, or docent, or security guard with keys and curiosity.

No, I am a dead-drunk New Yorker accompanied by a French preppy named Nico I met three hours ago and my best friend, Steve Duncan, a guy whose favorite place in the world is a two-hundred-year-old sewer tunnel underneath Lower Manhattan. And how we have managed to access the bell tower in the spire of Notre Dame is by using a combination of gargoyles, flying buttresses, and a makeshift ladder to scale the outside of the cathedral in the middle of the night. In the rain. For no particular reason other than we were down there, and the spire is up here, and this just seemed to be the best way to get from point A to point B. And after finally making it up, I just can't resist the urge to play Quasimodo. Now I'm hearing *"Bonsoir?"* from one story down below.

Over the last few years I've been to a lot of places, in a lot of cities, where your average tourist shouldn't be—and many more that your average tourist doesn't even know exist. I've become part of the world of people who break into national monuments for fun, put on movie screenings in storm drains, and travel the globe sleeping in centuries-old catacombs and abandoned Soviet relics rather than hotels or bed-and-breakfasts. A world where I party with people living in the tunnels under New York, squatters in an abandoned São Paulo mansion, and Ukrainian teenagers in Cold War bunkers and partisan hideouts under Odessa. Where I discover ancient Roman ruins in the sewers beneath the Capitoline Hill, dodge trains and the third rail in five of the ten largest subway systems in the world, and manage to avoid entrance charges for landmarks from Stonehenge to the minarets of the Bab Zuweila gate, built over nine hundred years ago to guard the city of Cairo. I'm part of a loose-knit worldwide network of artists, historians, adventurers, and other assorted nutcases sometimes called "urban explorers." All of it has been fascinating. And all of it has been completely illegal. And now I've gotten caught. I take a moment to assess the situation. I'm about to get arrested. In a foreign country. On top of the most famous cathedral in the world. Drunk.

When Steve and I first met Nico, three hours beforehand, we were fairly unimpressed. Decked out in an argyle sweater over a collared shirt, knit scarf, and designer jeans, he was sitting at a bar, drinking a glass of red wine with a posture that indicated he'd be more comfortable discussing the merits of

Foucault and Sartre than crawling through catacombs or scaling medieval stonework. He looked like a French version of Zack Morris from *Saved by the Bell*, not a daredevil urban adventurer. But then again, nobody we've met in the world of daredevil urban adventurers has really looked the part. Not the shy Korean girl from a wealthy family who takes naked pictures of herself in abandoned power plants. Not the London bus driver with a weakness for lager, mince pies, and well-endowed women who is halfway to his goal of visiting every abandoned subway station on earth. Not the flamenco dancer with the soft Quebecois accent who travels the world rappelling into storm drains. And certainly not me, a mild-mannered midwestern Jewish boy who got nervous sneaking cigarettes between classes in high school. So we sat down and introduced ourselves. A mutual friend, part of the underground world of French cataphiles with whom we had spent long hours exploring the tunnels that snake below the XIVe arrondissement, had set up the meeting. "I think you will have fun together," she had said in her halting English. "Nico likes to climb too."

After we meet Nico we decide to head out to see what we can find. It's still kind of early, so Nico suggests we hit the Canal Saint-Martin, an underground river constructed by Napoleon in 1802 to bring freshwater to the exploding population of central Paris. It's guarded by a locked gate, but Nico explains that this is no problem; he climbs up the gate, which isn't quite flush with the ceiling of the tunnel. Then he grabs the tiny ledge at the top, maneuvers around a corner, and goes hand over hand by his fingertips ten feet above the canal before swinging around the other side. Not a move your average preppy could do. Steve and I follow, and we're in.

This gets the night started. We walk down the ledge on the side of the underground canal, taking pictures and marveling at the point in space that we happen to occupy. To get to the canal gate where it enters the tunnel, we've walked along the side of a marina. This marina was originally dug as a moat—a moat whose purpose was protecting the fortress imprisoning the political opponents of the Bourbon kings of France. Three centuries ago we'd have been standing in a dungeon in the basement of the Bastille. We slowly make our way north along the canal, telling stories and making sure we don't fall in. Steve, as usual, has brought a flask of whiskey and breaks it open. I don't know if France has an open-container law, but it doesn't really matter: one of the side benefits of being in places outside the public realm is that you don't have to worry about the rules of the public realm. After about a mile and a half of walking, we encounter a tunnel that branches off to the side. This turns out to be a connection to Paris's 150-year-old sewer network. With some rubber boots and an air meter, we probably would have gone wandering off into the 1,200-plus miles of the system, but without these there's really only so long you want to hang out in a sewer. After a short time spent taking pictures, we figure the quickest way to get back to the street is to just pop open a manhole.

I've never popped a manhole before and feel embarrassed about it. It's the urban exploration equivalent of being a lawyer who hasn't ever argued before a jury, just sat with a stack of papers and whispered in the lead counsel's ear from time to time. So I tell Nico and Steve that I've got this one.

People look at the tops of dozens of manholes every day. But not many have actually been in the other side. Generally speaking, below that metal circle on the ground is a vertical cement tube, about the same diameter or slightly larger, with either a ladder leading down, or more often just a set of rungs set into the cement. This tube might go down five feet or fifty feet, and at the bottom is an entrance to the drains, or sewers, or telecommunication tunnels, or some other guts of the city. Our tube has the embedded rungs and is about fifteen feet deep and perhaps three feet in diameter.

Manholes are not designed to be opened, or "popped," from the bottom. When workers want to enter, they take a tool, yank off the manhole cover, leave it over to the side, and then set up safety cones or fences around the open hole in the ground. Once they're finished with whatever they're doing, they climb back out and use the tool to yank the manhole cover back into place. Popping them open from below is generally reserved for people who run around these places for fun. As such, there's no real proper—or safe—way to do it. But even if there was one, it's still a pretty bad idea. Best-case scenario in popping open an unfamiliar manhole from below is climbing out into a park with some curious picnickers giving you funny looks. Worst-case scenario is sticking your head up out of the hole and having your last sight be the tire of an SUV coming at you at fifty miles an hour. So I listen at the manhole for a while. When I don't hear the telltale *thunk-thunk* that indicates that traffic is passing over it, I determine we'll exit onto the sidewalk. Now it's time to get the thing open.

Over the years, urban explorers have figured out a few different methods of popping open manholes from below. I've just learned a new one, which is to stand with the rungs at your side, grab them with both hands, flip yourself upside down, and then shove as hard as you can against the bottom of the manhole cover with your feet. I haven't actually tried this yet, but it seems like a lot of fun, and I resolve to impress my companions with my mastery of this advanced manhole-cover-popping technique. Steve reminds me to grab separate rungs with each hand, the purpose being that in case one breaks or comes loose, I'll still have a grip on the other, and as such won't plummet fifteen feet headfirst down the shaft. This is important: when a physical structure is out of the public realm, the usual rules of safety and maintenance that we are all unconsciously used to don't apply. The manhole could have last been opened yesterday or never. The rungs could have been set into the cement fifteen days or a hundred fifty years ago. It could have a faithful civil servant doing inspection, maintenance, and upkeep on a regular basis, or be completely off the official map. I grab, flip, and start to push. Paris's manhole covers weigh about two hundred pounds. Ten minutes later I'm still hanging upside down and the manhole cover hasn't budged. The other two are losing patience. "Come on, let me do it," Steve says.

I am not letting Steve pop the manhole. The whiskey has given me an inflated sense of the moment, and getting it open has now become a test of manhood. But I accept that I don't have the technique to do it the cool way, so instead I flip back down, move up a couple rungs, place my shoulder against the manhole cover, and shove. The feeling in my abdominal muscles makes me question if I just gave myself a hernia, but I feel the metal disk budge. One more shove and it comes loose.

Now comes the scary part. The lid has been "popped," meaning it's not flush with the sidewalk anymore, and is now hanging at a shallow angle half in, half out of the hole. What

I'm supposed to do now is balance on the ladder rungs, reach up with my hands, and shove this thing off of the hole and onto the sidewalk so we can climb out. The problem is that I have heard stories of people who have had a lid settle back into place while they were trying this, crushing—or even severing—their fingers. So instead of gripping the edge of the cover and shoving, I try to nudge it along from the bottom, never putting my hands in a position where I could potentially lose part of them. The manhole cover goes nowhere. My companions become more and more anxious, because in addition to wasting time we are now hanging out below a suspiciously half-open manhole on a sidewalk. I finally give up and let Nico do it, feeling like a baseball player who's just stepped up to the plate in the bottom of the ninth, taken a couple pitches, and then headed back to the dugout and asked the manager to pinch-hit for him. And not even because he's a particularly bad batter but because he's scared of getting hit in the head with an inside fastball.

We clamor out of the hole. Nico has managed to shove the manhole cover halfway down the sidewalk in one try. I try to cover up my shame by insisting on putting it back, but after seeing my earlier ineptitude the other two are having none of it and quickly put the cover back in place themselves.

"What now?" I ask.

"There's a church I've been looking at where I think we can do a climb," Nico casually mentions in his Parisian accent. He motions south—"Let's walk this way." Steve and I follow, finishing off the flask.

Walking through the city at night is quite unlike doing so back home: Paris has a sense of peace that is wholly lacking from the twenty-four-hour energy of New York City, and we don't encounter another person the whole way to the Seine. As we walk across the Pont Neuf twenty minutes later, I wonder what church we're going to and how we're going to climb it. It isn't until we hop the short fence into the yard that I realize the "church" Nico's talking about is the Notre-fucking-Dame. I still have no idea how we're getting up.

"OK, so I come here last time and they are doing some work," Nico says as we walk across the yard toward the back of the cathedral. "I think there is, the metal parts they use when they fix something, what is this called?" I'm confused until I realize Nico is searching for the word "scaffolding," and while there isn't any constructed, we quickly find some unused parts lying on the ground. We fit two of the pieces together and form a rickety metal structure that we lean against the building. One person holds it steady while another gingerly makes his way up it, and we're on the first terrace. We haul up this makeshift ladder and repeat for the second terrace. Now it gets tougher: the ladder won't reach all the way up to the third terrace. Luckily, Gothic cathedrals such as Notre Dame generally make use of a structural reinforcement—the flying buttress—that in a pinch can also serve as a climbing aid. We use the ladder to make our way on top of one of the flyers, and then manage to scoot along it up to where it connects with the third terrace.

Now we're really stuck. The fourth terrace is at least thirty feet above us. Saying I had second thoughts about continuing would imply my first thought was something other than "Let's get the hell out of here already." We've gotten an amazing up-close look at a beautiful part of a landmark cathedral few ever get to see. Isn't that enough? Plus I've started to feel raindrops. "All right, guys," I say. "Get your pictures and let's bail."

"Hey, help me look for a way in," is Nico's response. Steve is off testing a drainpipe for climbability. I might as well have said, "Nice view, huh, guys?" For my companions, the thought of turning back now is so ridiculous my comment doesn't even register. I consider quietly slinking off, heading back down the cathedral, and getting out of here before we create an international incident. It is a sickening yet incredibly freeing feeling when I realize there is no way I'll be able to make it back down without at least one of the other two to hold the makeshift ladder steady. And neither of them seems to be going anywhere but up.

We find a door. I can tell the lock on the door is a warded lock, meaning that you use a specially shaped key that bypasses "wards," or small metal guards inside the lock designed to block an improper key from turning and triggering the latch. It's not a very effective mechanism, hardly ever found in the United States, and is mostly used in old European locks. I'm pretty sure that with some time, effort, and luck I can get it open. Then I notice the entire lockset is simply screwed onto the door. Nico has a Leatherman. It takes us about forty-five seconds to break into Notre Dame.

The door leads directly to a spiral staircase. We head up and find ourselves at another, similar door at the top of the staircase and exit onto a narrow stone walkway in what's now a steady rain. On one side of us is a low stone railing, and on the other side is the bottom of the slanted metal roof. The calm, light downpour takes the edge off the adrenaline buzz, and this combines with the menagerie of stone goblin-like creatures dotting our surroundings to add a creepy, gothic feeling to the night. I imagine I now know how Batman would feel if

Gotham City was "La Ville de Gotham" instead. The statues are not the restored sculptures that the tourists see up close; some are worn away to the point where you can barely tell they're supposed to have faces. The rain lets me see the difference between the statues that are actual gargoyles, which function as water spouts, helping to funnel the runoff from the rain away from the building, and the ones that are merely chimeras, which are solely decorative. After a couple of minutes of admiring the view and exploring the terrace, I hear a *thunk*. I look over and see that Nico has flung himself against the roof, slick with rain, and is somehow managing to inch his way up to the spire without slipping back down. The adrenaline kicks back in again.

I glance over at Steve. "We going up there?" I ask nervously. In return I get the straight-on look with the slightly crazed glint I've come to expect in these scenarios.

"Moe, I have no idea where you're going. But I'm certainly not stopping here." Steve finds an easier route where two sections of the roof meet and several statues can be used as handholds before a final short vertical climb up protruding gargoyles. I take a deep breath and follow. As I struggle up the last few gargoyles to the spire, I feel a particularly narrow and worn one sort of give a bit beneath my foot. I have a flash of complete panic. I'm going to break Notre Dame. But it holds, I make my next foothold, and as Steve and Nico help haul me up into the spire I start to let myself think that this was actually a good idea.

Once we've made it to the top, we start to relax a bit. The inside of the spire is circular and narrow, perhaps a dozen feet in diameter, with upper and lower platforms connected by a ladder. The interior of the structure is made entirely out of wood, which you can't tell by looking at it from the ground. Steve and I head up the ladder to the upper level and take a look around. To the west is a beautiful view of the back of the twin square towers that crown the entrance to the cathedral. I take a moment to appreciate the perspective: tomorrow there will be hundreds of tourists on the north tower looking right at where we are now. But none of them will know what it's like to look back.

After I have Steve take the obligatory vanity picture of me standing in the spire, I start to get bored. The other two are taking pictures, and Steve is the kind of photographer who is never quite satisfied with his last shot. Each long exposure is inevitably followed with "Cool, cool . . . Let me try one more thing here." I can tell it's going to be a while—because of the effort we've put in, and the overwhelming unlikelihood of ever returning, I know Steve is not leaving until he gets exactly the photos he wants. So I look around for something to do in the meantime. I chuckle to myself.

"What's so funny?" Steve says.

"This is going to sound really weird," I reply, "but I kind of wish I'd brought a book."

In lieu of reading, I decide to try to see if there's anything interesting up here that I've missed. The spire houses a few bells, and after a bit of poking around I can see that each one is operated by a simple pulley system. I give one of these pulleys a light tug, and a large bell to my right wobbles a bit. I figure a slightly harder tug will result in a soft chime—an appropriate celebration of our accomplishment, no? Unfortunately, the combination of being both heavily drunk and a completely inexperienced bell ringer leads my intended "soft chime" to sound more like a royal wedding has just taken place in the cathedral. In the silence of the winter night, it's probably the loudest noise between here and the Sacré Coeur two miles to the north.

Steve pauses his picture taking. "What the hell, Moe?" he says, staring at me with a mixture of disbelief and disgust.

Now, usually in these circumstances I'd be the first one to insist we blow the joint immediately. But Steve has really only just started taking photos, and Nico, who has wanted to get up here forever, is off enjoying himself on the roof somewhere. And as I feel like I've already acquitted myself so incredibly poorly on this excursion so far, I am determined not to let my stupidity completely ruin the night. So instead I put on a false bravado.

"Jesus, calm down," I say, trying to put a tone of smug condescension into my voice. "There's no way anyone in there would think anyone is up here. Chill out and take your pictures. I'm going to hang out over here."

I know this will convince Steve to stay. There's a fine balancing act involved in trying to get where you're not supposed to go, and that balancing act involves not giving in to your fears but at the same time not being a clueless idiot. It's a narrow tightrope to walk, and one that takes some practice to really get a feel for. If you're too scared, these nights usually involve staring at a fence for half an hour before convincing yourself that the bum on the corner is actually an undercover cop, and then going home. If you're too much of an idiot, they involve, well, climbing up Notre Dame and ringing the bell. Steve is always worried about being too scared. I am always worried about being too much of an idiot. So between the two of us, we've worked out a pretty good rapport that's let us get to, and more important get away from, a lot of places we're not supposed to be. By playing out of position, I know I've caused us to lose our balance and fall firmly onto the "idiot" side of things. It's a trick I reserve only for situations like these, where I'm feeling so particularly insecure about my place in the company of dare-devil international adventurers that it outweighs my desire to not end up dead or in jail. If I had just managed to open that manhole earlier, my response would probably have been something smart, like stealthily leading the way back down, or at least making an effort to hide. Instead I decide to play Brando.

Steve goes back to taking pictures. I relax again. My little speech has had a bit of an auto-hypnotic effect, and I've actually convinced myself that all will be OK. I am wrong. A few minutes later we hear voices. I peak down and see flashlights coming up the ladder below us. I make a silent vow to never again let myself think stuff like this is a good idea.

We see the first policeman's head pop up through the hatch. He looks around, sees us, and says something sternly in French that I assume translates out to "Don't move, assholes." He motions down for his companions, and as he steps up the last few rungs of the ladder to our landing, I hear Steve say dryly, "Well, I hope this isn't like the last time I got caught climbing a cathedral."

{ **PART ONE** }

ONE

New York City, 2001

It has been six years since Steve last got caught climbing a cathedral. Three months after the destruction of the World Trade Center, he decided it would be a great idea to scale the rusty scaffolding on the side of the Cathedral of Saint John the Divine on the Upper West Side of Manhattan. The 121,000-square-foot behemoth is best known for being the largest cathedral in the world. It's also home to something of a hero of ours, Philippe Petit, the man who tight-roped between the Twin Towers of the World Trade Center in 1974. Despite being open to the public for over a century, Saint John's has never actually been completed, undergoing continuous construction since 1892. This construction is on and off, but nowadays mostly off. In the 1980s, work was started on the south-side tower, but Saint John's soon ran out of money; in 1990 the workers went but the scaffolding stayed.

Eleven years later, this now rusty, decrepit structure was an invitation for curious Columbia University students such as Steve to climb up to the roof at night and take pictures. Once he was having such a good time, he decided to stay up there after the sun came up. An overly paranoid passerby saw him, mistook his camera's telescope lens for an automatic rifle, and called 911. Fifteen minutes later, a forty-person SWAT team was there for him. It ended up not being so bad. He spent the night in jail with a bunch of guys arrested for smoking pot, and the charges were dropped the following morning. Had he been caught on top of the George Washington Bridge, which he climbed September 9, 2001, it probably would have been a different story.

While Steve Duncan, urban adventurer extraordinaire, was out climbing bridges and getting arrested on top of cathedrals, I, like so many other bright-eyed recent college graduates, had just moved to New York City and completely fallen in love with it. In the summer of 2001, Leigh, the woman I would be marrying in four months, and I had scored a great sublet on Riverside Drive, about a ten-minute walk from Saint John's. She had just finished her second year of law school and had gotten an internship in Brooklyn, and I had a summer job with a local nonprofit doing outreach to city council candidates. Life was good: I was in the right place with the right person. What more can you ask for than that?

There are two separate human tendencies when settling into a new place. The first is to nest—to make your home comfortable and familiar. The second is to explore—to get a sense of your surroundings. It's probably evolutionary, something about needing to survey the territory for food, water, and enemies while also needing to fortify your home base against invaders. Everyone has both tendencies, but usually one is dominant. Some people are nesters, some are explorers.

Leigh was a nester. After unloading our meager belongings

on the corner of 116th Street and Riverside Drive, she stayed behind, eager to set up the new place. I could have cared less about unpacking a single box. I'm an explorer: the first thing I want to do is to know my surroundings, get the lay of the land. This was New York City; there was a lot of land to get the lay of. I started east on 116th Street.

"You! You, you!" I hadn't gotten halfway down the block when an elderly Asian lady started shouting at me. Thinking I should put on a "tough city-guy" façade, I attempted to ignore her and just continue on my way. Obviously this must be one of the many crazy New Yorkers I'd heard of. But I was wrong. This lady had actually judged that I was both a trustworthy and friendly enough young man that, despite my best attempts to ignore her, she could grab me walking down the block, press her car keys into my hand, and get me to parallel park for her. "You park! You park!" she said, pointing at a car angled awkwardly in the street—one of those classic bulky American sedans that seem like you're piloting a yacht when you're behind the wheel. Her voice indicated that the topic was not remotely up for discussion, so I hopped in, put the car in gear, and managed to squeeze it in between its neighbors. Expecting at least a "Thank you" upon exiting the car, I instead got a curt nod as I handed her back the keys. Well, that's just the way things were in New York, I supposed.

After this encounter I spent the next fourteen hours wandering the streets of Manhattan, just trying to take it all in. I can't remember where I went or what I saw. The details weren't important. The process was—the ability to experience my new surroundings, the chance to have encounters with stern ladies in need of talented parallel parkers. I finally staggered back to the Riverside Drive apartment at three in the morning, still in awe of my new home.

It was a great summer, one of the happiest times of my life. In August 2001, a couple months after arriving, Leigh and I were visiting a friend who was the manager for the Gap store in the basement of the World Trade Center. On a whim I took a trip up to the observation deck while they stayed behind. It was a beautiful day, admission was only ten dollars, and there wasn't even a line. They let us up on the roof, and I remember the amazing feeling of freedom. I looked down, and the huge sky-scrapers of Manhattan looked like Monopoly houses. I marveled at the fact that I lived in such a city and that I had the rest of my life to discover it all. A month later, I got a harsh reminder that I didn't necessarily have the rest of my life to see the city. Everything can be gone tomorrow. So I'd better start right now.

It all began innocently enough. New York is an amazing place, and like all new arrivals to the city, I had the fresh eyes to appreciate the wonder. Just by turning the corner on a non-descript Bronx block you come across Edgar Allan Poe's old cottage, the concrete playground where Hip-Hop started in the 1970s, or the tenement where your grandmother grew up. There are skyscrapers and shacks, slums and mansions, people from every country on earth, every walk of life. For someone with a healthy sense of curiosity, New York is a sort of drug. Every block you go, you want to see what's on the next one. Every interesting person you meet, you want to meet another. Every answer you get brings more questions. Every perspective of the city you can see just makes you try harder to see the ones you haven't. The questions just keep getting tougher, the new experiences harder to find. For most people, this thirst to see and discover is eventually satisfied or subsumed by life's other priorities. But for a scant few others, it just keeps getting worse. Eventually, if it gets bad enough, you can start to get yourself into trouble.

My problem was that I didn't know how to get myself into trouble yet. Like so many others, I didn't truly grasp that the "Do Not Enter or Cross Tracks" sign at the end of the subway platform is nothing more than a painted piece of metal that you can step right around, or that you can duck through a hole in the wall of a foreboding industrial hulk of a building and spend hours wandering inside, or that many times the only thing stopping you from sitting on the roof of a skyscraper and gazing out at the most magnificent skyline on earth is a bored guard at the front desk, a set of stairs, and a doorknob.

So for a short while I satisfied my curiosity in small, everyday ways: taking a subway ride to a new stop and heading up the stairs, turning left instead of right while walking home, talking to strangers I'd meet at a lunch counter in Flushing or a shop on the Lower East Side. I stumbled across many little corners of the city this way, and each was rewarding. But it wasn't enough.

Good medical students—the ones with true passions for being doctors—aren't content to just spend their education reading books and listening to lectures. They want to be in the operating room, examining the inner workings of the human body up close and personal. I felt that same need with the city. I enrolled in graduate school for urban planning, I got my tour guide's license, but I wanted something more. I wanted a knowledge and experience that went beyond what was normal and easy. I would cross the Brooklyn Bridge and wonder what the city looked like from the vantage point of the people who had stood on the massive stone towers a century and a quarter ago spinning its steel suspension cables—cables that looked maddeningly inviting to ascend. I learned about century-old abandoned subway stations, an empty brick aqueduct that ran for miles just a few feet below the streets of Harlem and the Bronx, a secret train platform underneath the Waldorf-Astoria once used by Franklin Roosevelt, and the half-dozen disused observation decks on our Art Deco skyscrapers. I would stay up nights wondering how in the world I could get to these places, how I could manage to see them for myself. I got a horrible itch—an itch that made me wake up in the morning thinking, "Someone else got to go there . . . so why can't I?" Everyone has an itch like this—a feeling that other people are living the dreams and doing the things that they want to do. Some people want to be rock stars. Some want to climb mountains. Some want to be the president. I wanted to see everything in New York City.

One day, a couple years after I had moved to the city, I was waiting for the train after a late-night poker game at a friend's house. I had won thirty bucks and was feeling lucky, and Leigh and I had been fighting so I didn't want to go home yet. A train had just passed and the subway platform was empty except for me. I made my way down to the end of the platform, where a dull red sign marked the end of the space freely available to each of eight million New Yorkers, twenty-four hours a day, seven days a week, and marked the beginning of a mysterious world known only to a few small subsets of the city: subway workers, graffiti writers, the homeless. I was sweating as I gazed down the tracks into the dirt and darkness. It was only one step past the sign, but the mental barrier was enormous. We live our whole lives as prisoners of artificial boundaries— boundaries put in place not by mountains, rivers, or walls but by people and institutions who simply tell us that they're there. Crossing these boundaries, realizing that this prison that has been constructed in our minds doesn't actually exist, isn't physically difficult. But for people like me—people who had spent twenty-seven years waiting for the sign to say "Walk" before crossing the street—it can take an unprecedented act of will. I had to steady myself on the "Do Not Enter or Cross Tracks" sign that marked this mental border and physically push my leg forward with my other hand in order to step around it. I went down the short ladder onto the tracks and started down the tunnel. Glancing back, I remembered the Woody Guthrie lyric from the fifth verse of "This Land Is Your Land"—the one they don't teach you in school or play on the radio.

As I was walking I saw a sign there
And on the sign it said "No Trespassing."
But on the other side it didn't say nothing,
That side was made for you and me.

Of course, Woody Guthrie's side of the sign probably had open fields and a nice cool breeze blowing, not striped "No Clearance" signs and 600 volts of direct current in the form of the third rail running next to him a foot away.

. . .

As I made my way down the tracks I noticed something interesting. Walking subway tracks and riding over them in a train are two opposite experiences in the exact same point in space. Riding is bright, crowded, noisy, and clean—well, relatively clean. And with the occasional exception of a crazed preacher, it's fairly relaxed. It's a familiar place, one that New Yorkers feel a certain comfort in and ownership of. If you would do it in the passenger seat of your car, New Yorkers will do it on the subway: nap, eat, put on makeup, clip their fingernails.

Walking is dark, solitary, quiet, and absolutely filthy. And I was very, very far from relaxed. As soon as I stepped around the sign it was like a switch had been flipped. I was instantly more alert. I got a strange, queasy feeling in my stomach, but one that instead of distracting me made me focus on my surroundings. I could almost feel my pupils start to dilate.

Since that first step, I've walked tracks on seven different subway systems around the world. I've gotten this same slightly nauseated feeling of nervousness, the same adrenaline-fueled alertness, every time. I never fight it; in fact, I've long since learned to welcome it. Subway tunnels are no place to get comfortable. In order for them to be certified to walk on the subway tracks, the MTA makes employees take an eight-hour safety course, and when they're actually on the tracks they have to have all the proper lights and equipment. Even then it isn't a hundred percent safe: since 1946 there have been more than 150 cases of workers being hit by a train or electrocuting themselves on the third rail. And that's just the professionals. Dozens of average citizens—drunks, graffiti writers, suicides—die on the subway tracks every year. I was aware of all of this but I still had to go.

That first time I didn't go far, or stay long, or really even see much I couldn't already see from the platform. But the sensation, the feeling of being in a new environment I'd only thought about experiencing, was there. The light, the smell, the air were all different. My curiosity had been satisfied, another perspective on the city gained. To me it was amazing.

When I got back to the platform, panting not from exhaustion but excitement, everything in the station was exactly the same. No alarms had gone off; no overzealous straphangers had "seen something and said something." No police had suddenly appeared, waiting expectantly for me to return before whipping out their handcuffs with a patronizing quip. The only thing that was different was me. It wasn't just the act. It was the opening of possibility, the realization that the boundaries that had kept me from sating this desire were totally in my head. In addition to the dozens of neighborhoods and thousands of streets above, more than a hundred miles of tunnels underneath New York City had now been added to my mental geography. And if these boundaries were a figment of my imagination, what other boundaries were as well? I had wanted more, and now I realized that I could have it. The experience was like giving someone who struggles with a small coffee addiction his first hit of cocaine.

TWO

New York City, 2005

OK, so you want to go out the window and I'll hold the elevator?" I do want to. But I freeze.

Three days ago I had met Steve Duncan on top of a small roof at the end of a hidden alley in an industrial section of Queens. In the couple of years since I had taken those first steps in the subway, I'd met a few like-minded people and spent a good deal of time in the tunnels, ruins, rail lines, and other nooks and crannies of New York. My favorite places became a beautiful derelict courthouse in the middle of a ruined South Bronx neighborhood; New York's oldest bridge, completely abandoned for decades, built in 1848 over the Harlem River; and an elevated rail line down the west side of Manhattan, overgrown with two decades' worth of shrubbery over the long-disused tracks.

The other people I'd met each had their own stories and motivations. There were rebellious high school kids wanting adventure and exploration, artists and photographers trying to capture their aesthetic vision, a couple of people who simply had a visceral love of tunnels—whether it was the space, the solitude, or some unresolved issue from the birthing process, I couldn't say. But Steve was the first guy I had met who I clicked with on an intellectual level. Chatting with this skinny, shaggy-haired blond hipster with the goofy grin and slight lisp was the first time I'd talked to someone where I didn't feel the need to ask—or answer—"So why do you do this?" We both happened to be at a small get-together for explorers. I had asked if he wanted to try to get to an abandoned observation deck.

Old guidebooks are the best history books. They give you a sense of the city as it was perceived in the moment, without the clouded judgment of historical hindsight. They're also a great way to glimpse back into the New York City of yesteryear and begin the hunt for the remnants of it today. By far the best of these old guidebooks is *The WPA Guide to New York City*, commissioned by FDR's Works Progress Administration and published in 1939. The WPA guide lists seven observation decks open to the public just in Manhattan, ranging in price from $1.10 (the Empire State Building) to free (the Bank of Manhattan Trust Building on Wall Street). Not listed is our goal—the 512-foot Williamsburgh Savings Bank Tower, the tallest building in Brooklyn, and for almost sixty years the tallest building between Manhattan and Paris. Through some research, however, I'm pretty sure that its uppermost terraces used to be open to the public. Built during the excesses of the 1920s, the building boasts a beautiful banking hall on the ground floor and one of those slender prewar towers, which in this case is crowned with a golden dome, giving the building a laughably phallic appearance. Compounding this, the dome also serves as the top of a smokestack, leading to occasional billows of white steam ejaculating from the tip of the priapism. Opened in 1929, it later became known as the "Tower of Pain" for its concentration of dentist offices.

I've been frustrated with observation decks in New York for some time now. The Williamsburgh Savings Bank Tower is just one of over a dozen buildings or structures that used to have public observation decks that are now closed or used for private space. In the 1920s, the owners of these skyscrapers had pride: they wanted to build magnificent buildings, wanted the public to get a chance to see how amazing they were. But things have changed now. There's no need to peacock. New York City skyscrapers are now so well-known and popular, the owners no longer feel any need to show them off. Social value that used to be derived from openness now comes from exclusivity. It seems like the city is conspiring to keep you off its heights.

In New York City, one of the top tourist destinations in the world, there is currently one public observation deck, on the eighty-sixth floor of the Empire State Building (although the reopening of a second one, the Rockefeller Center deck, would happen in a few months). While the view is great, the cost—not to mention the hours-long line—makes the activity an arguable value. The pattern for it, and for most touristy observation decks I've visited, seems to be to jazz stuff up with a lot of bells and whistles, charge a ton of money, and advertise it as an "experience." (A good tourist rule of thumb is to skip anything that is advertised as an "experience.")

Here's what people want from an observation deck: to be up high, have an unobstructed view of the city, and be able to snap a few pictures. They don't want $20 souvenir photos of them superimposed in front of the building. They don't want talking elevators. They don't want a tchotchke shop the size of

Rhode Island to walk through before getting to the deck. But these are the kinds of observation decks we have now. So if you want something different from this, you've got to find your own.

Steve and I meet at the entrance to the tower and head in. We're all ready with a fake story about root canals, but the guard at the entrance doesn't give us a second look. We head to the tower elevator and hit the floor we think the abandoned deck is on. We're right, but the elevator door opens into an active office whose workers give us mildly curious looks. Darn.

LADDER TO AN ABANDONED OBSERVATION DECK, WILLIAMSBURGH SAVINGS BANK TOWER, BROOKLYN.

Luckily we have a Plan B. The terrace is surrounded by masonry that reaches all the way up to the next story. Maybe there's a way to make our way down it from the outside. We hop back on the elevator and press the button for the next floor up. We're in luck: this office is empty, about the size of a large studio apartment. Steve holds the elevator for a quick getaway as I poke around. Looking out the window, I realize we're going to be able to do this: there's a ladder on the outside of the tower a couple feet away from the window. It won't be the simplest maneuver, but I'm pretty sure I'll be able to grab the side, swing around onto it, and climb down to the deck below.

I relay this info to Steve, who is still holding the elevator, and who suggests I get going. I go to lift up the window. There's no real reason to be scared. The building is an old prewar one, not likely to have any alarms or much in the way of security at all. Even if we get seen on the terrace by the people in the office, the worst that will probably happen is that someone will come to escort us off the premises. I know this window is just one more of those mental boundaries; that I can lift it up, swing onto the ladder, and climb down to the deck with no more difficulty than it would take to negotiate a simple playground jungle gym. I also know that after hemming and hawing for a while, I'll manage to do it. But I don't know how to explain it to the guy waiting expectantly at the elevator door. My hands are at the bottom of the window. I resolve to contract my biceps and force them to pull up on the ledge. Instead I hear myself say, "Uh, you want to check it out and I'll hold the elevator?"

Thirty seconds later I hate myself as I hear, "Come on, Moe, it's totally cool," coming from one story down.

I let the elevator go, the journey out the window now easy after the trail has been blazed. As I take the last step off the ladder and look around, I'm expecting some great views and maybe to hear a deep voice say something like "Excuse me, gentlemen, could you tell me what you're doing here?" What I'm not expecting is a history lesson on the Revolutionary War.

There are seven signs surrounding us, each one attached to one of the fences that surround the deck. They're numbered from 9 to 16, with number 10 missing. On the other side of the abandoned office there's another window with another ladder, which leads down to the second deck, which houses signs 1 through 8. Each sign has three components: an illustration, some text, and a photograph. Looking closer, I see that each

illustration and text is a short description of a specific action by
either the British or the Continental Army—the British landing at Gravesend Bay, Washington's night retreat from Brooklyn to Manhattan—in the Battle of Brooklyn, during the early
days of the American Revolution. As I read the description of
each event, I can see the entire terrain—from Staten Island, to
Flatbush, to the island of Manhattan—where it played out over
two hundred years ago. The photographs are of the view from
the deck itself, with a red dot pointing out where the event
in question happened. Sign number 12 reads "Washington Calls a Council of War." The illustration is of Washington
conversing with his advisers over a map. The text describes the
decision of the Continental Army to retreat from Brooklyn.
The red dot on the photo is pasted just to the left of the Twin
Towers. I later learn that these signs were put up to commemo-
rate the bicentennial in 1976, and that in 1977 the building was
landmarked with the signs still up.

New York City has one of the strongest historical preservation laws in the world, one where designation as a landmark
means (allowing for only a few small loopholes) that you can't
legally alter any part of the structure that is visible to the public. A short time after the Williamsburgh Savings Bank Tower
was landmarked, the observation decks were abandoned. Since
you can see the backs of the signs from the street, they're now
considered part of the landmarked façade, which means they
can't be removed. So they stick around the abandoned decks, a
lost little part of an older New York City, waiting to impart
their lessons as a reward to the lonely few whose curiosity leads
them to venture there.

Steve and I take our time. I examine the signs and admire

the view; he takes photo after photo after photo. We climb back up the ladder, shut the window, and head back down the elevator, through the lobby, and past the guard, who grunts at us as he reads the paper.

Once we're outside, I turn to Steve. "So are you into the subway?"

THREE

N ew York is a new city, relatively speaking. In cities like Rome and Paris the underground world is enormous: centuries-old (if not millennia-old) quarries, ossuaries, and aqueducts exist that catacomb huge sections of the underground. Archaeologists and underground societies spend years documenting these abandoned worlds, and are constantly discovering new offshoots and networks.

The underground world in the cities of the western hemisphere is different. There are a few unused nooks and crannies underneath New York, but for the most part anything underground is going to be part of the currently-in-use infrastructure of the city. Somewhere in between these two worlds lie the abandoned and never-used stations of the New York City subway system.

The most famous one of these is the gorgeous City Hall station, built in 1904 and abandoned a little over forty-one years later. It's the most architecturally noteworthy, featuring an arched tile roof, stained-glass skylights, and hanging chandeliers. It's also probably the trickiest one to sneak into,

BROKEN ANGEL.

© *John Hill*

involving running a single-track, no-clearance tunnel where you simply have to pray you've timed the trains correctly, although a more stress-free way to get there is to join the New York City Transit Museum and take one of its members-only tours. Another of these abandoned stations lies two miles north on the same line, directly below 18th Street under a posh neighborhood on the East Side of Manhattan. That's our goal tonight.

Steve tells me to meet him at his place, which turns out to be a shabby loft on a somewhat derelict industrial block of Bed-Stuy. There's a crazy house on the corner that looks like something out of a Tim Burton movie, with a sign that reads "Broken Angel" over the entrance in a dagger-like font. Later the block becomes semi-famous as the "Block" in the Dave Chappelle film *Block Party*, but my introduction to it is Steve's response to my request for directions: "So you go up Downing and then go around the bend when it ends. Don't worry about the idling cars. This is just where the hookers usually take johns because it's almost like a dead-end street."

I find the place, ring the bell, and head up the stairs.

"Hey, how's it going," Steve greets me with a smile.

Steve's girlfriend, Molly, is lounging in a chair. She's a

pretty, thin redhead with a cocky edge to her that's about three parts endearing to one part annoying.

"Oh, so you're Steve's new exploring lover," she says, her tone indicating that she harbors no jealousy and is just trying to needle Steve a bit as he looks sheepishly on. "God, he's been talking about you for the last week."

It's sweet how they interact. They have an easy pleasure in each other's company that Leigh and I have been missing for a while now. I haven't mentioned to Steve that I'm married, because I'm pretty sure I'm not going to be married for much longer. It's not the late nights running around subway tunnels, which have started to happen more and more. Leigh has actually always been encouraging of this—in fact I wonder how much of her encouragement is designed to simply get me out of my comfort zone, out of the easy but unfulfilling place that we're both in.

After chatting for a bit, Steve and I head over to the East Side of Manhattan. I want to do the station, but I'm also using this mission as an excuse to jump the fence into Gramercy Park. Gramercy Park is the last private park in Manhattan, restricting access to the gated-off green patch at the end of Lexington Avenue to the people who can afford the apartments that surround it—and even then they have to buy a key for $350. When I first passed it, I saw a solitary guy sitting on a bench, smoking a cigar with a very self-satisfied look on his face. It was enough to get me to vow to sit where he was sitting. I tell Steve this is first up on the agenda, but surprisingly he's not into it.

"You can see everything through the fence," he says. "I dunno, this seems like the kind of thing I'd only be into if I were really drunk." Still, he's a sport and indulges me as we quickly hop the fence and take a lap around the park, where I make sure to sit on the same bench I'd seen Mr. Cigar.

Happy with ourselves, we head down into the nearby active station at 23rd Street. After swiping through the turnstiles I glance over and see Steve pull out a silver flask and surreptitiously take a swig. I'm astonished.

"Dude, what are you doing?" I ask.

"Just having a drink to loosen up a little bit. Hey, you want one?"

I cannot think of a worse idea. "No, man, I don't want a drink. You're swigging vodka when we're about to go running in subway tunnels?"

"Not vodka, bourbon," Steve answers, looking at me like I might as well have suggested he's drinking paint thinner.

I can't believe it. I try to figure out my obligations to this guy if he drunkenly falls on the third rail as we're strolling down the tunnel. I make up my mind that I've got to be responsible, get us to come back and do this another time, but before I have time to argue, the train passes, the platform is clear, and Steve is hustling down the tracks.

It starts off pretty well. The tunnel is four tracks: two local tracks on the outside, and two express tracks on the inside. We're on the downtown local track. We stick close to the wall, on the opposite side of the track from the third rail, walking at a brisk but controlled pace. After a couple minutes we see the edge of an abandoned platform. And at just that moment we see a train on the opposite local track barreling toward us. We're not in danger of being hit, but there's nowhere easy to hide. We reach the abandoned station in a panic, sure we've been seen and reported. I immediately want to ditch the mission and bail back to the active station.

"Yeah, that's probably the best idea," Steve says. "Let me take a couple pictures and we'll get out of here."

"Pictures? We've got no time for that," I say, trying to keep the anxiety out of my voice.

"No, hold on, just a couple."

Thinking back on our earlier time in Gramercy Park, I realize that while our motivations are similar, our goals are slightly different. I want to go everywhere. Steve wants to photograph everywhere. He opens his backpack and takes out a black circular case, about eight inches in diameter, with two red wires coming out of it. I almost have a heart attack.

"What the fuck is that?" I scream in a whisper.

Steve's eyes light up. "Hey, I just got this—it works really great with my new camera for lighting photos underground. Basically, I was having problems with shadowing, and . . ." He starts to go on about lumens, ISO settings, apertures, and a lot of other stuff I don't understand.

I interrupt. "It looks like you just took out a fucking bomb! Please put that away before someone on the next train sees it and they send in the antiterrorism unit."

All I can think about now is the crazy drunk I'm with who's going to get me shot. I grab the light and shove it back in the pack. "Come on, it's stupid to stay here. If we get arrested they'll delete your pictures anyway. We'll get good ones next time."

We leave the abandoned platform on the other side, heading downtown toward the Union Square station. Big mistake. Union Square is an express station, which means it's a popular station, which means there are people. As we approach we can see the platform around the bend. Unless we think a few dozen upstanding citizens would ignore a couple young men with backpacks covered in soot coming out of the subway tracks, it seems like a pretty bad idea to exit here. We end up hiding in a little nook between the express tracks, about a hundred feet from the station. Steve, instead of planning our next move, decides the first course of business is to take another sip from the flask and roll a cigarette.

"I don't really smoke too much, but it just feels like I should have a cigarette right now," he says.

We start going over the pros and cons of heading out here versus going back to 23rd Street. As far as I can tell, the only pro to coming out here is that we'll have less walking to do. For some reason, though, this pro seems to be terribly important to Steve. Even though we've known each other for only a few weeks, we quickly start arguing in that exasperated way that old couples do when they know there's no hope of changing each other's mind.

We don't get to argue for long, though: our decision ends up getting made for us. When we glance behind us at the downtown tracks toward the Union Square station, we see flashlights. They're coming toward us. We look back down the uptown tracks and see more flashlights. Steve looks at me. He has that glint in his eye that I don't recognize yet but will come to soon enough. We start to run.

This is a lot different from the careful excursion coming in. The "brisk but controlled" pace goes out the window. We book it down the tunnel, sticking to the middle two express tracks, as late-at-night trains usually run only on the outer, local tracks.

Tonight is an exception. We see the lights of a train bearing down on us from the downtown express track; there must be a service change. We hop the third rail, hide, run some more, hop the third rail again, hide from another train, and hope the people with flashlights behind us are routine maintenance workers and not the police.

Finally we see the 23rd Street station come back into view. Normally it's best to hide, wait for a train, let the platform clear, and then jump back on up, but we don't have time for this. We scale the short ladder, swing around the red sign, and head toward the exit. A guy dressed in civilian clothes is staring right at us as we do this. I'm sure he's an undercover cop. But we can't very well head back onto the tracks, so we do the only other thing we can: pretend like we belong there and walk confidently toward him.

I am sweating bullets as we come up to the guy, ready to have him whip out a pair of handcuffs at any moment. But as we get closer I notice he's dressed pretty shabbily, even for an undercover cop; it's obviously just a guy hoping to bed down for the night in an out-of-the-way corner on a not-so-busy platform.

"Oh, thank God, man," he says to us as we pass him. "I was sure you guys were the police." We give him a quick smile and get the hell out of there.

As we exit the station up to Park Avenue South I notice that Steve is limping—badly.

"You twist an ankle or something?" I ask.

"No, it's my hip," Steve replies.

"Your hip? How'd you hurt that? Did you bang it on something running?"

Steve hobbles along a bit before he answers. "No, it's an old injury. It got messed up pretty good and I had to have surgery on it."

"What'd you do to it?"

"I was climbing in Yosemite and fell and broke it. It's still not great."

"How long ago was that?"

"A couple years or so."

I think to myself that it must have been a heck of a fall if he's still limping.

FOUR

New York City, December 2005

I'm sitting on a metal chair in an abandoned firehouse across from a power plant in industrial Queens. To get here, I've walked from the nearest subway stop, twenty minutes away. The stop is actually in another borough. I have to take the F train to Roosevelt Island, a long, narrow strip of land in the East River, and then walk north and then east across a metal bridge that goes to Queens. It's subzero weather, which means a subzero-degree walk across the bridge with gusts of wind that would blow me into the water if there wasn't a guardrail. It's also pretty close to subzero weather in the abandoned firehouse. There's no heat, although somehow our utilities total almost $500 a month. Instead, for comfort I have an old blanket and a cat my roommate smuggled back from Mexico. The cat is sweet and likes nothing more than to sit on my lap and drool.

I have just turned thirty years old, and this is my new home. It's a far cry from the nice-size one-bedroom apartment in Brooklyn Heights—complete with heat and 600-thread-count sheets—I have left to Leigh, who is now my soon-to-be ex-wife.

My new job is also a far cry from my old one—which is most of the reason why I'm living in the cheapest place I could find on short notice. After a stint in city government, I quit and got a job at a historic preservation organization on the Upper West Side last summer.

"Yeah, so this isn't going to work out," the executive director told me after a month of me rolling my eyes at the depths of her passion for preserving gabled dormers and maintaining the integrity of the cornice walls of the tree-lined side streets of the neighborhood. Luckily I have a backup. I've always renewed the tour guide license I got on a whim in the summer of 2001, more out of vanity than anything.

I'm sad, but it's not really because of the marriage or the job, both of which I suspect I'm ultimately better off without. It's because I feel like I've failed my twenties—like I've tried to grow up and blown it, gone through the motions of becoming an adult hoping it would all somehow stick, just to find myself here—shivering, covered in cat drool, thinking about my future as a divorced tour guide.

But I can't afford to just sit here feeling sorry for myself. I've got to get some sleep. Because tomorrow I'm getting up bright and early and spending the next twelve hours convincing everyone just what a great city this is.

Short on money, pride, and options, a few months earlier I take a trip down to the corner of 50th Street and Eighth Avenue in Manhattan, where I meet a gruff gentleman in a University of Wisconsin jacket who introduces himself as Geoffrey.

"Got a license?" he asks.

I say yes.

"You talk to Meyers?" is his next question, meaning Hank Meyers, the person in charge of recruiting new tour guides.

"Yes," I say again.

"OK, wait out here."

I'm eager to start work, want to get going, but since there's not a bus to get on at the moment, I wait. You get paid $10 an hour for waiting, $20 an hour when you're on the bus.

After a few minutes a blue double-decker tour bus pulls up. A heavyset guy, just short of elderly, slowly makes his way down the stairs. He's dressed in a blue button-down shirt with the name of the tour company embroidered on the pocket, a string of pearls, red lipstick, and a tattered pair of pink shorts. Otherwise he looks like a fat, balding Art Garfunkel.

"Remember," he says in a smoker's rasp, as the tourists descend the stairs, "'TIPS' stands for 'To Insure Proper Service.' Tourism is a *service* profession. It's customary to *tip* your tour guide and driver.

"The box right there sir," he says to the tourist currently at the bottom of the stairs, who in no way whatsoever is indicating that he's currently looking for the place to put a tip. The tourist begrudgingly fetches a dollar from his pocket and throws it in the box.

"Thank you very much. Have a nice trip." After the tourists leave, he splits up the tips with the driver and steps out of the bus.

"Nat! I need you on the next uptown!" Geoffrey barks at him.

"OK. I'm gonna piss. Back in five," Nat replies, and slowly waddles down the sidewalk.

"Hey, I can take that bus," I tell Geoffrey.

Geoffrey looks at me like I have three heads. "C'mere, c'mere," he says.

I come there.

"You know who that is? That's Shimlekowski. You know about Shimlekowski?"

Other than his questionable fashion sense, I do not know about Shimlekowski.

"Shimlekowski is one of my best guides." This is said in such a way as to convey that this is in direct contrast to myself. "He's been doing this since you were in diapers."

"So when am I getting on a bus?" I ask.

"Don't want to be here, go home," is the answer. Geoffrey gives me a look that says, "Any more questions, idiot?" and goes back to squawking into his radio.

So I wait. After an hour and a half, and several buses have come and gone, I'm richer by $15 but still haven't gotten to do a tour. Finally a downtown bus comes in and the tour guide on it tells Geoffrey he's done for the day. There's nobody else standing on the sidewalk except Geoffrey and me.

He sighs, motions to me, and says, "You, what's your name? Take that bus on the downtown loop. Wait, listen . . ." He pauses, and looks me in the eye with an expression that indicates he's getting ready to impart some valuable nugget of double-decker tour-bus guidance.

I pay rapt attention, dedicated to committing this pearl of wisdom to memory.

"Try not to fuck anything up please. Okay?"

After that, I'm on time and earn pretty good tips. Being on time makes Geoffrey happy. Earning tips makes the bus drivers, whom we split them with, happy. This happiness on their part leads to getting on more buses on my part. A lot more. It's not too long before I'm the guy who gets "I need you on the next uptown" while looking sympathetically at the new recruit standing on the sidewalk.

And to boot, it's now the holiday season, and the city is packed with tourists. My new life is going around and around and around, doing the same two-and-a-half-hour tour over and over and over, jabbering away in a down jacket and mittens on top of an open-air double-decker tour bus. I sometimes hear actors complain about the grind of doing theater—eight shows a week, six days a week. Please. Try being a tour guide: back-to-back-to-back-to-back-to-back solo performances, ten to twelve hours straight each day, outside in the rain, snow, or hundred-degree heat, all the while trying to figure out when you're going to be able to grab five minutes for a sandwich or a bathroom stop at Starbucks. During the busy season, tour guides don't talk when they're not working. Laryngitis is a constant hazard, and as there are no sick days, there is no making up the $200 plus tips you're going to lose to it. Your voice becomes your livelihood, not to be risked on trivial chats or meaningless conversations.

There are advantages to my new life, however. While business is currently hectic due to the holiday season, there are no tourists in January, and therefore no work. There's no family I have left in the city now. I absolutely have no obligations—not even to my two cats, whom I've also left with Leigh. I've got nothing to do and nobody to worry about me. And no reason to say no when Steve asks if I want to go to Paris for two weeks. The only thing Leigh and I had to split in the divorce was our airline miles, and I've got just enough to get me across the pond.

I'd been to Paris before: Leigh and I took an impromptu honeymoon there four years ago when airline prices plummeted after September 11. We took walks along the Seine, visited the Louvre and the Musée d'Orsay, discovered a great little restaurant in an out-of-the-way corner of the XVIe arrondissement, and spent three hours waiting on line to go up the Eiffel Tower. It was a great and perfectly standard honeymoon.

This trip will be very different.

FIVE

Paris, January 2006

Two flights, three trains, a hole in a fence, a slide down a muddy embankment, and a half-mile walk in the dead of night through a series of abandoned train tunnels later, and Steve and I have about five feet left to go to our destination. After a half-hour we've talked a lot but still can't quite bring ourselves to go any farther.

This is because this last five feet involve crawling through a hole in the ground. And entering this aperture is the closest thing to going down Alice's rabbit hole that you can get in the real world. That hole in the ground will lead to a huge shadow world below Paris—a web of abandoned quarry tunnels dotted with World War II bunkers, ossuaries, unofficial art galleries, and other assorted surprises colloquially known as "the catacombs," or "catas" for short.

Fifty feet above us will be the Left Bank of Paris. Fifty feet above us, if you want to see a sculpture garden, or a history museum, or a remnant of the French Revolution, you queue up, pay your money, and snap your photos from behind the ropes.

Fifty feet above us, if you don't have a map to these places, you ask for directions.

Down here, if you want to see these things, you walk down an abandoned train tunnel, squeeze through a hole in the ground, and go find them. And if you don't have a map, you might meet the same fate as Philibert Aspairt. One day in 1793, Philibert went down into the catacombs and his torch went out. His body was found eleven years later.

There are very few chances to see something truly astounding on your own terms anymore. Today we live in the world of historic preservation, mass tourism, and liability laws. How often can you spend days wandering one of the most amazing urban spaces in the world, without a ticket taker or security guard to be found? This is the thought that finally gets us to dig through the debris at the entrance, take a deep breath, and crawl down the rabbit hole.

The Night Before

We're greeted by a small group of cataphiles, one of whom had already met Steve in New York. She is an immaculately dressed young French woman who instantly earns the nickname "Rosie" from me: it seems to fit the pink skull on the shirt of her otherwise jet-black outfit. With her are a couple of artists from a squat on Rue de Rivoli and a surprise: our friend Miru Kim.

I'd first met Miru a few months ago outside an abandoned chemical plant along the Queens waterfront, right after she'd moved to town. A few explorers, including Miru, were meeting there for the night to check the place out and also paint some signs for an upcoming event. A homeless guy had seen one of us enter and called us in to the police. I've never been able to figure out his motivation for this; my best guess is that he was hoping to get a free dinner from the precinct out of it. As a result, our party was soon broken up by four burly plain-clothes officers with steak-thick New York accents. As they took us outside, I saw a slight Korean girl sitting dejectedly by the entrance; she had come late and gotten caught before she'd found us.

"So listen," the cops told us. "You guys were spray painting, which is also illegal, so technically we could take you in on burglary because you were committing a crime while trespassing. Handcuff you, run the paperwork, and we'd all get a shitload of overtime. But . . . hey, we were kids once too."

Since at least two of us in the group were old enough to be pretty surprised if we got carded buying a six-pack, I suspected this last sentence should have been something more along the lines of "But . . . my wife will kill me if I don't get home in time to put the kids to bed again" or "But . . . I'm supposed to meet the boys for drinks at the titty bar after my shift," but I sure wasn't going to open my mouth and point this out. The cops took our IDs, gave us pink summons slips ordering us to appear at the Queens County Courthouse for a trespassing violation, and let us go. When Miru handed over her ID, I remember wondering what in the world this nice girl was doing here with our degenerate selves.

Back in Paris, while Miru, Steve, and I are making our hellos outside the restaurant, Rosie interrupts. "So, you want to climb a tower?" The last thirty-six hours have consisted of two transoceanic airline flights, a night in Iceland, three bars, one impromptu climb up a construction crane, and zero hours of sleep. So of course the answer is "Let's go."

"Great," says Rosie. "Then we are off to see Saint- Jacques."

The Tour Saint-Jacques is the only surviving part of a sixteenth-century Gothic church, the rest of which was demolished shortly after the French Revolution. Nicolas Flamel, the legendary alchemist, is supposedly buried underneath its floor, and Blaise Pascal, the mathematician and scientist who first proved the concept of a vacuum, used it to conduct his experiments on atmospheric pressure (today it also houses a meteorological laboratory). It's located inside a small park in the IVe arrondissement smack-dab in the middle of Paris, and I can already tell it will afford a magnificent view. It's one of the highest structures in the central part of the city, only about fifty feet shorter than the towers of Notre Dame, which rise a quarter-mile to the south. It's on one of the busiest thoroughfares, and despite it being well past midnight, I have no idea how we're going to pull this off without getting caught.

The first part is easy: somehow, Rosie's got a key to the park, which is closed after dark. But there's still the problem of getting past the eight-foot-tall solid metal barriers that surround the actual tower. If it were just me and Steve, we could probably find a way over, but we have the added challenge of getting the other four folks across. After a bit of poking around, Rosie somehow finds a shovel. Steve gets to digging. I am absolutely amazed that no passersby seem to find this a particularly noteworthy situation. If it were Midtown Manhattan instead of central Paris, we'd be in handcuffs by now. when I first learn different cities have vastly different cultures and approaches to the impromptu and unsanctioned use of public space—and Paris's approach can basically be summed up as "whatever."

After about ten minutes, Steve has managed to create a hole under the barrier big enough for me to slip through. I take the shovel and clear out the other side a bit, so that it's big enough for the others—one of whom is about six-foot-four—to get through as well. Everyone wiggles under, and we head to the tower.

The Tour Saint-Jacques is currently being inspected and restored, so we have the advantage of the scaffolding surrounding the tower, which makes the climb pretty easy. We make our way up the metal staircases, stepping over protruding gargoyles, and stopping occasionally to admire the detailed stonework close up. But the real goal, as always, is the top.

Because of the scaffolding, we can get a close-up look at the giant statue of Saint-Jacques added to the top of the tower in the nineteenth century. Rosie claims that if you look into his eyes you can tell he's crazy, but I don't really see it. I'm content to hang out and admire the view while the others take photographs. Paris is a compact city, and it seems like I'm visually stumbling upon another world landmark every thirty seconds: Notre Dame, the Louvre, the Eiffel Tower, the Panthéon. I start to disassociate from my immediate environment, start to orient myself in my greater surroundings and form the mental connection with the miles and miles of urbanity spread out around me.

My mild fugue state is broken by Steve's voice. "Hey, Moe,

hop up on top of that thing, would ya?" he says, pointing to a statue of a winged Gothic creature preening at the corner of the tower. I balk at the request. A big factor in getting to climb the tower was the scaffolding. The scaffolding was erected to assist with the historic preservation of the tower. So I feel like anything that might damage the sculptures—like sitting on them, for instance—is kind of bad manners. Miru, on the other hand, has no such qualms. Her eyes light up at Steve's suggestion, and she's soon making her way over to the statue.

I know she's going to add her own twist to the pose. One of her current art projects is the Naked City Spleen, which involves photographic nude self-portraits in abandonments, bridges, tunnels, and other interesting places. Artistic vision is a powerful thing, and Miru is one of those artists for whom the vision is so overwhelming that any obstacle that might compromise it must be overcome by any means necessary. For example, one time, for some reason, she decided her next project had to involve nude photos in pigpens—so she spent months calling every hog farm in the county, and when this didn't pan out, she drove to the middle of Iowa, snuck into an industrial farming facility, took off her clothes, and spent the next few hours snuggling naked with a bunch of three-hundred-pound sows. That's the extent Miru will go to in order to scratch her artistic itch. So niceties like historic preservation—or the fact that it's about ten degrees out—don't really register with her once she's hooked on to something.

You might think it strange to all of a sudden see one of the people you're hanging out with just up and take off her clothes, but it's all business: artists need models, and for this project Miru is both. It's kind of like watching a player-manager in baseball put down his clipboard, pick up a bat, and hit the on-deck circle. My main thought upon seeing this is: "Jesus, she must be cold as hell." Miru perches on top of the statue and manages to somehow hold her pose while riding the creature through three or four long-exposure shots. After the shoot she's shivering terribly, barely able to stand, but has a look on her face of pure satiation—the enjoyment of a job well done.

I've been to a lot of crazy places with a lot of crazy people: people who will climb thousand-foot rock walls with no safety gear, people who will fly halfway around the world to rappel into an abandoned hydroelectric tunnel or climb a national land-mark, people who will walk for miles through waist-deep, shit-filled sewers for no other reason than to see what's there. But if I really, really want to get somewhere, really want to do some-thing, give me two people with two things: Five-foot-nothing, ninety-eight-pounds-soaking-wet Miru with an unfulfilled artistic vision. And Steve with a full bottle of Jim Beam.

We descend the tower through the interior spiral staircase and then go out a small passageway back onto the scaffolding. We clamber back down to the park, attracting the glancing at-tention of a couple of people on the sidewalk. When we return to the scene of our excavation under the gate, the gang de-cides to try to fill the hole back in. I know that we'd been seen climbing down the scaffolding, and all I can think of is the irony of getting caught at the end of this excursion filling up the hole we dug to get in. I wait nervously while two of the others pack in dirt and debris, eventually creating a mound of detritus that looks exactly like someone is trying to hide a hole in the ground. Still, fifteen minutes later when we're safe, sip-ping tea back at the artist squat, I can forgive our new friends

SECTION OF THE MAP.

anything. It's been the most wonderful welcome to a city that I've ever had.

When we wake up the next day, Rosie gives us what will become our most precious possession: a flash drive containing the pdf of the highly detailed catacomb map, which we print out at a nearby shop. We also arm ourselves with plenty of food and water; rubber boots, dry socks, and an extra pair of shoes for the tunnels that are flooded; and an assortment of head-lamps, flashlights, and an open-flame carbide torch affixed to a hard hat. Feeling like Magellan about to round Tierra del Fuego, we hop on the Métro, disembark at the Porte d'Orléans station, and make our way down the tracks, through the tunnel, and into the rabbit hole.

After a little bit of crawling, the tunnel opens up enough for us to stand. We consult our map, get our bearings, and set off for our first destination. It's an easy decision. When you first gaze over a map of the catacombs, it's tough to ignore the areas marked by a skull and crossbones.

SIX

Most visitors to Paris know the catacombs as a forty-five-minute, eight-euro tour through the main Parisian ossuary—basically a giant underground boneyard. The Paris of the late 1700s was one of the densest urban areas in the world. There are many things about managing this kind of urban environment that we just take for granted nowadays—like what happens to what you flush down the toilet, or how freshwater suddenly appears after turning a handle on a faucet—that were developed as ingenious solutions to once intractable problems. Waterborne diseases like cholera would devastate urban communities, a result of sewage mixing with drinking water. Sewer systems, aqueducts—these were inventions of necessity, not convenience.

The ossuaries were another of these inventions of necessity. In the eighteenth century, Paris was the largest city in the world and, along with London, well along its path as the forebear of the modern metropolis. As such, it had to start dealing with one of the great problems of the modern metropolis: pollution. In addition to garbage, sewage, industrial waste, and all the other things we might think of as "pollutants" today, Paris had another pollutant that had to be dealt with: dead bodies. The main burial ground, Saints Innocents Cemetery, was smack-dab in the center of the city, right next to the main market. The size of Paris had exploded in the seventeenth and eighteenth centuries, tripling in population—and potential cadavers—during this time. The mass burials, each of which the parish church took a fee for, quickly overwhelmed the embattled cemetery. The smell of corpses was dominating the city center, with the putrefied remains causing disease. A solution was needed. Burials in the city proper were banned, new grounds were set up on what was then the outskirts of town, and Saints Innocents and other central cemeteries were exhumed, the bones treated and transferred underground to the old quarries.

Some of the remains of these six million or so dead Parisians can now be viewed on the official catacombs tour. There, the bones are neatly stacked, with the skulls sometimes being used to form patterns. It's a great tour, and an easy way to see an interesting part of the city. It's a little over a mile long—about one-half of 1 percent of the total length of the catacombs. We're headed to the ossuaries that aren't part of this tour. But first we have to figure out just how the hell to get there. The catacombs have almost two hundred miles of tunnels.

The first thing I notice in these tunnels is that I can see my breath. But it's not because of the temperature. While it's freezing out on the train tracks, this chill fades almost immediately upon the first turn after entering the rabbit hole. The reason I can see my breath is because of the humidity: it feels like we're almost swimming in the tunnels. I later learn that the catacombs, like natural caves, have a consistent year-round climate:

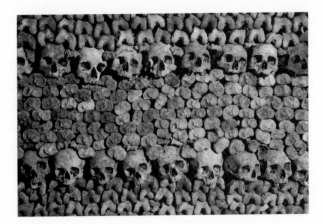

OFFICIAL TOUR BONES.
© *Lucinda Grange*

in this case about fifty-five degrees Fahrenheit and 98 percent humidity. The practical effect of this climate is weird: as we're traipsing through the tunnels we're sweating profusely, but when we stop to rest or take pictures we immediately start to get cold. We're constantly pausing in our activities to take off and put on layers. At one point, having been on the go for a while and not wanting to soak my pants in a tunnel flooded up to my thighs, I find myself running around in my underwear.

The second thing I notice is that I can't read the map—as I should have suspected, it's entirely in French, which I don't speak a word of. Steve has been reviewing his high school French by reading *The Three Musketeers* in the original, and has actually been managing to passably communicate with locals. Still, despite my linguistic disadvantage, I insist on being the navigator.

"What's a *chatière*?" I ask, after seeing that one is coming up ahead.

"Here, let me see," Steve says, making a grab for the map.

I don't let go but hold the map out to let him take a look. A *chatière* turns out to be a narrow passageway or other opening, specially dug to connect one part of the network to another. Essentially, it's a wormhole. There are dozens of *chatières* marked on the map. After an hour or two of arguing and winding our way through the tunnels, we find a narrow *chatière* in the tunnel wall, a few feet off the ground. We pull ourselves up and through, and find ourselves crawling on a bed of bones.

The remains of these departed souls didn't get the nice, neat treatment of the ones you pay to see. Instead of being neatly stacked along the wall, they're flung haphazardly into small rooms and tunnels. In one tunnel, the shaft that the bones were thrown down was never fully sealed up, and they reach from the tunnel back up into the shaft, somehow stuck to the wall. The result is eerie: crawling in the tunnel and looking up the shaft, it seems like you're about to be buried in an avalanche of centuries-old dry bones. There are almost no skulls—we were later told that pretty much all of them had been taken for souvenirs.

It's easy to forget the humanity involved in these tombs when the bones are all that's left of the people they belonged to, just random Parisians from centuries past. I imagine that this isn't what most people would want with their remains—to be buried with thousands of others, dug up as a public health hazard, and randomly thrown underground without even being stacked up nicely like some others. But there are other, more specific resting places in the catacombs, ones for people whose individual stories are pressed into service as stand-ins for the countless others who've been forgotten.

After leaving the ossuaries behind, we decide to seek out one of these, the tomb of the aforementioned Philibert Aspairt. Philibert is a legend, often referred to as one of the first cataphiles. When he disappeared in 1793, it was rumored he had entered the catacombs underneath the Val-de-Grâce military hospital, one of the oldest parts of the tunnels, and was looking for the wine cellars of the monks of Chartreux when his torch went out. When his body, reduced to a skeleton, was found in 1804, it was gripping a ring of keys, minutes from an exit. After hearing this story, I didn't feel silly for carrying three extra flashlights around with me.

After our time navigating around the catas, I can't imagine how Philibert ever had a chance at that wine. Even with the benefits of LED lights and an annotated map, it takes us hours to wind our way over to his tomb. The catacombs are incredibly mazy, with myriad dead ends, offshoots, intersections, and splits. It's not difficult to walk in most of the tunnels: they're a comfortable height, or close to it. But there are times the height of the tunnels suddenly lowers and we find ourselves crawling or doing what we deem the "cata walk," a quick crouching stride through tunnels about five feet in height. After about fifty feet of this, your ass and thighs feel like they've been lit on fire, but it's better than crawling. I'm a little concerned about Steve during these stretches, remembering his broken hip and limp after the tunnel run. I'm worried I sound like his mother when I bring it up, but he doesn't seem to mind.

"Yeah, the hip thing kind of comes and goes," he tells me. "Sometimes it really bothers me, sometimes it's totally fine. A lot of it depends on if I'm doing a lot of climbing and my leg muscles get really strong. That seems to help a lot. And of

FLOODED CATA TUNNEL.

course this doesn't hurt," he adds, holding up our half-drunk bottle of whiskey.

The variety of rooms we pass seems endless, ranging from little more than caves to elaborate multilevel structures that wouldn't be out of place in your average nineteenth-century Parisian aboveground building. But the variety of tunnels is even greater: two feet high to ten feet high; lined with concrete, brick, neatly stacked blocks of stone, and rough, naked limestone; boasting graffiti, carvings, and disused utility cables. These tunnels are the backbone of the catas—all of the different types forming an interconnected network.

That's what the catacombs are: a network. About the same time poor Philibert disappeared, what used to be an unrelated collection of quarries—mostly limestone and gypsum—was slowly and systematically being discovered, mapped, and stabilized in a process known as "the consolidations." Belowground uncertainty affected aboveground development: you never knew when you might start excavating for your dream house and hit a sinkhole caused by an improperly stabilized, long-forgotten limestone mine. When large-scale development started above what today is the XIVe arrondissement, these "consolidations" became needed. The result is a comprehensive network of stabilized tunnels dug mostly in the pursuit of these abandoned quarries. To this day it's overseen and maintained by the Inspection Générale des Carrières (IGC), the municipal agency that was first charged with the task of the consolidations. The IGC is actually the oldest government agency in France, surviving two empires, three monarchies, five republics, a Nazi-run military administration, and the seventy-one days of the socialist Paris Commune in 1871. Making sure the city doesn't fall into a hole in the ground is a fairly nonpolitical function.

Another result of this consolidation is the map we're using, which is essentially a version of one developed two centuries ago by the IGC, annotated and updated by various cataphiles over the years. And finally we make our way into a small room in the upper right-hand section of this map marked "Tombe de Philibert," where poor Philibert is memorialized by a tombstone set into a wall, with a short inscription telling his story. It reads:

> *À la mémoire de Philibert Aspairt perdu dans cette carrière le III nov^bre MDCCXCIII retrouvé onze ans après et inhumé en la même place le XXX avril MDCCCIV*
>
> (In memory of Philibert Aspairt, lost in this quarry on November 3, 1793, found eleven years later and buried in the same place on April 30, 1804)

Nobody really knows if his bones are actually buried behind the wall with the tombstone set into it. Cataphiles aren't shy about breaking through walls; they do it all the time to create the *chatières*. We later learn the wall behind the tombstone has been dug through twice. But nobody has ever found Philibert's remains.

LA TOMBE DE PHILIBERT.
© Eric Ruggiero 2012 –
www.ericruggiero.com

By the time we make our way over to Philibert, we're exhausted. We thought we had prepped correctly for the trip but didn't count on the sheer amount of time we'd be down there. It's not my fault. I've done a great job navigating, with Steve's impromptu half-hour photo sessions the main culprit. After a quick hello to the remains of our predecessor (and another twenty minutes taking photos), we start heading back south to the entrance. We still have plenty of time in Paris. We can afford to leave further exploration for another day.

Steve and I emerge from the same hole we went in about twelve hours earlier. What I really want to do is crawl up out of the abandoned railroad tracks, hail the nearest cab, and say, "To the Louvre!" Crawling out of the tracks is accomplished without incident. Then I try to hail a cab. The driver takes one look at us, covered in dirt from our twelve hours underground, mumbles a few words, and continues on his way. I catch the eye of another cabdriver. This one doesn't even slow down. Defeated, we take the subway, arriving thirty minutes later down the street from the Louvre. I walk in wearing the same clothes that I've just tried to hail the cab in, although I do ditch the helmet with the carbide torch attached and send it back to the hotel with Steve, who wants to head back rather than go see an art museum. The ticket taker doesn't look at me twice.

This is the best idea I've had in Paris so far. There are two juxtapositions that make this so. The first is that during the entire time in the catas, the foremost thing on my mind was: "Don't get lost." At almost every turn we were stopping to check the map and make sure that we knew where we were. When I get to the Louvre, I don't even glance at a map. After twelve hours of pinpoint navigation, I want to just wander and see what I run into.

The second is the fact that in one day I can see the best of what two vastly different cultural worlds have to offer. In order to truly get to know a city, you have to try to obtain the broadest experience possible. We have a great opportunity to visit a side of Paris few get to see, and I am determined to make the most of it. But I also want to spend some time visiting the highbrow side of Paris, the side everybody gets to see. Both kinds of excursions have equal importance in my mind: they're flip sides of the same coin. And when I think about it, I realize this interpretation could quite possibly be literal, just substituting "ground" for "coin." Much of the underground world we were in had been created as an effect of excavating the stone used in constructing the world on the surface. I wonder if some of the walls of the Louvre are made of the stone that used to fill some of the hollow spaces of the world that I had walked through a short time ago—the world that's the side effect of the creation of buildings like this one, one that houses such incredible works of art and beauty. But that underground world also has art; much of it has been turned into something beautiful too. We've only just started our exploration of the catacombs, haven't yet seen any of this beauty firsthand. But we're about to.

SEVEN

The more we saw of the catacombs, the more we wanted to see. The main attraction that we had missed on our first trip was the "Times Square" of the catacombs: the main rooms not too far from the entrance where most of the young Parisians will go to meet up for parties or longer excursions. It's also the only part of the catas that's regularly patrolled by police, although getting caught in the catacombs is not a huge deal, with a civil fine—along the lines of a parking violation—and perhaps an escort to the surface being the only real consequences.

We meet up with Rosie and her friends again the next day to get some pointers. This time they have us meet them at another squat, this one an abandoned bank. A young, well-dressed guy greets us at the door.

"So how are you able to live here?" I ask. The bank is right in the middle of the city, in a tony neighborhood that did not seem like it would easily let real estate go for free to a bunch of squatters.

"Oh," he tells us in English, "so it is like this. There is a bank, yes? And the bank does not want to be in the building here anymore. So they sell the building to a man to do condo. But instead of condo, we come do squat." This sentence is said with a certain finality to it—similar to how you might end a story about renting your last apartment with "So then I signed the lease."

Later I ask Rosie how long they've been there, thinking it's a temporary crash pad until the developer's ready to get going.

"Hmm, maybe six months?" she replies. It turns out that not only are the laws on squatting incredibly liberal in Paris, the whole can't-be-bothered attitude extends well beyond recreational trespassing to that of the more permanent variety as well. Later on, we'd meet another guy who would manage to live rent-free, complete with electricity, running water, and Wi-Fi, in his own two-bedroom house on the Left Bank for almost a year before the city caught on and politely asked him to move.

We start to talk about the catacombs again: what there is to see and where to see it. It's now Friday. Rosie tells us that there are usually more people—and therefore more cops—on the weekends, so we decide to take Saturday off and prep for a longer trip starting Sunday afternoon.

Our previous trip seemed short, like we didn't really see much but still took twelve hours. We know that if we want to do a truly comprehensive excursion, we are going to have to sleep down there. I tried to take a nap once on our earlier trip. But no matter where I lay down, whether on limestone, dirt, or the solid stone benches that line some of the rooms, it was like the floor was sucking the heat right out of my body. I need a sleeping bag anyway, so we hit a camping store to pick up some gear.

Steve does not get a sleeping bag. "The dollar's at 1.40 to the euro. This is way too expensive," he says. He instead opts for a cheap emergency foil blanket and a sleeping pad.

We set out from the hotel mid-afternoon. The trip doesn't start out so good; we try to get to the abandoned tracks that lead to the entrance a different way from usual. A couple hours, a locked gate, and several confused passersby later, we decide to forget our bright idea, walk about a mile to the entrance we know, and go from there. By the time we get down onto the tracks, it's dark already. Still, despite this false start, we're determined to spend as much time as it takes to see what we want to see.

Most of the noteworthy areas in the catacombs are specifically indicated on the map, using the names for the places that the cataphiles have come up with. The general area we're headed to on the map is dense with these annotations, with rooms bearing names like "Salle Marie Rose," "Le Cellier," "La Plage," and "La Chambre Egyptienne." It takes about thirty minutes of walking to get from the entrance to this "Times Square" area. And like the real Times Square, when you first arrive, the visual overload is stunning. Entire underground caverns are covered with murals, sculptures, and art—works of incredible quality despite being done on a stone surface, in 98 percent humidity, and completely without the benefit of natural light. It takes a special kind of artistic vision, one Miru would no doubt appreciate, to spend this kind of time, energy, and skill for an audience of pretty much yourself and some random people who happen to enjoy going into tunnels. Just for starters, you have to spend at least an hour getting there before you even reach your potential canvas, first lugging your paint, lighting, and provisions down some abandoned train tracks and into a hole in the ground, and then winding your way through a tunnel network to your destination.

But the art isn't the only thing covering the walls in the catacombs. Much more frequently found throughout the tunnels are graffiti tags. It's interesting: a stretch of tunnel or cavern wall will generally be either spotless or completely covered in tags. There seems to be a certain social agreement down in the catas: people get to enjoy the freedom to paint and write graffiti to their hearts' content, yet some of the tunnels are left to be enjoyed in their natural state.

It's not just the catacombs that the cataphiles graffiti, though. For instance, when we went up the Tour Saint-Jacques, it was tough to miss the seventy-foot-high letters on the netting surrounding the scaffolding reading: *"Sexe, Drogues et Catas. F.C."* F.C. stands for *Frotte Connard*, which translated literally is "Rub, asshole," but which Rosie told us should be read as something more like "Erase this, you asshole!" It's a challenge to the anti-graffiti crowd to try to erase their stuff. Still, as rude as that message on the scaffolding might be, the tower itself is untouched—again, a nice balance of expression and respect.

Steve spends hours taking photos of the art in these rooms, but I don't mind at all. It would take days for me to get bored in here. Finally, we pack up the photo gear and get going. We're off to our bedroom: the bunker used by the Germans during the Nazi occupation of Paris.

. . .

There were actually numerous bunkers used in Paris during World War II. A few connect to the catacombs, including a large one used by the Nazis, and another, slightly smaller one that was used by the French Resistance. We couldn't get into the French Resistance bunker: the entrances had all been sealed up by the IGC. Rosie told us that about a week ago there was a way in, but it had just been filled up with concrete. That's the way the catas are: parts are sealed up by the IGC and (less often, unfortunately) parts are opened back up by the cataphiles. For tourists like us, what we get to see is pretty much just the luck of the draw.

The German bunker is in the northernmost part of the catacombs, with the "Times Square" area, where we currently are, near the south. We have a better idea of how to get around the catas than on our last trip, but it still takes us hours of navigating before we get there. This bunker is open—but just barely. The only way in involves squeezing through a tiny *chatière*, which scrapes both of my shoulders at once. Despite being thoroughly exhausted at this point, I refuse to make the place our bedroom. I just can't handle the thought of three inches being the difference between waking up tomorrow and enjoying a nice meal and a glass of wine after finishing our trip, and being buried alive.

We take a while to check out the bunker. There's nothing to indicate it was ever a Nazi quarters, with the only things even being German the words *Notausgang* ("Emergency Exit"), which is written on the metal doors, and *Rauchen Verboten* ("No

Smoking") and *Ruhe* ("Quiet"), which are stenciled on the wall in several places. I wonder what happened to the Nazi symbols or relics: if the Free French or the IGC or even the cataphiles destroyed them, or if there even were any to begin with.

After leaving the bunker, we head to a nice-looking room not too far away. It's strangely reminiscent of an old bathroom, with what looks like a stone sink filled with water. Unfortunately, while nice and roomy, it smells like an old bathroom as well. We decide not to sleep there, either, and end up bedding down in a humble sanctuary a short distance away.

You would think after several hours of trekking, it would not be too difficult to fall asleep in a cave with no natural light. But there's a problem: it is absolutely freezing. Even with the sleeping bag, which is supposedly good for temperatures down to just above the freezing point, after about ten minutes I feel like I'm Harry Potter having my soul sucked out by a Dementor. I end up wearing my coat, hat, and two pairs of socks to bed. Steve shivers all night, wrapped in his pitiful-looking foil blanket. I know it's fifty-five degrees, and am pretty sure there's no real danger of hypothermia or anything, but I still feel kind of bad. Not bad enough to offer to share my sleeping bag, though. Later we learn the trick is to bring a hammock; there are several places where the cataphiles have set up hammock hooks. As long as your body isn't actually making contact with the ground, it's not so bad.

Despite tossing and turning all night, we still somehow end up sleeping for twelve hours. But that's OK: our big constraint isn't time but water. We decide we're staying down and seeing what we can find until we run dry.

We spend the day just wandering, exploring the amazing array of spaces that the catas have to offer. The Class Galleries, where for decades each graduating class of the Mineralogical Institute has painted a new mural on the wall of an out-of-the-way stretch of tunnel. The Salle Z, with its huge archways and twelve-foot high ceilings, a welcome relief from watching our heads in the tunnels all day. The Abri Laval, with its tiled floor, and a nameless room that's painted as a night scene—entirely in a calm dark blue except for a moon and stars (and an *F.C.*) on the wall. We also run into a mural of the Statue of Liberty during our meanderings. It makes me just a tad homesick.

We run out of food, and water, and dry socks, but still can't tear ourselves away. It's only after the lights on our headlamps start to dim that we decide we had better start making our way back to the rabbit hole. Finally, on our backup lights, we feel the cool air of the outside world, and a couple minutes later crawl out onto the abandoned train tracks. We've emerged from our entombment after about thirty hours. Steve catches a cab (learning from our last excursion, this time he's taken both a clean jacket and pair of pants with him), but I want to walk home. The route back to our hotel takes me directly over the amazing area where we have spent the last two days. I don't need a map. My time spent figuring my way beneath Paris has somehow given me an almost instinctual sense of navigation and understanding of the city streets. I realize Paris has clicked for me: I completely understand its geography. I may not know all the shortcuts, but I know I'll never really be lost again.

The moment when you realize you truly know something

on a deeper level than before is an almost mystical experience. It's one of those things that make life worthwhile. My goal on this trip wasn't to spend a certain amount of time underground or walk a certain length of the catacombs. My goal was to get to know Paris: the Paris above and the Paris below. As I turn the last corner back to my hotel on Rue Saint-Jacques—where yesterday I made the exact same turn fifty feet below—I realize I can leave the city with no regrets.

We end up taking one more short trip into the catacombs with a different friend of ours, David. There's plenty written about the catacombs—in fact, David has contributed to some of the books—but unfortunately for me they're all in French. So while our hours spent exploring on our own were great, I'm excited to go with an expert guide who can actually explain to us in depth what we're seeing. And instead of having to schlep down the train tracks again, this time we're going the fun way.

"Yes, this is it," David says, looking at a manhole in the sidewalk. Using a "popper"—basically a piece of metal attached to a strong piece of cord—he yanks the cover up and off. It's about noon, on a moderately trafficked commercial street. We head down, and David asks a couple of passersby to kick the manhole back into place. Apparently this is par for the course in Paris.

There is only one place we haven't seen that we want to: underneath the Val-de-Grâce, the church turned hospital where Philibert used to be the doorkeeper. David sets the pace.

Throughout the convoluted, hours-long journey he doesn't glance at the map once.

On this excursion we get one of those surprise glimpses into history that make these kinds of trips so worthwhile. Every time a tunnel was inspected, stabilized, and mapped, notes were carved on the wall, including the initials of the head engineer and the year of the work. Most large tunnels also have the name of the street they run under engraved on the wall—a great help when trying to follow the map.

But on this trip, we're running into engravings without a year, instead having a one- or two-digit number followed by an R. But David explains: these are also years, just using a different calendar. The French Republican calendar. We already knew that the memorial on Philibert's tomb was inscribed well after April 30, 1804, the year of his burial, but if we didn't we'd know now. This is because there was no April 30, 1804, in Paris. Philibert's burial date would have been written as the tenth of Floréal, Year 12R—or the twelfth year of the French Republic.

Finally, we duck under some cables, navigate a shallow archway filled three-quarters of the way with water, wiggle through a *chatière* that never seems to end, and emerge into a raw, cavern-like space. A carving on the wall reads *"Grande Cour du Val-de-Grâce"*—Grand Courtyard of the Val-de-Grâce.

During the revolution, many of the old symbols of Church and monarchy were ransacked and appropriated for more public uses—Notre Dame was looted and then did a short stint as a warehouse, for instance. The Val-de-Grâce escaped this fate. Even though it was built as a church and convent, it was left untouched by the Republicans, probably due to the fact that the

REPUBLICAN CALENDAR DATING.

resident Benedictine nuns also served as nurses for those in-
jured in the revolution. During the Republican era it was officially converted into a military hospital, which it still serves
as today.

The French Revolution took place shortly after the IGC
was formed and the consolidations began. But that doesn't
mean there aren't stories and history from these quarries that
predate this. The stories of the area we're in reach back to over
a century before the formation of the IGC, to Queen Anne of
Austria and King Louis XIII (you might know them best as
the king and queen in *The Three Musketeers*). David tells us the
story of how the Hapsburg queen conspired with her Spanish
relatives against the French king in these old quarries, later
building the church above in thanks for bearing a son after
twenty-three years of childless marriage, and retiring to this
building after this son, the future king Louis XIV, came of age
and ascended to the throne.

Still, while tales of subterranean royal intrigue are all very romantic, the most interesting thing we come across is much more mundane. It turns out we get to see where the queen's other dirty business ended up. In a small room we see the bottom of a well—a well that David tells us was dug as repository for the queen's chamber pot.

EIGHT

Amsterdam, January 2006

We've got a couple days left before our flight back, and after our marathon trips we're pretty catacombed out. So we decide to hit Amsterdam, mostly just to relax and see a new city. Stumbling around on our last night, we see a bar that looks friendly and not too touristy. Each beer comes in a different-shaped glass. I order two beers of the coolest-shaped glass variety, for which I have to leave my ID as a deposit, and we sit down at one of the large wooden tables.

I have just read *The Game*, a popular book about a society of "pickup artists." It's been years since I've been single, and the last time was in college, where I lived in a hippie Jewish cooperative house that threw parties where making out with the person next to you was treated as just slightly more forward than shaking hands, and the merits of non-monogamy was a regular conversation—in short, not a place where you had to try too hard. So when a friend insisted I borrow the book shortly after I separated from Leigh, I figured, sure, I could probably use a few pointers. While it's very, very heavy on dudespeak, which can make it a tough read for someone such as myself, who had grown up in a household where *Free to Be . . . You and Me* was a present on my fourth birthday, the basic point of it is fairly universal, involving how to make yourself a generally more attractive person. But there's also a bunch of advice and pointers about how to interact with girls and quickly get them to like you—aka "game." I decide I am going to impress Steve by putting my newfound "game" to work on the cute Dutch girl who is part of the group that has sat down next to us. I am normally way too shy for stuff like this, but the combination of alcohol and a foreign country serves to ease my trepidation. I mentally review some of the pointers and lessons from the book. "Here, watch this," I whisper to Steve.

To my utter amazement the shit actually works. I read her palm, making up some stuff about how "intuitive" and "driven" she is. I guess the number between 1 and 10 she's thinking of (if it's not 7 it's 4. If it's not 4 it's "Wow, you know how unusual you are?"). I stop paying attention to her and charm her friends for a while with stories about New York until she's nudging me to pay attention to her again. This girl is into me. I slowly see what the book describes as a "doe-eyed deer" look come into her eyes. She tells me she has a boyfriend. As we leave, about five beers into the night, I somehow gather up my nerve and tell her to kiss me good-bye anyway. She does.

Steve's response to this is to jump into an open construction ditch in the ground. I'm confused. I wait for him to stop monkeying around and climb out. "What was that all about?" I ask.

"Arghhhh. God damn it!" he responds. "How did you do that?"

"Do what?" I reply.

"Get that girl to kiss you?"

"Dude, why are you so upset? You have a totally hot girl-friend."

"Moe, I had to beg Molly to go out with me for, like, six months. That girl is just as hot and you made out with her after two hours." I suppose this explains the frustration, but not why he responds to it by jumping into a hole in the ground.

But Steve has not even come close to working out his issues. As we walk through town we come to a building covered in scaffolding, which Steve starts climbing up without even pausing to look around for cops. I don't really want to follow, mostly because I'm pretty drunk, but I feel obligated. We've been equal partners on this adventure so far, and I don't want to end it by being the one hanging out on the ground waiting for Steve to finish the last climb. So I start up the scaffolding.

And it's wonderful. Everything is easy. There's no freezing, no nervousness affecting me physically. It turns out there really is something to the expression "Dutch courage." I can't imagine why I haven't done this before.

Climbing while inebriated is something I really shouldn't recommend, but I will anyway. Now, I'm not talking about drunkenly trying to scale a rock wall at Yosemite or anything, but in those instances when the mental barriers are significantly greater than the physical barriers, the combination of booze and adrenaline can be magic. The mental barriers are washed away, while the physical barriers are still a long way away from being truly tested. I don't always like doing it—as with all drugs, it can serve as a cheap shortcut for something that would be much more satisfying if accomplished naturally— but there have been so many times I've indulged, I can't in good conscience make judgments.

Still, I can understand the disapproval. The first time I let it slip to my grandmother Ethel that I had done this, I received the following admonishment by e-mail: "You know, Mose, I hope you have gained some common sense since this. Are you trying to give your poor grandmother a heart attack? You know you should not drink and climb, just like you should not drink and drive."

Steve ends up on one tower while I end up on another. We hang out for a bit and then start the descent. We're both exhausted when we get down. I notice the church is actually called the Mozeshuis, or "Moses House," in Dutch. It feels like a sign.

Steve seems to have gotten whatever it was out of his system, and we walk down the street for a bit, heading into a bar on the corner.

"So how the hell did you do that?" Steve asks after we sit down.

"I just climbed up after you. It wasn't that tough. You aren't that much better of a climber than me, you know."

"No, you idiot, I mean the girl. How'd you get her to kiss you? You know you acted like a complete asshole to her half the time."

I don't really know how to respond. I don't want to tell him I learned it in a book. I delay by taking a slow sip of my beer, affording me a bit of time to plan my response.

"Dude, I wasn't an asshole. I just acted like I knew I was cooler than her. Really, that's it. Just pretend like you're the coolest guy in the room. You probably are the coolest guy in the room anyway."

Steve thinks for a minute and then busts me. "Oh, come on. I don't show people I'm cool by reading their palms and shit."

"Yeah, but that's just so I have an excuse to talk about feelings and personalities and stuff like that. You've got to break the 'Hey, what's your name? Where're you from? Come here often?' kind of mold."

"Yeah, you know, I guess that makes sense. I dunno, I love Molly, but sometimes I wonder if I'm wasting the years I should be doing this stuff on one girl."

"Yeah, I get that. I mean, I remember being in the exact same situation a couple years ago when I was about your age, thinking the exact same thing."

"What? You're great at this. I mean, you just got some totally random Dutch girl to kiss you. And you haven't combed your hair in about a week and a half."

"Nah, this is kind of recent. I haven't really been single for that long."

"Oh, yeah? How long were you going out with your girlfriend for?" Steve asks.

"Awhile," I reply. "And, uh, it was more like a wife than a girlfriend."

"Wait, you were married? When was this?"

I realize that despite spending countless hours sharing adventures on two continents with this guy, I haven't ever mentioned the first thing about my personal life. I remember reading somewhere that women bond by talking and men bond by doing. I don't know how often this particular rule actually holds true, but I do think that anyone seeking to prove it could do worse than looking at the last six months of Steve's and my friendship.

"Uh, well, actually up until the middle of last year." I don't mention that I'm still technically married—that if I had happened to misjudge our climb and drunkenly plummet from the church tower, Leigh would be the one inheriting my student loan debt and the beige pullout couch I picked up off the sidewalk.

"So why'd you do that?" Steve asks.

"What?"

"Get divorced. Well, actually, wait a minute. This is kind of blowing my mind. Let's start with why you got married."

Why I'm getting divorced is easy. Leigh has decided she's fallen in love with a coworker almost two decades her senior and who is, most creepily, a dead ringer for her dad. To be fair, if this hadn't happened it would eventually have been something else—Leigh and I had been unhappy with each other for a while without either of us really realizing it—but the overall repulsiveness of this particular situation made it easy to finally effect the split.

But why I got married is tougher. There was never any romantic reason, any real spark between us. When we first met in college we were great friends, but I never thought of pursuing a relationship with Leigh. She pursued one with me, though, and we eventually started going out. And from there I just gave into inertia and insecurity. I got married because I was scared—because I needed security, stability, support. Because I just didn't know what else I was supposed to do, because those same invisible boundaries that kept me off the places I wanted to go also kept me in a place I didn't want to be—at least, not at that time and not with that person. I ended up traveling down a life path I just didn't know how not to follow. I was going to grow up, get an office job, and marry a nice, nonreligious Jewish girl. So I married the first one I came across who made me laugh.

As I lay out the story to Steve, I realize it's my first time telling it, even to myself. I realize how constrained I've been, and how free I am now. I don't just have the whole city to explore. I have the whole world. I have churches to climb, *chatières* to crawl through, strangers to kiss. There's tourist season and a semester of grad school to get through back in New York, but that's a matter of months. There's no doubt in my mind what's coming after that. I look at Steve. "So where're we going next?"

NINE

New York City, 2006

New York has the largest and greatest variety of bridges in the world. Cantilevered bridges, arch bridges, swing bridges, lift bridges, drawbridges, and our seven huge suspension bridge masterpieces. We have bridges for trains, pedestrians, automobiles, bicycles, trucks, and aqueducts. We have bridges that are overused, underused, and completely abandoned. We have bridges built as engineering marvels from before the Civil War, bridges built as engineering marvels a century after it, and plenty of simply good, functional, plain old bridges. We have four of the former longest suspension bridges in the world, two of the former longest steel-arch bridges in the world, the former longest cantilevered span in the world, the former longest vertical-lift bridge, the largest vertical-lift bridge, the strongest steel-arch bridge, two of only four retractile bridges in the country, and arguably the most famous and recognized bridge in the world. I've always thought New York, not Pittsburgh, should be nicknamed the "City of Bridges." I've walked numerous times across almost all of the nineteen different bridges that lead into the island of Manhattan. I've never been on top of one. But that's about to change.

Steve pours us a drink at his loft, and we plan out our approach. Our goal is the Manhattan Bridge—a tall, slender structure north of the Brooklyn Bridge that carries seven lanes of traffic, four subway tracks, and two bike and pedestrian paths between downtown Brooklyn and Manhattan's Chinatown. We're due to meet up with Dsankt, an adventurer and photographer currently in town, to make the attempt. Dsankt runs the website Sleepycity.net, which details his adventures in storm drains, subways, catacombs, and other assorted off-limits places around the world.

There are a lot of different types of people involved in urban exploration—I've met everyone from artists to ironworkers to doctors—but at its essence, the urban exploration subculture is a branch of greater nerddom. An adventurous branch, to be sure, but a branch nonetheless. You can readily tell this through the most common day job among the crowd, which is (like Dsankt) far and away computer programmer; in fact, sometimes urban exploration is referred to as "reality hacking" or "place hacking." The creative problem-solving aspect, the search for small holes in security to exploit and infiltrate, is what attracts a lot of these people to the hobby. Or it might just be the chance to come as close as you can to playing Dungeons & Dragons in real life.

But another way to tell this is by the amazing array of goofy monikers explorers have taken, which they will refer to themselves as with a complete lack of self-consciousness. I'm not just talking about a silly nickname used among their particular group of friends—there are grown men who will introduce themselves with names like "Shadowstalker," "Geronimo-X," or (far and away my favorite) "Spungletrumpet." Some of these monikers come out of the graffiti or art worlds, but most are just the same online handles people use on the urban exploration message boards. Discussing this with Molly once, she told me, "Oh, yeah. If Steve called himself, like, 'Dr. Infiltration' or something, he'd never have gotten to first base."

Generally the folks who are trying to gain some artistic or academic credibility from the hobby (like Steve, who is constantly trying to sell his photographs) will start using what's on their birth certificate or at least a reasonable derivative, but not always. One of the most influential people in the scene, the late Jeff Chapman, was actually appointed a director of the board of the Toronto Architectural Conservancy despite being best known as "Ninjalicious."

Another one of these exceptions is Dsankt. Notoriously secretive, he guards his face and real name with a zealousness usually reserved for supervillains and turncoat mobsters in the witness protection program. His bio on his Facebook page is of a child with Down's syndrome taken on a worldwide adventure by the Make-A-Wish Foundation. If I let slip so much as his first initial or the color of his hair, I'd never hear the end of it.

Dsankt is one of urban exploration's heavy hitters—and like most of these heavy hitters, he's a young, itinerant Australian and a member of the Cave Clan, a group formed in Melbourne, Australia, in the mid-eighties. The Cave Clan's primary purpose is to go in drains—their unofficial motto is "Go in Big

Drains!"—although they're usually game for pretty much any-where interesting and off-limits. This isn't the first time we've hosted one of their members. A guy who goes by the name Sio-logen came to town earlier. Silo is largely considered the good-will ambassador for urban exploration and one of its main trailblazers—someone who's been in five hundred storm drains around the world and needs very little prompting to go in one more. He travels around the world going in drains because he just loves drains—the same way some people love to travel around visiting baseball stadiums or ancient ruins. He has a nearly incomprehensible accent, a product of some strange mix of his childhood in Canada, Scotland, Trinidad, and Australia. Silo's favorite topics are storm drains, tits, abandoned subway stations, and booze, in that order.

One time we're talking about the hazards of exploring storm drains. Silo can rattle off a list of them, as well as stories of near-death experiences involving each one—rain, bad air, accidentally falling in a collection pit, which is a giant hole in the ground filled with a combination of sewage and storm drain runoff. This is all par for the course, part of the standard prattle that explorers have over a beer. I've heard some of these stories before and am tuning out a little bit.

Then I hear, "Yeah, the only part of this that really bothers me is the itchy bumhole problem."

I know of no such problem. This gets my attention.

Silo explains. "You know. The itchy bumhole problem. You're always having to keep yourself from scratching at it or you'll spread the worms."

Silo sees the expression on my face, which causes him to

adopt a tone like he's trying to explain to a four-year-old that there's no monster in his closet. "Look, mate, I'm not talking about some huge African tapeworm here. Just your average pinworms. You're always picking them up in the drains. Nothing really awful—they just make your bumhole itch."

I'm a pretty novice drainer. I've been in a few, looking forward to being in a few more. I'm even looking forward to being able to trade some near-death stories with the likes of Silo someday. But the casualness with which he mentions intestinal parasites as a standard hazard of the trade makes me reconsider pursuing this particular side project.

Luckily, Dsankt doesn't have much interest in an easy drain trip, parasites or no. He's already spent the last week running through live subway tunnels and exploring underground rivers. After he gets done with New York, his plan is to infiltrate a semi-abandoned power plant in Niagara Falls, rappel into a gigantic, century-old drainage tunnel over one hundred feet below the surface, make his way through this tunnel to the back of the actual falls themselves—and then somehow manage to get back out. We don't want to disappoint the guy: it's time to step it up a bit and shoot for something new. The Manhattan Bridge.

We're spooked. I've never climbed a suspension bridge before, although one bitterly cold night Steve, another friend, and I summited the Hell Gate Bridge—an arch bridge that's part of a rail viaduct between Queens and the Bronx. The Hell Gate is a beast. Opened in 1917, it consists of twenty thousand tons of steel, and according to *Discover* magazine, if all humans disappeared from the earth tomorrow, a thousand years later the Hell Gate would be the last human-made structure still standing in the city. It's the direct inspiration for Australia's Sydney Harbour Bridge, a similar, if somewhat larger, version of the same design, completed sixteen years later. The Sydney Harbour Bridge is the most famous landmark on the continent, and the most famous bridge in the entire hemisphere. The Hell Gate, if I'm being generous, is perhaps the fifth or sixth most notable bridge within a ten-mile radius. This is how head and shoulders above the rest of the world New York is when it comes to its bridges.

People have been climbing the bridges of New York City ever since they've been built, and even before. Prior to the completion of the Brooklyn Bridge span in 1883, thrill seekers were, for a short time, permitted to ascend one tower via a temporary spiral staircase and take a footbridge, constructed for the use of the bridge workers, over the East River to the other tower. Perusing newspaper archives from the turn of the twentieth century turns up headlines like "FIGHT WITH MADMAN ON BRIDGE TOWER: Demented Russian Walks up Cable of Williamsburg Bridge," "WOMAN'S DARING FEAT ON BRIDGE CABLE: Climbs with Man 335 Feet to Williamsburg Tower," and "TERRIFIED BRIDGE PAINTERS: A Finnish Sailor Walked up the Cable, Stood on His Head on the Tower and Waved His Legs." (This last article ends with the sentence "To-day Hingrend will be examined as to his sanity.") In more recent times, there was a secret society formed in San Francisco in 1977 called the San Francisco Suicide Club, which, among other clandestine activities, made a sport in the 1970s and 1980s of getting up the type of bridges that, since September 2001, have been subject to the kind of security usually found in federal prisons.

John Law is a former Suicide Club member, one of the founders of the Burning Man festival, and the author of *The Space Between*, four short stories about bridges. For over two decades, from 1977 to 2001, he scaled dozens of bridges from the Golden Gate to the Verrazano-Narrows. He recalls how he first fell in love:

> *I was the best climber in Big Rapids, MI. Possibly the only climber. There were no cliffs or really much in the way of rock walls anywhere about, and the culture of climbing that one might find in, say California or any other state with mountains, was nowhere to be seen in the area. I could climb things like nobody's business: trees, buildings, telephone poles, swing-set structures. . . . . maybe a bridge? Nobody else much cared. Not only was climbing things NOT cool in Big Rapids, like say, being good at football or maybe hockey was, but it was actually a bit frowned upon by my peers. They thought I was kinda nuts. I could care less. I had liked climbing things, anything really, ever since at age five I had climbed the tall swing-set pipes, all the way to the top. Then, sliding down, legs wrapped tightly around the pipe, I experienced a fabulous tingling in my crotch. It was the first time I felt that particular sensation, one I still identify with climbing . . .*
>
> *The attraction of the Maple Street Bridge was then, two fold for me. Just getting out onto those mysterious, heavily overgrown islands was part of it. Maybe no*

one had ever been out there! Also, the idea of climbing onto that massive, imposing structure was very enticing. Knowing how climbing made me feel, well . . . you can imagine. Could it really be done? I determined to find out. I was eleven years old and that was how I saw things.

Steve has already climbed a few of the suspension bridges, and had actually been up the Manhattan Bridge before, but now there's a new obstacle: security cameras by the four possible starting points to the climb.

Now, security cameras are not the end point of discussion when it comes to getting somewhere other people think you shouldn't be; they're more like the first, tentative salvo of the security state. It's pretty unlikely anyone is watching them consistently, if at all. Instead, they're usually there to record evidence in case a crime is actually committed. These cameras are covered by an opaque dome and are pretty high up, so I can't tell what they're pointing at. Probably they're just recording the pedestrian pathway in case there's a mugging. And even more probably, nobody will ever even check the footage unless there's cause to, which we certainly don't intend to give them. But they weren't there a few months ago, and I can't help worrying that my conventional wisdom has no bearing on things that might be considered terrorist targets.

"So why do you want to do this bridge if you've been up it already?" I ask Steve. I tend to be very goal-oriented about these adventures. Once a particular place is checked off the list, I don't much see the point in going back.

"My pictures from the last time suck," he answers. "I've

actually been wanting to climb it to get better ones for a while, but I was away and then I was out of commission with that hip thing for a bit. But what I really want to climb is the Brooklyn Bridge. That one I've never done. I can't really imagine I'd get away with it, though. But I've thought a lot about it."

I've thought a lot about it too. There's only one way up the Brooklyn Bridge: to climb up on the suspension cables, navigate around the suicide guards—metal gates on the cables designed specifically to keep people from scaling them—and then balance on the cables, hang on to the guide wires for dear life, and hope a gust of wind doesn't come along. It's no laughing matter: in 1999, Robert Landeta, a twenty-seven-year-old who wanted to set a Guinness World Record for most bridges climbed in one day, decided to start with the Brooklyn Bridge that morning. He made it about two-thirds of the way up the cable before he fell to his death. Landeta did the climb in broad daylight, had a friend videotape it, and even attracted a small crowd of curious onlookers egging him on. But this was a different time. Before 2001, people bungee jumped off bridges in the middle of the night with a "Don't ask, don't tell" understanding with the police. But now we're deep into the security age. Not long ago three guys were arrested after being seen coming down from the top of the Williamsburg Bridge, another suspension bridge, about a mile north of the Manhattan Bridge. Our plan to get up the Manhattan Bridge tonight seems risky enough. Climbing the Brooklyn seems insane.

"You know there's no way to get up without being seen, right?" I say to Steve. "But maybe you could get away with it if you pretended you were crazy or something."

"Yeah, I thought of that. But the thing is I really want photos. So my plan's to take an old camera, get my pictures, and then toss the camera off the side, swallow my memory card, and pretend I'm a potential suicide. I'm guessing I'll just get sent for a psych evaluation and get out of the mental hospital after a day or so."

Hey, sounds like a plan.

We meet Dsankt on a side street in Brooklyn and head to the Manhattan Bridge. I'm incredibly jittery. Steve and I banter back and forth about the pros and cons of taking a shot at the climb, or our backup plan of ascending the construction site just north of the approach. This debate is peppered with talk about girls, traveling, and anything else we can think of that will take our mind off police SWAT teams and Rikers Island cellblocks. But despite our attempts, I can't manage to make my thoughts stray very far from these scenarios.

"Dude, we're totally going to get arrested," I say.

This does not deter Steve in the least. "C'mon Moe. If you don't get arrested every once in a while, you're not really trying hard enough."

Once again I marvel at the casual insanity of the situation I've put myself in. I do, however, realize Steve's actually right. You'll never know when you've left the artificial boundaries completely behind if you don't run up against the boundaries of harsh reality every once in a while. I just hope I don't run up against them the way Robert Landeta did.

So why risk death and jail just to be able to rise a few hundred feet more above where you already are? Not only "because it's there," George Leigh Mallory's great rationale for climbing

Mount Everest, but because it's there and you're being told you can't climb it. There's something about exclusivity, about not being allowed to go somewhere interesting, about being told "No, that's not for you," that can drive a person mad. I had become palpably jealous of the workers I saw on top of New York's great bridges every once in a while. I wondered if the best thing to do wasn't maybe to just grab a vest and hardhat and head up one some random weekday afternoon.

But it won't come to that. It's happening this night. Something feels different, unfamiliar, as we three walk back and forth across this bridge that I've walked countless times before. It takes me a bit, but I realize the difference is that I know I'm going to be on top of it soon. I don't know how I know this, but I know.

"We're going to do it," I say, mostly to solidify to myself what I've just realized. Ever since that night I've found I can intuitively tell if these adventures are actually going to happen, or if I'm just involved in an elaborate process of bullshitting myself. This intuition doesn't, however, make anything easier, or calmer, or even give it that sense of inevitability that allows me to disconnect from my anxieties and enjoy the moment. In fact, after saying these words out loud, I almost throw up.

Finally, when there are no people on the pedestrian path, we make a break for it. Luckily, bridge workers have left the camera partially covered by some black netting. There's a short section of climbing up the superstructure, perhaps twenty feet, where we're exposed and can be seen from the pedestrian path or by oncoming traffic. We navigate this as quickly as we can and reach a catwalk where we're able to hide. That's the easy part. Now comes a two-hundred-foot climb up an exposed ladder. It's the kind of thing you wouldn't think twice about doing if it were on a conveyer belt contraption at the gym where you're never more than a few feet off the ground. But it's a lot different when one misstep and they'll be scraping you off the top of the D train.

"OK, let's chill out here for a while, see if everything is cool," Steve says. This is easily the worst idea I've ever heard. We're already committed, already where we shouldn't be; there's no sense in stopping now. If we're going to get caught, it's going to be after accomplishing our goal, not sitting here within spitting distance of the roadway, relaxing and rolling cigarettes. Besides, I'm in the zone. I can't let myself stop and think about this. I wait for a short break in traffic, hit the ladder, and start climbing.

You wouldn't think there'd be a whole lot of technique to climbing a ladder. And there isn't for about fifty feet. But after that my grip starts to go, my forearms start to tighten, and I start to repeatedly bang my knees into the rungs while climbing as my body compensates for my deteriorating upper-body strength by shifting my weight forward into the ladder. I switch my hands to grip the outside of the ladder instead of the rungs, which takes some of the strain off my forearms, and point my feet slightly outward as I ascend the ladder. This helps. Now I'm about halfway up. Even if I wanted to go down now, it wouldn't matter: gripping the ladder in order to keep from falling backward is what's tiring me out, and I have to do this no matter if I'm heading up or down. Adrenaline and the obvious unfeasibility of letting go to rest my arms propel me on my strange, panting shuffle the rest of the way up. Eventually the ladder reaches a narrow catwalk. I'm actually inside the structure now, and the only source of illumination is the bridge lighting coming up through the grate of the catwalk I'm standing on. I, of course, have forgotten to bring a flashlight. I carefully fumble my way along the catwalk, coming to another, diagonal ladder. Despite the fact that Steve and Dsankt aren't here yet, or that I can barely see my hand in front of my face, the need to be on top of the structure has completely overtaken me. Up, up, up, is all I can think. I manage to navigate this last climb, doing pretty well until I bang my head against the hard metal roof. There's a hatch. I pray it isn't somehow alarmed, push it open, and I'm on top of the world.

The top of the Manhattan Bridge is, perhaps, six and a half feet wide. A football field's distance above the East River, I can lie down across the top, dangle my heels off one edge, and reach my arms above my head and grab the other. If you were to build a ten-foot-tall scale model of the bridge, the part we're on now would be slightly more than two inches wide. It's amazing to me that something so ephemeral can carry more than seventy thousand vehicles and several hundred subway trains a day. There aren't any guardrails, unless you count the narrow tension wire that runs between the ornamental globes that dot its towers—nothing to keep us from falling if a nice gust of wind kicks up and we lose our footing. After a few minutes Dsankt pops his head out of the hatch, takes in the surroundings, and turns to me with a look of utter amazement on his face. I glance down and notice traffic is still running smoothly across the bridge, a sure sign we've made it up without being seen.

As Steve and Dsankt start taking pictures, I gaze out at the city. I can make out downtown, midtown, the bump disturbing the symmetry of Manhattan where the Lower East Side juts out into the East River. Uptown, the Empire State Building is dark, but the Chrysler Building is still lit up in white. Downtown I can see the hollow part of the sky where the Twin Towers should be. The Brooklyn Bridge stands solidly, majestically, and tantalizingly to the left.

I realize that at this moment we are more tenuously connected to the city than any other human being within its borders. We're hundreds of feet away from the nearest person, about a quarter of a mile from the nearest inhabited building, physically attached to the city only by a thin piece of metal rising hundreds of feet above a narrow span to its shore. Out of the million and a half people crowded onto the thirty-four square miles of the island of Manhattan, none of them—not David Rockefeller, not Donald Trump, not Michael Bloomberg—have the sheer vastness of space to themselves that we have right now. But even with this removal I feel intensely, electrically connected to the city. Counterintuitively, these two feelings—removal and connection—aren't at odds, instead reinforcing each other. It's an amazing, almost spiritual experience.

Think of your favorite place in the city—any city. There are five things about it I'm willing to bet are true.

First, it's not monetized. You might be able to buy something there—a beer, a hot dog, a memento—but it's nowhere you pay to go. It's not hard to understand: How can a favorite place be somewhere that's merely borrowed for a price?

Second, it has a story. It's not just a random street corner in the middle of nowhere. It's somewhere at least modestly noteworthy, somewhere that has some kind of history.

Third, it has a personal story. It's special to you in some way. If someone asks you how you found it, or about your first time there, the answer is more than one sentence.

Fourth, it's a refuge. Somewhere you can go to get away from it all: the hustle and bustle of the city, the people and problems of everyday life.

Fifth, and last, it has a vista—a view. Maybe it's of a skyline, maybe it's of a streetscape, maybe it's just of the people walking back and forth on the sidewalk, but it's somewhere with a visual appeal. And places that offer both refuges and vistas are some of the most magnetic places in the urban environment, allowing you to both interact and be away from the city at the same time. Think of gazing at a skyline across the river while lounging on a rock in a secret nook by the water, or watching a sunset on a city rooftop, or sitting in a corner office high up in a downtown skyscraper long after everyone else has left work. It's this simultaneous feeling of removal and connection, this feeling I'm experiencing right now, that people crave.

Climbing to the top of one of New York's great suspension bridges provides all of these things in spades: a refuge and vista together, a story both personal and universal, and a place that's completely devoid of monetization. It's what makes the activity so appealing, even for those who haven't been. If you asked one thousand New Yorkers if, all things being equal, they'd like to sit alone, unmolested, where we are now, I can guarantee you that one thousand of them would unhesitatingly say yes. Well, at least those who aren't afraid of heights.

After twenty minutes or so at the top, the other two wrap up their photos and it's time to leave. New York City is rightfully known as "The City That Never Sleeps," but there are some narrow windows of time when it dozes off just a bit. At about four-thirty a.m. on weekdays, the city starts to rise from this light slumber and, quite rapidly, regains the energy and dynamism of its daily routine. It's now well past four, and we want to be safely on the pathway by the time this happens. Dsankt and Steve disappear back down the hatch, but I have one more mission. I'm still ten feet from the top. Next to me is one of the huge ornamental metal globes, and I know if I leave without climbing it I'll never be satisfied. I take only a few seconds to pause at the summit, but they're a few seconds that, untaken, would have weighed on my head for years. There's something about being at the pinnacle of a structure that's so much different from merely being up high. You can turn 360 degrees and see nothing in your way for miles, the last vestiges of restraint eliminated.

On the way down we take a more roundabout way through the bridge girders that, while slower, allows us to rest. We reach the first catwalk, navigate the final climb down the superstructure, drop back down onto the pedestrian path, and start walking back to Brooklyn. After about thirty seconds of walking, I suddenly feel like I've been punched in the gut with a ray of pure sunshine. The sunshine expands throughout my body until I can't hold it in anymore. I start to laugh. I start to scream. I jump in the air. I have a shit-eating grin on my face all the way back to Steve's loft. In fact, I have a shit-eating grin on my face for most of the next week.

"Addiction" is a strange word, a word that implies you're doing something you don't really want to do. It's generally reserved for drugs, alcohol, and other things that affect the body chemically, and negatively. Graffiti, running, sex, rock climbing, bungee jumping—I'd heard all of these described as "addictions" before and had always dismissed this definition as crass hyperbole. I still don't know if I would use that word, but after climbing the Manhattan Bridge, I understand. Every bridge I've climbed since then, I've been chasing the feeling from that night, chasing that explosion of light deep in the pit of my stomach, chasing that first high.

Dsankt heads back to his hostel, and Steve drives us back to his place, where we relax with some more whiskey. I don't have to be up tomorrow, and it'll take a while to wind down from the adventure. As we're sitting and chatting, I notice Steve's laptop on the table. It's open and has a picture of a rocky landscape with sentences in large type across it. It reads:

Skydiving
go to Tibet
do peyote in the mexican desert
go to Alaska
buy a good backpack
climb with corwin
travel with corwin

"Who's Corwin?" I ask.

"That's my younger brother," Steve says. "He's pretty cool. He's really into fencing. I'm pretty sure he's ranked somewhere in the top five in the nation in his age group right now."

"So what's the climbing with him about? And going to Tibet and Alaska and doing peyote and all that other stuff?"

Steve hesitates a bit. "Uh, so you know how I've got a bad hip?"

"Sure, from breaking it when you fell rock climbing."

"Yeah, uh, well, the reason why it broke when I fell is because I had bone cancer in it."

I don't quite know what to say to this, but luckily Steve doesn't seem to expect an answer, instead continuing:

"So, uh, for a while there the doctors said I was probably going to die. So I made a list of all the stuff I wanted to do before then."

I glance back at it. "Climb the Manhattan Bridge" isn't on there. "Climb the Brooklyn Bridge" isn't even on there. Instead it's "climb with corwin."

"They thought you were going to die?"

"Yeah. For some reason they stuck me in the pediatric ward of the oncology unit. There's kind of nothing like spending a week in a pediatric oncology ward to make you appreciate life a little more."

I'm a bit baffled. All this stuff, this adventure, I'd always thought Steve was just ever so slightly insane, had just enough of a case of "don't-give-a-fuck-itis" to let him take the risks that he takes. Realizing that he had come so close to dying—and

not even in a blaze of glory, getting lost in the catacombs beneath Paris or falling off the Brooklyn Bridge, but in such a
mundane way—makes me reconsider my assessment of him.
I start to think that there's something to going through that
which makes you fundamentally change how you view your
personal risk-reward ratio in life. Something that makes you
view bad luck as fundamentally uncontrollable and unavoid-
able—so that instead of trying to minimize your risk, you focus
on maximizing your reward. I think of what I'd do if some
doctor came in and told me something that got me thinking
about making a list like the one on Steve's laptop. I think of
where "Climb the Brooklyn Bridge" would be on the list. I
can't tell.

A few months after the climb, I check Sleepycity. There's
a new post, titled "Who Are You Midnight Wanderer?" I start
to read . . .

> *We're closer than you think, you and I. We've passed
> within grasp upon the streets, late at night when the
> misty clouds of warm breath momentarily hang in the air.
> The paths of two wandering strangers intersect then di-
> verge, threading through the thick shadows which creep
> from every crack and crevice; drifting like ghosts through
> the dim yellow islands that float below the sparse street-
> lights. There comes a familiar uneasiness as our faint out-
> lines bolden and we approach each other. The distance
> closes and our heartbeats quicken, rising with the nervous
> pace of our feet. Maybe you dig your hands deeper into
> your pockets, or puff out your chest slightly, a quick intake*

*of breath . . . the streets are dangerous around here, right.
Anyone may be prowling, lurking, waiting.*

*Our bodies pass unflinching, for all the build up there
is no crescendo. I wish just once to validate that building
tension. As we drift apart upon this cobblestone dotted
sea of shadows, I consider where are you walking this time
of night? Is it midnight cravings, an illicit rendezvous
or something so innocent as missing the last train home?
I peek around to catch the last glimpse as you're envel-
oped by the city and my curiosity grows stronger. Perhaps
for you this is a journey rather than a simple destination. If so, for what purpose do you roam? Your quiet,
clean appearance may belie a host of secrets and ill in-
tentions. As Tolkien penned, "not all those who wander
are lost." I have no answers to any of these questions,
they come unbidden with each passerby and depart
unanswered.*

*I crave to ask of you whether you ask these same ques-
tions of me. I fight the urge to turn and yell into the empty
laneways, to know what you're thinking. Are you even
curious at my passing? Surely you silently query my nocturnal ambitions. I wish to scream aloud my plans, to
engage the world with my bold scheme and say This Is
What I'm Going to Do And This Is How I'm Going To
Do It. I've learned my lesson from the supervillains of old
though and dispel such self-destructive notions, drop my
head and march on. My meandering route conceals a
carefully chosen path, a planned approach to the venue of
nefarious deeds. I pass no others while tracing my path to*

the base of the towering spire. Am I the only one to embrace my human frailty and venture high above the city this night?

MANHATTAN BRIDGE.

sleepycity.net | sewerfresh.com

TEN

On Halloween, I go out with Steve, Molly, and a few other friends. I'm dressed as a burglar, a quick and lazy outfit I threw together in about five minutes. The others we're with also all have generic costumes. Only Steve's is creative.

Steve and Molly have gotten to the place in their relationship where marriage is beginning to be discussed. It's not quite shit-or-get-off-the-pot time yet, but there is a lot of tension about where the relationship is headed. Molly is looking for a left turn down happy matrimony road. Steve is not. They've recently had a serious fight about this, and are currently on something in between a "break" and a "breakup." In addition to the fight, Steve has chosen another way to make a statement about his feelings on the subject, which is through his Halloween costume. He's dressed as a groom, complete with tuxedo, large gold band around his left ring finger, and ball made out of thirty pounds of sheet metal about a foot in diameter that he's attached to his ankle with a chain. That's the bride—not Molly. Molly is dressed as a cheerleader.

When I question Steve about the sheer assholery of this

costume, he tells me he wasn't counting on Molly showing up after their fight, that he thought this breakup was actually for good this time. Still, despite the costume, she somehow puts up with him for the night. At about two a.m. we get a text from Shane Perez, a Miami native who's just moved to town and become part of our adventuring crew. Shane's e-mail has the word "Hyposomniac" in it, which is an apt description of his personality: he's a ball of endless extroversion and energy, one of those guys who seem to be happy only when they're doing some kind of activity with somebody else.

His text reads, "There're too many girls for me at this bar. Come help out!" Steve, Molly, and I head over there and when we arrive we find Shane is right: there are too many girls. Shane is currently making time with one who's dressed as Alice in Wonderland. I find another, costume-less girl, and quickly settle into flirting with her. Steve, with Molly in tow, can't do likewise. Instead he plays pool in the back.

While Shane and I are off with our respective ladies, six guys come into the bar, obviously spoiling for some kind of confrontation. I notice them acting up at the pool table where Steve is screwing around. As the lady and I have moved past flirting and are now making out in the corner, I figure I've got better things to do than get involved in this. But when I start to hear a scuffle and raised voices, I head over. I get one sentence out—namely, "Hey, what's going on over here?"—before a heavily tattooed guy with a blond crew cut punches me in the face. I take a couple of shots before I even fully comprehend what's going on: I haven't been in a fight in ten years. I wing a half-decent right hook that hits the guy on the jaw, then get dragged off in a chokehold and thrown out of the bar. A minute or two later Molly comes out in tears. She's followed a little while later by Steve, whose face is now covered in blood. The six guys have really done a number on him. The fact that he had smoked a king-sized joint on the way over probably didn't help his chances. And of course neither did the fact that he was trying to fight while literally tethered by a ball and chain. Still, I learn that despite this insult to her dreams of settled couplehood, Molly had jumped headfirst into the fray brandishing a beer bottle. Shane, who is dressed as Wolverine, complete with two-foot metal claws, sat clueless in the corner the whole time.

Strangely enough, Steve really isn't upset as he comes staggering out of the bar. In fact, he's absolutely ecstatic.

"That was awesome!" are the first words out of his mouth. "Where are we going now? Hey, let's go climb a bridge."

Molly, understandably, does not want to go climb a bridge. Amazed at my friend's interpersonal cluelessness, I hail them a cab and shove them both in against Steve's protest—"No, come on, I'm up for more stuff." It doesn't matter that he had received a pretty nasty stomping for absolutely no reason, or that he didn't even land a punch, or that six guys against the two of us and a girl in a cheerleader outfit wasn't exactly a Marquess of Queensbury kind of matchup. Climbing something is Steve's way of responding to any kind of emotional scenario—joy, anger, frustration, celebration. Just got dumped? Let's go climb a bridge. Just won a Pulitzer? Let's go climb a bridge. Just got your ass handed to you by five meatheads and a guy who looks like a reject from the Yakuza? Let's go climb a bridge.

I remember another time he'd had this response, a spring night some months previous, around midnight. Steve called me up to commiserate after he and Molly had had a fight. It was a weekday, and already late, but I was itching to go adventuring. After a few minutes of relationship counseling, I decided to see if I could talk Steve into a quick trip.

"You want to go do something? Maybe a little bridge, something like that?" I asked, expecting to have to slowly and carefully wheedle him out of his self-pity and into adventure mode.

But instead I got an excited "Yeah. Fuck yeah." Steve picked me up, frustrated and scattered from his confrontation, almost crashing the car in distraction as we headed up to the very northern tip of the island of Manhattan.

Broadway is the longest street in New York City. Starting almost at the southern tip of the island, it heads north, with a gradual slide to the west, until thirteen miles later it passes 220th Street and heads over the Broadway Bridge into the Bronx. We parked the car and took a look at the bridge. It's a lift bridge, which is a type of movable bridge. Most people think of drawbridges when they think of movable bridges, but lift bridges are more common in New York City. Instead of the bridge deck splitting in half and opening up in order to let boats through, the entire deck stays horizontal while it's raised into the air by huge cables, which are anchored in the two towers that rise above either end of the deck. The Broadway Bridge actually has two decks, a lower one for auto traffic and an upper one that the number 1 train rumbles across. What we wanted to do was get to the rooms at the tops of these towers where the cables are anchored, and then hopefully find a way to get above them, out onto the very top of the structure. The first part looked simple enough. There was a staircase on the pedestrian walkway that led from the lower deck to the upper deck. From

the upper deck, a series of ladders led up to the top. The staircase had a cage around it, boards around the cage, and a door
secured with a heavy padlock. This, I supposed, was meant to
keep people from ascending the staircase to the train tracks
above. So instead of the staircase we used a ladder-like girder
next to the cage, which took us about ten seconds to climb.
After scaling this we crawled along a beam over to the ladders,
and soon were starting to make our way up.

We headed up the ladders until we were within sight of the
lift room. It had been almost a hundred-foot climb and I was a
little exhausted. We stopped to rest on the last landing, excited
at soon getting up, in, and on top. Steve's mood had completely
changed: he was smiling, in the moment, enjoying life.

As we headed up the final ladder, something started to
smell. It was a familiar odor, but one I couldn't quite place. I
opened the hatch to the top and the odor got stronger. Then I
heard a strange sort of breathy, fluttering sound. As I popped
my head up into the lift room, it all came together in a split
second, but that didn't stop me from screaming and almost
falling down the ladder when I felt something hit me in the
side of the face.

The entire lift room was filled with pigeons. Not one or
two—colonies. And they were not happy to see us. They were
flying onto our faces, landing on our bodies, scratching and
pecking at us. One pigeon landed directly on top of my head
and started needling away at my scalp. It didn't actually seem
malicious, more like it was combing through my hair for a tasty
bug or two that it thought might happen to be hiding in there.
The pigeons were so thick we couldn't even see where we were
going. We had headlamps, which helped us get a slight sense of

the surroundings, but the light was also serving to startle and confuse the pigeons into fluttering madly around our heads. I felt like I was in one of those cartoons where a kid accidentally kicks open a beehive, except the bees were actually huge flying rats. We felt around, continually shooing off the birds, until we found the huge gear that operates the cables that lift the bridge deck.

Trying to navigate a climb up rusty machinery in a swarm of pigeons is a bit tricky. Eventually we managed to make it up on top of the gear, reach above our heads, and grab onto some loose fencing that guarded the entrance to a catwalk. There was about a one-inch toehold as we scooted along the edge of the catwalk, hanging on to the fencing, trying to find a gap where we could get through onto the catwalk proper.

It was much more of a mental test than a physical one. Lots of seemingly scary climbs aren't really scary once you realize the secret is simply "Don't let go." That's what this climb was like. As long as we didn't purposefully relax our grips, we weren't really in any danger of falling. The problem was that not letting go meant we were completely at the mercy of the birds. We had to use our hands to hold on, which kept us from using them to shoo away the pigeons instead, and had to endure the pecking, flapping, and clawing while navigating the ledge. Climbing this bridge should have been a challenge on an episode of *Fear Factor*. But not the last challenge, where the "fear" usually involves something like falling off a cliff or crashing a car. The second challenge, the one where they make you eat bugs or bob for pig testicles in a vat full of bile. The lift room was easily one of the most disgusting things I have ever encountered in my life. Finally we found a gap, made it onto the catwalk, frantically beat back the swarm, and spotted the hatch to the top of the bridge.

Despite this ordeal, as we crawled out onto the top, Steve was buzzing with happiness. His mood started to rub off on me, making what we had just endured fade from my consciousness. There was a full moon, and the view was great. I chuckled in a self-satisfied manner as I took it in, slowly turning clockwise: the Hudson River to the west, with the George Washington Bridge not too far away, the curve of the Harlem River as it swings around the northern tip of Manhattan and heads south, Yankee Stadium off in the distance. As I finished enjoying the panorama and looked downward, preparing to start the descent back into the hatch, I had to hold back a retch. I was completely covered in pigeon shit.

ELEVEN

The New York City subway system is the most complicated in the world. Actually, it's not a system at all. It's three separate, independent systems, built over the better part of four decades, which were eventually consolidated into the single network that exists today. Since then there have been various additions to this network, a handful of new stations and tunnels, some track modifications, and the remnants of a few failed attempts at expansion. There are express trains, local trains, hundreds of emergency exits, and dozens of strange nooks and crannies. London's system is longer, Tokyo's and Moscow's move more people. Many others run better. Many more smell better. But there's no underground rail system in the world that can rival New York City's for sheer complexity.

Still, the geography of exploring the system is usually straightforward. You step off the end of the station platform and follow the tracks until you reach the next one, seeing what's there to be seen along the way. I once read a newspaper article about a civilian found wandering "deep in the subway tunnels." I almost laughed: there is no "deep in the subway tunnels." It's rare that you can find a spot in the system that's more than five hundred yards from the nearest open station, and the places that are are usually almost impossible to visit with any degree of safety. And if you need to bail, there are generally at least three exits immediately available to you: a station on either end, and an emergency exit between them, which is usually a set of stairs leading from the tracks to a hatch set into the sidewalk above. After all, the subway was designed to carry people—a lot of people—not to be a lonely, mysterious labyrinth to explore.

There are, however, a few exceptions to this. One exception lies underneath the Lower East Side of Manhattan. There you enter a netherworld where active tracks, long-disused tunnels, and half-abandoned stations all flow together. This netherworld has ebbed and flowed—active tracks become abandoned, decommissioned tunnels become reactivated—and during 2006 is at its zenith. You can step off a platform into this network and walk underneath four zip codes interchanging between the three subway lines serviced by nine different trains before reentering an area open to the public. And when you do, you have the option of exiting at one of seven different stations, three different emergency exits, or out onto the pedestrian path of the Manhattan Bridge. It's the only part of the system where I would say it's realistically possible to get lost underground, to drift through the tunnels below New York until you don't know what's above you.

One day, just before New Year's, I'm walking through this world, planning out the coming year in my head. This year, 2006, has gone by quickly—the days spent on the tour bus, the evenings in class, the nights adventuring through the city. I've gotten up half a dozen bridges, done countless trips into the subways and storm drains, made it into long-abandoned courthouses, hospitals, and factories. My favorite trip has been to walk for more than a mile underneath the streets of Harlem through the remnants of New York's first reliable water supply system, the Old Croton Aqueduct, abandoned for almost a century.

Steve and I have figured out where we're going next. Steve owns his own small business producing and selling maps of New York City, and does freelance photography on the side. As such, he's got a good amount of travel flexibility. He's already in Europe, back in the catacombs to get some pictures he'd missed out on during our first trip. I've worked nonstop on the double-decker tour bus since getting back from Paris, and have saved up enough money that I can take the rest of the winter off to join him in Italy next week for an exploring trip through Europe before heading by myself to South America for a couple months. I originally intended for the South America trip to be a more standard backpacking excursion, but now I'm not so sure: after our trip to Paris, I start to think what else might be out there to discover that doesn't make it into the guidebooks. I'll get back in the spring, do the tour guide hustle, and try to finish up grad school. Then I can start in on the traveling again in the fall. In the meantime, though, I'll make do with what's in town. And what's in town is over a hundred miles of subway tunnels.

Some people are drawn to the tunnels, connecting with them for their own sake, the environment itself being the attraction. These people have existed for as long as there have been subway tunnels in New York City. Exactly one week after the original IRT subway opened in 1904, a Bronx man by the name of Leidschmudel Dreispul was hit and killed by a south-bound express train. An article in *The New York Times* described the aftermath: "the down-town express service of the system . . . suspended for half an hour, no trains running until 6 o'clock, at which time all the down-town stations south of the Grand Central Station were packed with a shoving, grumbling crowd of men, women, and children anxious to get home." Because of this and other early fatalities from civilians on the subway right-of-way, the IRT had to put up signs—the signs that read "Do Not Enter or Cross Tracks" that we see on the end of each platform to this day.

I'm not usually the type to visit the subway tunnels just to be there. When I go, I almost always go with a goal: an abandoned station I want to visit, a stretch of track I want to walk, some piece of graffiti I want to see. But tonight is different— I just miss the tunnels. I want to wander them the same way I sometimes get the urge to just aimlessly wander the city streets with no destination in mind, no particular place to go.

There's a lot written in the tunnels of New York City, and everything written on the walls tells you something. Many times it's something practical, something about the train routings or the latest maintenance. Sometimes this isn't even written in words. The most important thing in the tunnels is told by two alternating colors, diagonal stripes of red or orange and white, colors whose message is, "Stand here when a train's coming and you'll die."

More often, though, it's a personal message, written by a pseudonymous author. It's not a very long message, just a single sentence consisting of one subject, one verb, and one object: "I was here." That's not what's actually written, of course: the message is implied, the author's signature all that's needed to convey it. These signatures are most often written in spray paint, or sometimes with a white-oil-paint-based marking implement called a Mean Streak. Many of them are completely illegible to the layperson.

But on occasion longer, more literal writings are also found. These are stories, usually written in black letters on a swath of tunnel that's been whitewashed, although sometimes the background is a dull faded yellow or light grey. Almost all of these are written in the same aggressive font where the letter O has a slash through it and the letter A looks more like an equilateral triangle, are dated sometime in the 1990s, and bear the signature REVS or a variation. I don't remember a lot about these. I'm always alert, even anxious, when walking subway tracks, always have my adrenaline going. One of the side effects of adrenaline is that it wreaks havoc on your short-term memory. The same way you can't remember the blow-by-blow of a bar fight, instead having only vague recollections of emotion, reaction, stress, and violence, you can't really remember more than a few words strung together that you read while in an adrenaline-fueled state. I would go line by line over these stories again and again in the tunnels, each time sure I would remember exactly what they said, only to forget everything but an isolated snippet or two when I exited. I remember reading one once, being sure I'd gotten it, and only ultimately recalling something about a "fat Greek kid."

REVS has left dozens if not hundreds of these longer stories, each one waiting to tell me something I'll soon forget. He's left plenty of short messages around as well, the ones marked only by a signature. And he's left some things that fall in between. This night of wandering, as I come around a bend, I see a stark white four-word sentence painted in large block letters about seven feet above the track. It also tells me something. It's something I won't forget, because it's something I already know. It's something I've never admitted to myself, but now the four words are staring me right in the face. They read "None Of This Matters."

I have always operated under the conceit that exploring the city is somehow important, something that has some sort of professional value. Sure, it might not have a direct impact on the job one might be doing at the moment, but it matters in some other indirect way. Urban planners work with cities, and cities are a combination of the social and the physical. The two shape each other: people create our urban environment, and our urban environment affects much of people's lives. In order to be a good urban planner, you have to know both sides. Planners understood long ago that the social side of the city—the citizens, the communities, the neighborhoods—cannot be learned in the abstract, from on high. Planners need to be in the community, need to talk to the residents, need to learn how what they're doing affects the citizens of their municipality. They need an up-close, hands-on knowledge of the people they're working with—and working for. Ever since the days when a neighborhood activist named Jane Jacobs led the fight in the 1950s against the routing of buses through Washington Square Park by New York's powerful "Master Builder," Robert Moses, the planning community has learned this lesson fairly well. The days of engineering giant highways through the hearts of neighborhoods, focusing on transportation times and not people displaced, are long over, as they should be.

© *Eric Ruggiero 2012 – www.ericruggiero.com*

But the urban planning community has not learned this lesson when it comes to the physical side of the city. We plan drain systems without so much as gazing down a manhole, subway systems without ever walking the tracks. We leave this nitty-gritty to the engineers who design it, the contractors who build it, the members of the Laborers' International Union of North America Local 147, better known as the Sandhogs, who dig the tunnels. I always thought that what I was doing—seeing the city in an unmitigated way, raw and up close—was important. That doing this would somehow infuse me with a knowledge and perspective that would trickle out in my professional life and end up having some social value, contributing something positive to the city. I might not be getting course credit in my grad school program for these nocturnal adventures, but I still consider them an integral part of my education.

But when I see this four-word message, all the insecurities

that I've neatly hidden away in the back of my mind sud
ram their way forward. I know I'm fooling myself, simply trying to justify my loneliness, my obsession, my desire to be different, exclusive. Adventure and exploration of all stripes are
inherently egocentric hobbies, to the point of being colonial.
The first person—or at least the first colonial explorer—who
climbs a mountain gets to name it. This tradition's been followed to some extent in all cultures of exploration, even ours:
in the draining world, the person who finds a drain also gets to
name it. But it's silly: that drain's been visited countless times
before—constructed by laborers, inspected by engineers, maintained by sewer workers. Like all colonial pursuits, urban exploration is making the noteworthy for the newcomer out of
the ordinary for the old-timer. Abandoned subway stations are
just convenient places to store equipment for the track workers.
Old observation decks are where the office nicotine addicts go
to grab a quick smoke. Climbing up bridges is all in a day's
work for the guys who change the lightbulbs on their cables.
And kids have been running around the tunnels of New York
City for decades—exploring, writing graffiti, or just as a rite of
passage. Plenty of people have even called them home. What
the hell was I, a thirty-something divorcé, doing in an abandoned tunnel under the Lower East Side? What was I looking
for? What did I hope to accomplish, to prove by this? Did any
of this mean anything at all?

{ PART TWO }

TWELVE

Naples, January 2007

There are few feelings in life like waking up early, drinking a cup of coffee, going downstairs, and having an entirely new City at your feet. And Naples is just that—a City. Capital C.

Naples is loud, chaotic, and incredibly densely populated. Vespa scooters are the preferred mode of transportation through the narrow streets of the city center, sometimes carrying an entire family—and sometimes driven by children who look barely out of diapers. Add to this cars, trucks, and of course people. A lot of people. Stop signs and even traffic lights are taken as loose suggestions at best. Yet despite all of this, I never feel the least bit unsafe walking anywhere in the city.

Naples has an amazing amount of flow. The chaos isn't chaos at all, not once you figure out a few things. You can walk out into the middle of traffic blindfolded in the center of town and you'll be fine. Cars will slow down, the scooters will swerve around you, nobody will even honk at you. Eye contact isn't necessary: the drivers know you're there and always have one foot on the brake. But you've got to keep moving. No hesitating for a small break in traffic, or taking a tentative step out into the street; it breaks the flow of the city.

The best thing about this flow is that there's no anger involved. Honking is used to say "You might not be able to see me, but I'm here," not "Screw you, buddy!" or "Hurry up, asshole!" If you walk out in front of a car and the guy has to slow down, that's just the normal flow of things. Nothing to get upset over, not a personal insult, nothing to think about past the moment. Traffic is crazier than it is in most cities in the Western world, but there's no road rage. There isn't the pent-up anger you find in a lot of places in the United States that sometimes comes out in everyday activities like driving. And there isn't that sense of testosterone-fueled competition and defensiveness simmering on the streets and lingering below the surface of every mundane social encounter. Which I think is why, despite having several people tell me Naples is a dangerous place, I feel more at ease there than in other, supposedly "safe" cities back in the United States.

This ease started on the subway ride over to my hostel in the center of town. I was sitting in the far right-hand seat of a four-seat bench. The doors opened and a father and his son, who looked to be about seven or eight years old, got on. The father sat on the left side, and the son in the middle. Without a trace of self-consciousness, and despite not being crowded, the kid leaned his head against my shoulder and put his elbow on my leg. The father, I think because he noticed I was reading a book in English, eventually apologized and pulled the kid over to him, giving him a big hug and holding his hand the rest of the trip.

This scene turned out to be perfectly normal in southern Italy. To a large extent, I think it explains that lack of macho territorial energy that is so prevalent in countries with a more Anglo-Saxon heritage. I have no way of proving it, but it just seems to make sense to me that kids who grow up hugging their dads are generally much more chill. Naples is crowded, chaotic, energetic, and might be dangerous, although I never experience it. But it's not mean.

The reason I'm in Naples, though, isn't to figure out how to cross the street or marvel at the wonderful familial relationships. I'm here to explore the *sottosuolo*, the vast and varied underground of the city. I meet up with Steve and five other people upon my arrival in the city. There are two Australians from the Cave Clan, Guru and Nivelo, who's the main planner of the trip, and also three Americans: Gabe and Ashley, two college students from the Twin Cities, and Jim. Jim's an engineer currently living in Iowa whose interest in underground mazes and labyrinths borders on obsession. And Naples is just the place for him to scratch that itch.

Naples has one of the most extensive and varied undergrounds in the world. The city is a port surrounded by hills. Because of the proximity of Mount Vesuvius, large veins of yellow tufa, a durable, light, volcanic rock that is easily mined, run beneath the whole area. The hills surrounding the old port of Naples, as well as the central city itself, are riddled with huge bottle-shaped tufa quarries, often hundreds of feet high.

Over the centuries, many of these quarries have been converted for other uses, including storage or even parking garages. In addition to the quarries, the easily worked tufa was also used

TUFA QUARRIES, NAPLES.

© *Gabe Emerson*

to excavate burial chambers by the original Greek settlers, and later, early Christians honeycombed the hills above the city with their catacombs. The Romans dug huge tunnels hundreds of feet long through the hills. Pedestrian traffic, as well as fully loaded military wagons and carts belonging to royalty, used these passageways as shortcuts from the city to the sea—shortcuts that were also useful for a quick escape should the need arise. At the entrance to one of these tunnels is said to be the tomb of the poet Virgil, author of the *Aeneid*.

And as with most ancient Mediterranean cities, much of Naples is built on the ruins of what came before. So any digging is going to unearth the remnants of the previous settlements. We can even see it in action. A few subway stations are being constructed using the cut-and-cover method, where the street is dug up, a shallow ditch is excavated, tracks are laid, and the street replaced above it. We take a peek down into one of these. Gazing ten feet down takes us back about two thousand years as we see the diamond-shaped *opus reticulatum* brickwork of the Roman Empire.

Add to this ancient underground the modern underground networks—steam tunnels, subways, sewers, and storm drains— all of which have been built through and around two separate ancient aqueduct systems, one Roman, one Greek. Water from these ancient aqueducts was diverted to huge underground cisterns beneath the villas and palaces above, providing them with fresh drinking water. During World War II, Mussolini's civil defense corps converted hundreds of these various cavities beneath the city into air-raid shelters. Well shafts were converted into spiral stairwells, leading down into the hollow spaces below. Tens of thousands of Neapolitan residents survived the Allied bombardment in the shelters. After the war, these shelters were converted to yet another use: repositories of the discarded rubble from the construction and excavation during the huge postwar building boom. It's only since the 1970s that efforts by the local urban speleologists have spurred interest in the reexcavation and documentation of the underground of Naples. Meeting some of the pioneers in this exploration, survey, and mapping is what enabled the group's first expedition.

The head of this excavation and documentation effort is colloquially known as "the Don." The day before I get to Naples, the Don and our contact from Napoli Underground, Fulvio, took our group on an extensive journey through the ruins of one of these ancient aqueduct and cistern systems. When I arrive and see the pictures of body-belays into enormous abandoned caverns, I immediately regret my decision to spend the day before with my cousin, who lives in a small town a couple hours north. The other underground network I had visited extensively, Paris's, had been documented and stabilized during the eighteenth and nineteenth centuries. Seeing that process in action in another city was a rare chance that I've missed. Still, we have a week left in Naples. We know there's a lot to find. But Naples is not a city that gives up its secrets to outsiders easily.

THIRTEEN

New York is a Jewish City. It's an everyday thing. It's in the shrug the Korean grocer gives you, the casual colloquialisms of the Haitian cabdriver, the joking comment made by the Dominican guy whom you ask for directions on Ninth Avenue. For someone who grew up in a Jewish household, fitting in in New York is the easiest, most comfortable thing in the world. Who you are is in the air, in the streets, in the fabric of the city.

It's easy for me to feel this character, because it's the character I know intimately. But the Jewish character of New York is only one part of it. Numerous immigrants from every corner of the globe have made New York home, and each has contributed something indelible to its landscape. Few of these groups have come in greater numbers, or been there longer, or contributed more to the cultural landscape, than the Jews of Eastern Europe. But one group that has is the Southern Italians. And one of the main sources of this Southern Italian immigration has been the city of Naples. Before arriving there, I wondered how much of the character of the city I see every day in New York and just don't notice. I wondered how much of this character I would be able to recognize in Naples, not having grown up in an Italian-American household.

The easiest part, of course, is the food. Pretty much everything you think of as "Italian food" in the United States is specifically Neapolitan cuisine. The best example of this is pizza. Gennaro Lombardi brought the stuff from Naples to Little Italy around the turn of the twentieth century, establishing Lombardi's pizzeria, which is still on the corner of Spring and Mott streets over one hundred years later. And Little Italy should in reality be called Little Naples. The area of Lower Manhattan centered on Mulberry Street was a specific Neapolitan neighborhood. You can still see evidence of this Neapolitan heritage today every September during the Feast of San Gennaro—the patron saint of Naples.

But it turns out there's much more to it than just food and festival. In Naples, I notice I can see shadows of New York in the faces of the old men, in the gestures and body language of the citizens, and especially in the way people talk with their hands. Naples has almost an entire language based on hand gestures. Our hostel manager, an Australian named Jenny, tells us this comes from the hilly terrain, as people couldn't simply walk down the block to see a neighbor. Combine this with the inevitable noise that comes from a densely populated city, and sign language shorthand becomes the best and most efficient way to communicate with your neighbors across the valley.

I can also see New York in the flow of the city, in the general atmosphere. I wonder how much the jaywalking culture in New York comes from Naples. I can't know for sure, but I suspect the Lower Manhattan of fifty years ago bore a startling resemblance to the Naples of today.

I wonder how much there is that I miss. Probably a lot. But I can see the soul of Naples in New York. I may not know the specifics, I may not be able to articulate the similarities with any eloquence, but as sure as I can tell you New York is a Jewish city, I can tell you that it's there.

A nd there is one more New York trait that I suspect, and hope, is a residue from its Neapolitan heritage. Which is that even in our current age of terrorism paranoia, people in my city are really, really good about not sticking their noses in other people's business. A lot of other Americans think this is rude: after all, if you saw a person, say, sobbing her eyes out on the subway, wouldn't you ask what's wrong and try to comfort her? But doing so would be considered a breach of the careful etiquette New Yorkers have developed for these situations. That lady doesn't have anywhere else to cry at the moment. She's got to get to work, and that involves taking the subway with a bunch of strangers. So the strangers give her that personal bubble she'd have in another city, where she'd grab a few minutes of catharsis in her car before reapplying her makeup and heading into work to face the day. In a city so crowded, where privacy is always at a premium, a respect for privacy is taken as the default position, given priority over other tranches of proper etiquette. This isn't to say we can't be comforting and friendly, just that we need a cue—the lost-looking tourist to inquire about directions, the crying woman on the subway to ask for a tissue—before we do so.

This default setting of minding your own business extends itself to a lot of facets of life in New York, and gives us some advantages when it comes to our more illicit activities. I've been seen by strangers coming out of manholes, subway tunnels, even descending from suspension bridges. In almost all instances, the people have followed the tried-and-true New York practice of simply continuing along their way while studiously avoiding eye contact. The longest exchange I've ever had with a stranger in these circumstances was coming down from my first time on top of the Williamsburg Bridge, when an aging hippie riding a bike down the path asked us, "You go all the way to the top?" After hearing our affirmation, he replied, "Fuck yeah!" and biked off.

Trying to get the lay of the land in Naples, we ask Jenny what might happen if we're seen coming out of a manhole in the middle of the night by your average passersby. My suspicions are confirmed.

"Oh, no. This isn't a dobbing kind of culture at all," she tells us, using the Australian slang for "snitching." "People mind their own here." Seeing as Naples is the home of the Camorra, one of the most feared and powerful organized crime syndicates in the world, this isn't too hard to believe. But this could also work to our disadvantage: Naples is not the kind of city that's about to let a bunch of arrogant outsiders who've just rolled into town in on its secrets. Still, we decide to see if we can have a few adventures on our own.

Jim has a topographical map. He's very excited about this. The rest of the group is kind of beat, leaving Jim to go comb the hills of Naples alone in the middle of the night, looking for tunnel entrances. I am not optimistic: I can't imagine wandering around town looking for holes in the ground, especially in a city like this one, is going to yield much in the way of results. I go to sleep.

I wake up the next morning, and the topo map is spread out on the hostel's kitchen table, the gang crowded around it. Somehow, Jim actually found something, an abandoned building with a small network of quarries below it. Heartened by the fact that there is apparently stuff out there to discover, we make more of an effort. We schlep out to the northern outskirts of the city and manage to find an entrance to a drain that we follow for a while. Later on, some of the group pops manholes until they find a network of utility tunnels near downtown. We hear about an old abandoned industrial park from the 1960s and spend a few hours checking that out. A couple of small barriers jumped, scaffolding climbed, and "Employees Only" doors opened lead to some lovely views from the old castle downtown. Interesting, but only a scratch on the surface of what Naples has to offer.

Our experience in Naples is best summed up by our attempt to walk the ancient Roman pedestrian tunnels, known locally as *grotte*, through the mountains. There are two of them we know of. The first is the one by Virgil's tomb, the second a bit farther west by the coast. We scout them out during the day and see a pretty climbable iron fence guarding the entrances. Jim, Steve, and I wait for nightfall to make our attempt on the first grotto. We get over the fence unseen, only to encounter another one right behind it. This one isn't remotely climbable: it stretches about thirty feet to the very top of the tunnel, completely barring any and all access. We hop back over the first fence and decide to try the second grotto. This time the entrance isn't so obvious. We wind through the hills of what seems to be a very rich residential part of town, the kind of neighborhood where you definitely don't want to be caught accidentally wandering into someone's backyard instead of an old Roman tunnel. Still, we eventually find what we think is the entrance. Over the fence we go—with the same result as the first tunnel: a ceiling-to-floor gate that makes it impossible to continue.

The "extralegal" way, which is what we term our attempts at exploration without official sanction, isn't a complete bust, but it's close. In quite a new development for our motley crew of international urban adventurers, the straight and narrow will turn out to reveal more of the city. But of course it isn't quite as much fun.

FOURTEEN

Indiana Jones!!! Da-da-da-*daaaah!!!*" The short, elderly, and extremely energetic guide is shouting this nonstop while nimbly racing through the two-foot-wide ancient Greek aqueduct tunnels one hundred feet underneath the city. Steve and I are the only two participants on this particular tour—offered by candlelight, Saturday mornings only, from an obscure address in the Spanish Quarter.

The Spanish Quarter itself is one of the more interesting neighborhoods in Naples. Geographically, it lies directly west of the city center on a gently sloping hill. Its narrow and compact cobblestone streets form a grid, the only part of the street layout that comes even close to following a regular geometric pattern. Socially, it's a densely populated working-class neighborhood, and somewhat eccentric. This is the area of town where you're most likely to see a six-year-old riding backward on a Vespa motor scooter being driven by his nine-year-old sister, or be propositioned by one the *femminielli*, as members of the venerable Neapolitan transsexual community are called.

Below the Spanish Quarter is even more interesting: it's

home to an extensive network of underground aqueducts and cisterns, many of which were turned into air-raid shelters during the war, one of which we're currently touring. Tours are in Italian only, other than "Look, look!" and "Ooh la la!"—two phrases our guide uses every couple of minutes. Steve wants to take pictures, which means it's my job to pay attention to the guide and try to ask questions, serving to distract and delay him from rushing us along. This will give Steve the time to get the shots he wants. I'm doing pretty good at this job, combining the various things that are pointed out with a basic knowledge of Romance languages and the copious use of hand gestures from our guide to get a sense of the stories he's trying to tell us.

From what I gather, the house above where we entered was the house our guide and his brother had grown up in. During World War II, when they were children, they hid in the old cistern below that had been turned into an air-raid shelter. After the war, illegal dumping from construction filled in much of the old air-raid shelter and underground network. Later on, when they were adults, they reentered and reexcavated the former air-raid shelter and surrounding cisterns and tunnels, and started giving tours.

"Illegal" is actually a strong word when used to describe the dumping of construction materials; again, "extralegal" is probably the better term. In a city like Naples, bureaucracy, building codes, and paperwork are basically taken as, well, one of the many different ways of doing things. And postwar building almost never followed this official way. We had already encountered an interesting example of this in our journey through one of the underground tunnels we had found on our own. From what we could tell, it was designed and meant for use exclusively as a storm drain. However, every once in a while we ran into small pipes—often only a few inches wide—discharging sewage into the drain. During the postwar building boom, if it was easier and cheaper to just connect nearby buildings' sewage systems to this storm drain instead of an actual sewer, a way was found to make it happen.

Among our guide's other stories that I manage to semi-understand are ones about a pregnant woman giving birth on the stairs down to the air-raid shelter, about the damp air being used for the development of penicillin, and about how the toilets were right next to the bottom of the stairs. Why? Well, if you're in imminent danger of having a bomb level your house, what's the first way your body might react?

We emerge out of a nondescript door into a nondescript alley, with a nondescript middle-aged Italian woman staring at us. These are the entrances to the underground world of Naples. Not manholes, not anything you'd ever guess. In Naples, not just for the underground but for everything, knowledge and access are gained through people and relationships, not through academic research or random poking around. While developing those relationships in one conversation is certainly not unheard-of (Steve managed to talk his way into a Greek and Roman excavation site beneath a church, for instance), they can often take lifetimes, if not generations.

Luckily for us, there are a few organizations, institutions, and just quirky individuals (such as our aforementioned Indiana Jones impersonator) who give us a great look into the fascinating underground infrastructure of the city. We get to see old air-raid shelters, catacombs, crypts, aqueducts, archaeological sites, and even the tomb of San Gennaro legally—a great deal more than we got to see during our extralegal excursions.

I love Naples. I feel comfortable here. I think it's the kind of city I could eventually even feel at home in. But I know I'll never truly know the city. Not if I live here the rest of my life and magically become fluent in Italian tomorrow. It's too deep.

Some cities are shallow, some are deep. It's not a value judgment, and it doesn't have much of a bearing on how much I like a town. But it's there. Paris is a shallow city. Despite not knowing French and having spent only a few weeks there, I can tell you I know Paris. Maybe not all the nooks and crannies, not all the shortcuts, but I know the city. New York is different. It's deep, but in a very different way from how a city like Naples is deep. New York is almost defined by its transience. This is especially true of Manhattan. Even before colonization it was transient: the local Lenape Indians would set up shop in the summer, do some hunting, and then leave for the winter. More than any other city I know of, knowing New York is a choice: it's all there if you want to put in the work, but it's going to be a heck of a lot of work. And the work never ends. New York changes so fast that you're constantly playing catch-up. Because of this, it's actually the newcomer who knows the city best at any given moment; old-timers are always looking at it through the distorted lens of a city that's no longer there.

Naples has none of this history of transience. Well, it does, but only in one direction—out. Over the last 150 years or so, it's been one of the main emigrant points of the world. You can find people of Neapolitan descent from Alaska straight through to Tierra del Fuego. But with a few small exceptions—West African street merchants, Australian hostel managers—this migration hasn't been returned. As a result, the vast majority of its residents share a generations-long culture and understanding that goes exponentially beyond that of a more transient city.

What makes this glaringly obvious for me is that I can't pass. I'm one of those people that everyone always assumes is a local—at least before I open my mouth—anywhere where it's plausible someone of my particular appearance might live. I'm not quite sure why this is, other than that I feel comfortable in cities and probably project that sense of comfort. I got asked for directions twice my first day in Paris. Not in Naples. Despite my feeling that same comfort, nobody ever mistakes me for anything but an outsider. Nobody even starts speaking Italian to me. It's not tourist season, to the extent there even is one in Naples, and the way I'm dressed isn't particularly out of place. But it's obvious I'm standing out in some way. This doesn't happen anywhere else in Italy, or even anywhere else in Europe for that matter. It's not me. It's the city.

Steve and I catch a train to Rome, with Jim, Ashley, Gabe, and the Australians all going their respective ways. I leave feeling like we can't really crack Naples. I'm frustrated but somewhat resigned. In some cities that feeling of frustration is much worse, because you know if you stayed a little longer, prepared a little better, took a few more chances, you could have had it. Not Naples. I think I could stay forever and not really get that much further. It's just too deep.

FIFTEEN

Rome, January 2007

Ancient Rome had a problem: a lot of people, even more animals, and no way to get rid of their poop. To cope with this problem, a rudimentary sewer system was dug around 600 BC, flowing out to the Tiber River. True to Roman form, it even came complete with its own goddess, Cloacina. The marshy area it ran through was drained by this system and would eventually become the Roman Forum.

This sewer became known as the Cloaca Maxima, and a little research leads us to the location of its original outflow. A couple of Gypsies are camped out in front of it, obviously making it their home. After trying, and failing, to initiate a conversation, I turn to walk away, and hear some very rapid, very angry Italian being hurled at me by one of them. After repeated *Non parlo italiano*s on my part, I hear, "OK you speak English? You have made a very big mistake!"

I'm not quite sure of the big mistake I've made, but apparently I have gravely offended some sensibility of his in our brief exchange. I have no idea what to do. More important, I have no idea what he is going to do. Luckily, after a good deal more berating, he takes my apologies enough that I can walk away without fear of further offense. Well, here was another obstacle I'd put in our way. Instead of manholes and fences, now we have angry Gypsies to contend with.

The next morning Steve and I try to talk our way in, armed with peace offerings of pastries and beer. The guy who yelled at me isn't there, but his friend is. He doesn't speak English, offering Russian as an alternative. I counter with Spanish. He and Steve settle on a mangled conversation in French, and a couple beers later we're in. Imagine our disappointment when the tunnel ends in a brick wall after twenty feet.

We head down the river to see if there are any other entrances. A bit farther is another outflow, close enough that it might lead to the Cloaca. This time the obstacles are different. The first is a heavy metal gate. The second is an obstacle one might associate with sewers: namely sewage. While the other outflow is kept fairly clean by the Gypsies, this one has no such caretakers. Flies are swarming all over us as we're up to our ankles in muck, trying to pry open the gate. This time it takes a little elbow grease and a strong stomach instead of two beers and half-decent French to make it in.

Once we're in, it's a little better: most of the sewage is caught on the gate at the entrance, and there's only a trickle down the middle of the tunnel. The tunnel itself is huge and looks relatively new, constructed at least a millennium and a half after the fall of Rome. It begins to curve toward the direction of the entrance to the Cloaca, but stops at a massive concrete floodgate before very long.

With the Cloaca this close, we have to go on. Luckily for us, there's a ladder. Up the ladder, into the gatehouse, across a

STORM DRAIN GATE, ROME.

catwalk, and down another, much rustier ladder and we find ourselves in the sewers beneath the Capitoline Hill. These sewers make the first one look like the Sistine Chapel. We're on a slippery catwalk maybe two feet wide right next to the bodily waste of millions. One wrong step and we will literally be up shit creek without a paddle.

The deeper in we go, the more I worry. We've brought an air meter, which will tell us if the atmosphere ceases to be safe. But we're not really worried about air; we're worried about water. The catwalk is only a few inches higher than the effluence next to us. If it rises just a little, we'll be swimming back out. And if it rises a lot . . . well, let's just say I can think of a lot better ways to go. Offering up a quick prayer to Cloacina, we press on.

After a few hundred feet we come to an archway on the side of the tunnel leading to a smaller tunnel. It's not the kind of tunnel you'd find in the drains of newer cities, a side pipe that's obviously part of the system. It's older—much older—and not made out of the same dull concrete that forms the walls of the tube we're in. Instead it's made out of brick—the same kind of long, flat bricks that we've seen in the ruins of the ancient Roman forums.

It also doesn't lead directly to the catwalk, instead opening a few feet above. We crawl up and in and start down the tunnel. There's no sewage, just a muddy floor, and after a few hundred feet we find out why: it dead-ends in a complex suite of brick arched chambers. We are directly under the oldest part of the city. Could this be a remnant of the Cloaca?

After exploring this strange offshoot, we continue down the original tunnel. A little farther and the catwalk ends at a split. The right fork has no catwalk, and the left fork has a six-foot gap until it picks back up. Jumping it is out of the question, but we're both heavily invested in our quest for the Cloaca.

"You think maybe we can wade this?" I ask Steve, trying not to think of the diseases that must be floating next to us.

"I don't know. How deep do you think that is?" We test the water with Steve's camera tripod. The river of shit swallows the five-foot tripod with room to spare. We're not that invested. And so we're out of options.

It's hard to leave without knowing for sure if we've accomplished our objective, but we can't very well expect a big sign saying "Welcome to the World's Oldest Sewer!" While we're fairly sure we've failed to find the main channel of the Cloaca, we wonder if our side tunnel is one of its branches that was closed up over time as the city grew. But even if it isn't, it's a fair bet that it's at least a couple millennia old, host to the kind of history we've only read about—a solid find for a morning of traipsing through the sewers. Walking alongside the Tiber back to town, we give a friendly wave to the Gypsies and are honored when we get a slight nod of the head back.

That night I go out to dinner with a couple of people from our hostel. Coming back afterward, I find Steve despondent, and minus a good chunk of the bottle of whiskey I'd left him with. "I don't think we did it," he tells me. "I don't think we made it to the Cloaca."

We have a limited amount of time for our trip, and I'm not about to go breaking back into the sewers in search of something we may or may not have found already. There's another option though: pay 500 euros (about $650) to go officially with the Rome Underground society—Roma Sotterranea—the next day.

Now, while I generally find official tours restrictive and frustrating, I am not above doing it the official way if the risk/reward ratio is sufficiently in its favor. I would have much preferred being able to freely wander the Colosseum by myself, for instance, but instead of trying to hop the fence in the middle of the night, I queued up, got my ticket, and stuck to the beaten path.

Paying 650 bucks to go into a sewer, however, is ridiculous. But this is the culture of Rome. Different cities have different cultures. In Paris, for instance, people almost always just do things the extralegal way, but it isn't actually all that "extra." The police have a relationship with the people who do this stuff. They're content to play a cat-and-mouse game, with a civil fine being the biggest stick they've got. In return, the cataphiles can be counted on to report anything really bad down in the underground: structural dangers, smugglers, or anything else out of the normal course of things.

New York is different. Tolerance is less—much less. There are several interesting places that, if you are caught there, will most likely result in a night in jail, and there are a few others where there could be considerably worse consequences. But it's necessary—there's no other choice. There's simply no way regular people can get permission for certain things, which leads some people to take the risk of doing them without permission.

Rome is different from both of these cities. Most of the interesting underground stuff is part of well-guarded archaeological sites, and the local exploration groups are more on the academic side, are heavily cooperative with the authorities, and generally enjoy official access, as opposed to the "Don't ask, don't tell" policy that's prevalent in Paris, and the "Pray you don't get caught" attitude that exists today in New York.

Steve is actually considering paying the $650. Finding the Cloaca is a big reason he's come all the way to Rome, and he is apoplectic over the fact that he might leave without seeing it. Fortunately, I have just the solution for his malaise—a free solution. Walking around the city earlier, I noticed that next to Saint John Lateran—a building most noteworthy for being the official ecclesiastical archbasilica of the bishop of Rome (aka the pope) and, as such, the ecumenical Mother Church of all of

Roman Catholicism—there's a giant obelisk currently surrounded by scaffolding. It looked pretty easy to head in and up, and I know that a good drunken climb can work wonders for the psyche. Plus, Saint John Lateran legally isn't part of Italy, instead being an exclave of the sovereign Vatican state. I'm betting Steve, as a rebellious lapsed Catholic, won't be able to turn down the chance to do some extralegal adventuring in an area technically governed by the Holy Father—and right next to his official seat nonetheless.

Surprisingly, one of the people staying with us at the hostel, an Australian girl named Chi, says she wants to come along. It's not to climb, it's just for the walk, she tells us, but I already know she's heading up top. I recognize her mental state immediately because I've experienced it so many times myself. She's in the process of dealing with appealing things that lie outside her comfort zone. The logical part of herself is telling her that it's a ridiculous idea to climb up scaffolding in the middle of the night with two random drunk Americans, and is proceeding to come up with all the reasons not to do it. But a spark has been lit, and it is now our job to fan that spark into a flame—a flame strong enough to overcome the mental reservations. Certain things can help with this, booze being not the least of them, but another big one is other confident people around. Ultimately, I know that if we make the situation comfortable enough for her, provide a steady presence, and maybe give her a gentle push when the time is right, she'll listen to her gut and go with the flow. The three of us swig the last of Steve's whiskey from the bottle and head southeast to Saint John's.

"Who's cooler, James Bond or Indiana Jones?" Steve asks

her as we walk. The correct answer is Indiana Jones. This is one of the questions we ask to determine if we've encountered a kindred spirit. James Bond's only advantage in this argument is that he always got the ladies without having to fight off sadistic Nazis or nihilistic cult leaders first. Other than that, he's an uneducated thug, a blunt, humorless tool blindly following the orders of an antiquated colonial regime. Indiana Jones, on the other hand, is an intellectual, a professor who pursues his own interests, on his own terms, in the service of knowledge and human understanding. We also both, not so secretly, want to be Indiana Jones.

"James Bond," Chi answers without hesitation. This might explain why she has been completely unresponsive to our attempts at flirtation.

The climb is easy. I go up the scaffolding ladders with Chi while Steve works out his issues by doing a Spider-Man up the side. The scaffolding covers the whole obelisk, and we use the cross at the top of it to boost ourselves up to the final crossbeams. We've chosen a great climb. Unbeknownst to us, in the late sixteenth century the city of Rome was actually designed to give us a spectacular view.

Rome, like most old European cities, is a jumbled mishmash of streets and alleyways that have mostly evolved organically over time. There are a few exceptions, however, like in 1936 when Mussolini carved a grand boulevard called Via della Conciliazione out of the alleyways between the Tiber River and Saint Peter's Basilica. Another exception occurred 350 years earlier. The pope at the time, Sixtus V, decided that all roads shouldn't just lead to Rome—they should also lead to the seat of the pope. Sixtus cleared out radial boulevards from Saint

John Lateran to link it with the other major basilicas. As a result we have great, unobstructed views right down the main roads of Rome. The Colosseum is down one street, with Saint Peter's off in the distance behind it. Santa Maria Maggiore is down another. From our perch on the obelisk, we can also make out the dome of the Pantheon and, of course, right next to us, the magnificent roof of the Mother Church of all Christendom.

The night is misty, and Rome is not heavily lit up at night like Paris or New York. Even if Steve had brought his fancy camera, any decent shots are out of the question. Chi does her best with her regular point-and-shoot digital, mostly photographing the carvings on the obelisk, but I'm perfectly content with nothing. A good climb, a great view, an epic city—I don't need anything else. Photography is great, but oftentimes it can be a distraction from the experience itself.

Sitting back in the hostel, winding down from our impromptu adventure, I notice a change in both of my compatriots. Steve is no longer so despondent. While not completely mitigating his frustration, the climb has taken the edge off enough to let him leave the city in peace, Cloaca or no. And the flame that's been lit in Chi is there to stay. I feel kind of proud—I've helped create a fellow traveler.

"I can't stop thinking about it. It still gets my pulse racing," she writes me later. She doesn't have to explain further—I remember this feeling well. It's the same one I had for days after climbing the Manhattan Bridge.

There's another reason to celebrate. I do a little research, and it turns out that we haven't just climbed some random thing covered in scaffolding. The Lateran Obelisk is the oldest in Rome and the tallest in the entire world. The Egyptians constructed the 105-foot monument in Luxor approximately 3,500 years ago. It was brought to Rome by Constantius II in the fourth century and erected at the Circus Maximus. After having fallen sometime during the Middle Ages, our old buddy Sixtus V—who is now my front-runner for best pope ever— had it reerected next to Saint John Lateran, adding the cross on top that we had used to boost ourselves up in order to depaganize it. This was no mean feat. The obelisk weighs almost a million pounds.

Setting a goal and pushing yourself to achieve it is always rewarding, even if you ultimately fail or, as in our case of the Cloaca, even if you don't know if you succeeded or not. Rewarding in a very different way is learning you've accomplished something you didn't even mean to, just by seizing a random opportunity. I had helped one friend feel better, I had helped another unlock a part of herself, and I had seen a magnificent view of the Eternal City afforded only to a scant few. As I pack up to catch our train, I think back to a year ago and our climb up the Tour Saint-Jacques. I realize that, somehow, welcoming in the New Year with a climb up a landmark in a European capital seems to be becoming a tradition.

SIXTEEN

London, February 2007

I am blessed with good health. Doctor's visits are a routine thirty minutes. My eyesight has been 20/20 and my blood pressure 120/80 for as long as I can remember. I haven't had a significant injury since I broke my arm jumping off a picnic table when I was five, and the worst disease I've ever gotten was a bad case of poison ivy. It might be genes, it might be good immune system development, it's probably more than a bit of luck. One time I fell eight feet backward down a hole in the ground onto solid concrete in an abandoned courthouse and didn't even end up with a busted rib.

Steve has not had such good fortune. In addition to the bone cancer in his pelvis, he's had strep, staph, enterobacter, and *Aeromonas hydrophila* infections bad enough to hospitalize him. He's dislocated his right shoulder four times, dislocated his left shoulder once, broken his hip, broken his ankle, and had two concussions. He's taken a metal shard straight through his index finger after falling through a collapsing staircase in an abandoned hospital on an island in the East River, and had to have his forehead stapled shut after being mugged in a park in Upper Manhattan. He was once six hours away from having his left arm amputated when he got an infection after cutting open his hand in an underground river, and when he had the bone cancer he almost underwent a hemipelvectomy, which would have removed his right leg along with most of his right ass cheek. For twelve days in 2003 the doctors told him he was probably going to die.

Therefore, I'm not really that surprised when we're sitting in our hotel about six hours after arriving in London and I hear "Ummm . . . hey, Moe. I don't think I'm going to be able to go check out that drain with you guys. I'm pretty sure I broke my leg."

It's been about a week since we left the others behind in Italy to their own travels, and headed from Rome through Central Europe to Berlin before flying from Berlin to London this morning.

"You broke your leg between getting off the airplane and now?" I ask Steve, somewhat puzzled.

"Yeah—you know that cancer? It left part of one of my hip bones about this thick," he says, holding up his pinkie finger. "A bad knock at the wrong angle will crack it. Hey, uh, do you mind seeing if you can get some painkillers anywhere? I'd do it, but I don't think I can walk."

It's tough to explain the relationship between men, friendship, and pain. Emotional pain is easy to deal with in a male friendship; in fact, it's one of the main benefits of having friends. You know instinctively when to make a joke, when to commiserate, and when to just shut up, let the guy down a few whiskeys, and pretend like you never heard anything the next morning. But physical pain is different, especially for someone like me whose most agonizing memory is along the lines of slamming my finger in a door—not trying to grit out a broken leg without so much as a Tylenol PM.

I feel awkward. Steve is already apologetic about the situation, and I can tell he's bothered that his frail constitution has cost us a chance to go see a great part of the underground. That's why we're here, after all. London is the home of one of the first modern sewer systems in the world, designed by Joseph Bazalgette during the Victorian era in response to the "Great Stink" of 1858, when Central London filled with raw human waste to the point where one could walk from Buckingham Palace to the East End without escaping the smell of shit. The sewers are beautiful, featuring Victorian brick arches that would be at home in a posh house in Soho. Most are actually an infrastructure double dip, also serving as drains to carry the excess storm water runoff into the Thames River. This system incorporated many of the old tributaries of the Thames, which had already been submerged to varying degrees over the centuries. The group of London explorers we know are currently on a "lost river" kick, which involves examining old maps, heading to where these rivers used to be, looking for nearby "lids"—hatches or manholes—that lead down into the sewers, and then navigating underground until they've found the submerged waterway. This is the main reason we've put London on the itinerary: Steve is an underground rivers geek of the first magnitude. He can tell you every underground stream in the five boroughs of New York City, when it was buried, and prob-

© Eric Ruggiero 2012 – www.ericruggiero.com

SITTING ON THE
SHOULDERS OF EAGLES—
CHRYSLER BUILDING, NYC.
© Simon Yorkston

LONDON'S LOST RIVER FLEET.

© *Silent UK*

ABANDONED 18TH STREET SUBWAY STATION, EAST SIDE OF MANHATTAN.

© *Shane Perez*

UNDERGROUND ART—CATACOMBS OF PARIS.

UNDERGROUND ART—SUBWAYS OF NEW YORK.

Photo by Joseph Carnevale

CLIMBING NEW YORK CITY'S BRIDGES . . .

THE BROOKLYN BRIDGE

© *Simon Yorkston*

THE MANHATTAN BRIDGE

THE WILLIAMSBURG BRIDGE

© *Shane Perez*

THE GEORGE WASHINGTON BRIDGE

RIVERSIDE PARK TUNNEL MURALS.

© Shane Perez

AFTER THE BUFF.

RIVERSIDE PARK TUNNEL.
© *Allison Davis*

CATACOMB BONES, PARIS.
© *Eric Ruggiero 2012 –*
www.ericruggiero.com

NEGLINKA RIVER, MOSCOW.

ably what manhole cover to pop to find it. Plenty of nights when I've called him up, looking for a bridge or tunnel adventure, I've gotten, "Hey, actually do you want to go pop a couple sewer manholes? I'm looking for this stream that got submerged in the 1800s and I think I know where it might be." Steve's dream is to get a doctorate in history and become a professor of subterranean urban hydrological development.

Steve's shared academic obsession with lost watercourses is how we'd gotten in touch with the Londoners. So far they've had some success in finding many of London's lost rivers, and in their quest have found a lot of less historical but no less rewarding parts of Bazalgette's system. We'd just gotten an e-mail from two local drainers with the message "Found a new drain mates! You have to come check this one out, it's huge!" Huge drains are kind of like the burger and fries of the urban exploring world. Not exactly rare, but very satisfying.

I know Steve doesn't want me to see how hurt he is, and it seems like sticking around and making him feel obligated to put on a brave face is just adding to his misery. But what kind of person tells a friend, "Hey, sorry about the broken leg and all, but I'm off to see the town. Chin up, guv'nor!"? I have no idea how to navigate this scenario, so I'm pretty happy when Steve suggests I go try to find some drugs, which lets me leave the room but still be helpful. Luckily, in West London, drugstores are both open late and sell codeine over the counter. Steve somehow manages to not down all the pills in one gulp and follows the instructions to the letter when it comes to dosage and timing. When I tell him I'm pretty impressed by this restraint, I get a grim reply: "Yeah. I'm used to this."

The next day Steve somehow manages to hobble out of the room, and we take a cab to the Lord Wigram Ward of the Chelsea and Westminster Hospital. There they give him real drugs, stabilize his leg, and luckily have an Internet connection. Steve finds a cheap flight on Air India back to New York. I get him to the airport, watch the stewardess wheel him through security, and I'm companionless in London for the next three days. I take the first day just to walk around and sightsee, resolving to get going on the exploring tomorrow.

London in 2007 is dangerously close to an Orwellian surveillance world. Cameras cover the financial district, also known as "The City" or "The Square Mile," along with signs proclaiming things like "Do Not Engage in Anti-Social Behavior." Now, I certainly don't consider my mission—a climb up the old stock exchange tower under renovation on Threadneedle Street, in the heart of the Square Mile—antisocial behavior, but I figure the London cops probably would. So I'm nervous. After pacing back and forth by the building for a while, I hit the pay phone. Thirteen digits later, Steve is on the phone in his hospital bed on the East Side of Manhattan, exhausted and doped up on morphine but still ready with a pep talk.

"Hey, no, you should definitely go for it, Moe. I'm pretty sure it's a good idea. It'll be totally chill. Hey, c'mon, you should totally do it."

I leave the phone with a new resolution. Unfortunately, while this pep talk was going on, two road workers have parked themselves right in front of the spot where I planned to jump the fence. Fine, I'll take a walk around the block. After an hour they're still there. More walks around the block for me. Another hour later, they're *still* there. Steve's pep talk is wasted as I manage to navigate the night bus back to the hotel.

I have one more day in London, and figure I'll take the time to see Stonehenge. But since I don't want too much time to kill between seeing Stonehenge and trying the climb again, I take in a couple museums in the morning and head out on an afternoon train. Big mistake. It turns out Stonehenge is in the absolute middle of nowhere. And in the winter it closes at four p.m. I roll into the nearest town with a train station, Salisbury, about nine miles away, at three forty-five.

Well, I'm not about to just turn around and take the train right back. I figure something like Stonehenge, out in the countryside, probably isn't surrounded by a metal wall. If I can manage to get out there, I can at least see it from the road. I have two problems: how to get there, and how to get there before dark.

It turns out there's a smaller city, Amesbury, about three miles from Stonehenge. A few pounds and a twenty-minute bus ride later, and I'm in a little shop reminiscent of what you'd find in a regular U.S. roadside gas station, just with a significantly outsized dose of quaintness. I pick up a map of the town. It doesn't extend as far as Stonehenge, but I do see a line on the edge labeled "Old Stonehenge Road." That seems promising. I head out, hoping I can make it before dark.

Old Stonehenge Road eventually turns into a highway. I'm on the south end of it, between the road and a field. As the sun is setting, I can just make out the giant rocks off in the distance. Stonehenge sits in a field on top of a hill. The hill is in the crotch of a Y, with highways forming the Y. By the time I reach it, it's grown dark, and I realize there is no way to get there without crossing the highway. I look across the highway. There's a barbed-wire fence on the other side. By itself it would be no problem to navigate—it's not more than chest-high, consisting only of three strands of barbed wire running horizontally between the fence posts. The problem is that there's no gap between it and the road, and it's only about five-thirty—prime rush-hour time. I can't believe it. An hour and a half on the train, twenty minutes on the bus, and at least an hour walking, and my choice is: being stopped within spitting distance of my goal or playing Frogger with highway traffic in the dark. This time I have no pay phone around, no pep talk, nobody to push me along on that last step. I think about it, waiting for breaks in traffic and resolving to go when the gap is just a little bigger. Several minutes later I'm still standing by the side of the road.

I start to think about how I'll tell this story to people back home—think of how I'll reply to the inevitable "So then you just turned around and walked back to the bus station?" This leads me to suck it up and take a step out into the highway. I quickly see a car coming and step right back. I force myself to imagine that look on someone's face when they are unsuccessfully trying to hide their disdain for the person across from them. I think about how this is just like going around the red sign at the end of the subway platform, something that's as simple as putting one foot in front of the other, albeit very quickly. I look around, see no headlights, and dash across. I end up doing a sort of front roll/flop over the top strand of barbed wire, ripping my jacket and jeans but keeping my skin—and pride—intact.

This is it. I stand up, quickly assess myself for any injury, and start to climb up the hill that leads to Stonehenge. As I climb, I keep thinking that there has to be some sort of catch. But there isn't. Once again, there's no physical border, nothing real keeping me from where I want to go. I simply get closer and closer until I'm touching the massive bluestone megaliths that make up the complex. I have the place all to myself and it is amazing. No tourists, no fences, nothing but history and me. I take a few minutes to just wander around and marvel, softly touching the rocks. They're smoother than they appear—much too smooth to try to indulge my initial instinct of trying to climb them. They're also slightly warm to the touch, contrasting with the cold winter evening. I figure a couple of pictures are in order.

As I take the third photo, I see someone walking toward me. The guards must have seen my flashes go off. I'm not that surprised; I can't imagine that they leave the place completely deserted after hours.

"Hello," I say, deciding the best course of action is just to play the dumb American tourist who doesn't know you can't just walk right in.

"You know we're closed, mate," the guard replies. He can't be more than nineteen years old. "I'm going to have to escort you out. This way, please."

A few other teenage guards join us on the way out, and I surmise that this must be the local after-school job for the youth of Amesbury. I want to ask if they take their girlfriends here, or have clandestine midnight parties every once in a while. What I really want to do is ask the guards to take a few photos of me before we leave. But in these kinds of situations where you seem to be getting off the hook, the best course of action is just to shut up, count your blessings, and get out of there as soon as possible.

As they take me out through the gaudy tourist entrance, I'm happier and happier that I went the way I did. There's a huge difference between walking up under your own power, seeing your goal appear off in the distance, and being rewarded with getting to wander it unmolested—and rolling up in the SUV with the kids, forking over fifteen quid, going through the turnstiles and past the souvenir shop, and snapping your photos from behind the ropes. Until the guard showed up, I could almost believe it was a hundred years ago, with Stonehenge untouched by postcards, tickets, and official paths. How many people get a place of such historical importance freely to themselves to interact with, even if only for a few minutes, in this day and age?

I get back to London from Stonehenge at about nine-thirty. I'm already pretty happy with myself, but there's still a reason I stayed one more day. I catch the last Underground from my hotel near Earls Court and am in the Square Mile, walking down Threadneedle Street to the old London Stock Exchange building at one a.m. I don't call Steve this time. I don't even hesitate like I did at the highway. I've been having a pretty serious conversation with another partner—a partner by the name of Jack Daniel's. A quick look around and I boost myself up and over the wooden barriers. Sometimes it pays to just take the shortcut.

Once I get on the scaffolding, I'm reminded of the unconscious cultural assumptions our brains make. In the U.S., scaffolding is almost always erected according to the same pattern each time, so scaffolding climbs are usually pretty simple affairs: you find your way in, circle around until you find the ladder or staircase, and head on up; the ladder or stairs will be in the same place on each level. But this is different. There are various bits and pieces of scaffolding kind of scattered around the building—on different stories, in different locations. I can't figure out how to get more than a few flights up. I'll find what I think is a ladder up to the top, it'll dead-end after two flights, and I'll have to head back down and find something else to try. I'm conscious of the fact that there's probably some form of security patrolling the place, and as a result I feel like I'm in one of those 1980s video games where you have to navigate around a simple maze while avoiding running into one of the bad guys wandering around. Finally, after about twenty minutes of drunkenly climbing around the scaffolding, I get the bright idea to try the building itself. I maneuver through an open section on the third floor, find an internal fire staircase, and twenty-six flights later I'm on top of London.

I've chosen a great focal point. The old London Stock Exchange is right on the fulcrum of the old part of the City of London and the new part of the City of London. To the east is the brightly lit postmodern skyscraper city. To the west is the

ON TOP OF LONDON.

centuries-old classical London, anchored by Saint Paul's Cathedral. I take in the three hundred years of progress in one of the world's greatest focal points of civilization just by turning 360 degrees. Nothing antisocial about that.

London in early 2007 turns out to just be finding its groove. Siologen and Dsankt soon arrive in town and, along with some others, set off a chain reaction of urban exploration. Everything falls. First up are the rest of the lost underground rivers, and when those are found, the crew starts in on the abandoned Tube stations. We all considered these next to impossible, especially after the Tube bombing that July, but over the course of the next four years every last one is infiltrated. It doesn't stop there. They summit every major construction site, including the Shard, which is slated to be the tallest building in Europe. They get up onto the dome of Saint Paul's Cathedral, down into Winston Churchill's subterranean bomb shelter, up the chimneys of the old Battersea Power Station. They even manage to take a ride on (and crash) the queen's personal underground mail delivery train. All the surveillance, all the "Do Not Engage in

Anti-Social Behavior" signs, all the paranoia, turns out to be for show, a muscle-bound bouncer who can barely throw a punch. I visit London a few more times during this blitz, each time tagging along, essentially as a tourist, to something I'd thought impossible on my previous visit.

SEVENTEEN

Paris, February 2007

After London, I take the train to Paris to visit some Parisian explorers before heading back to New York for a day and then on to South America. My second night there I meet up with one of them on a street corner in the XIVe arrondissement. There is a public toilet not fifty feet away from this corner. And even if I couldn't make it that far, there's a fairly well-concealed public park right in front of me. But no, here I am peeing directly into the middle of the street. Why? Well . . .

"What? We are in France!" my companion for the night, Eric, replies when I tell him I'm going to head down the block to the public toilet. "Here, I have to take a piss too.

"You know what the most Latin country in the world is?" he continues as he lets a stream go right in the gutter of Rue Daguerre. "Not Italy, not Spain. France." My companion knows well of what he speaks. He's been relying on that relaxed Latin "Can't be bothered" attitude for quite a while now.

Paris is absolutely unlike any other city in the world when it comes to urban exploration. Combine large, dedicated, fairly well-coordinated core groups of adventurers with an incredibly relaxed attitude toward recreational municipal trespassing—or really anything that would lead to a hassle on the authorities' part. What you get are things like a clandestine movie theater—complete with open bar—that operated completely unknown by the authorities in an abandoned rock quarry about five minutes from the Eiffel Tower. Or a group that spends a year, totally illegally and completely unnoticed, repairing a clock in the Panthéon, one of Paris's national landmarks and the burial place of such luminaries as Voltaire, Marie Curie, and Jean-Jacques Rousseau. After the repairs were completed, the administration of the Panthéon was so embarrassed that they ended up taking this group to court, where the prosecutor called the charges "stupid" and the tribunal head was flummoxed as to why they didn't simply thank the repairers and start operating the clock again. That's Paris for you.

After peeing, we wait for our companions. "Where's the manhole?" I ask.

Eric looks at me sideways and chuckles. "No manhole," he says, in a tone that doesn't invite a follow-up question.

His companions arrive a short time later. "OK, come with me," he says. "I think we'll use the easy way." That's when I notice we're right by the entrance to the museum that leads to the official catacomb tour. One rule of Paris is that oftentimes secrets are hidden in plain sight. Eric simply takes out a key ring and tries a couple, and the door opens. "Stay along the wall so you don't get seen," he says, pointing to a solitary security camera in the corner. "I don't mind the eight euro," he continues, "but going this way is much better: you don't have to worry about tourists, you can take tripod photos, you can—"

I can't take it anymore. I have to ask. "How did you get the keys?"

He chuckles. "What, you don't have people working on the key problem? Or the alarm problem?"

Well, no, we don't. Maybe we should. But it's not just the attitude of the authorities that's the problem. Paris is a very old and very stagnant city. New York has a few interesting nooks and crannies but doesn't have nearly the history needed to create a subterranean network like the one that exists in Paris. Places get closed up and reopened in Paris all the time; it's just part of the game. Our first time in the city we heard of an entrance to the catacombs, only to find it welded shut when we got there. We assumed the game was over: the police had found it, sealed it, and that was that. I ask Eric about this entrance during our time on the street together. It turns out the entrance has been reopened and closed back up half a dozen times in between my visits. There's always more than enough stuff in Paris to occupy everyone from hard-core explorers to casual cataphiles. In New York, if one of our favorite underground niches gets closed up, it's a blow. There's a very limited number of these that are regularly accessible by your average curious urbanist, especially in this day and age.

Paris has also not changed much for about 150 years. Nothing new really gets built in the city proper, and historic preservation laws are draconian. In New York, you can't count on an interesting space being there tomorrow, much less for the time it takes to transform it into a movie theater. The town is always changing. Old things go, new things come, spaces get filled in, or dug up, or sealed off. Every once in a while someone manages to pull off a good, extralegal event without getting the place shut down. But for the most part it's still a few folks, a nutty idea, an impromptu adventure, and that's a wrap.

Maybe it's laziness. Maybe it's fear. Maybe it's the dregs of the post-9/11 paranoia. Maybe it's just the fact that we don't have the positive feedback loop France has: the more you pull off, the more people get into it, the more attempts are made, the more it becomes just a part of the city.

After heading into the museum, we turn out to have a pretty nondescript excursion, at least for this group. A secret passageway, an illegal key, an undiscovered tunnel below the XIVe arrondissement, some wine and cheese. Just your average night out in the City of Light.

New York City, February 2007

After I finish my trip to Europe, I have one day back in New York before leaving for South America, which I use to visit Steve in the hospital. Molly is there taking care of him, and he seems in reasonably good spirits.

"Hey, Moe. Welcome to the other half of my life," Steve says by way of greeting, and I feel honored that I've been invited into this half as well.

"How was the trip back?" I ask.

"It was OK. The plane wasn't too full, and the attendants let me lie down across three seats since I couldn't really bend my leg. And on the way to the plane I got to ride on one of those little carts you sometimes see in the airport terminals." He looks lovingly at Molly. "And then when I landed, it turned out this wonderful lady had managed to mobilize half the airport staff with her worry about me. I got carted through customs at JFK in about three seconds. Except for the fact that I was in blinding pain the entire time, the whole thing was actually fantastic."

"How long's it going to take for the break to heal?" I ask.

"Well, actually it turns out my leg isn't broken at all," he says.

"Really? So what's the deal?"

"So I went to the emergency room the night I got back. But apparently, in New York, if you go into the emergency room in blinding fucking pain but with no readily apparent source of that pain, they think you probably just want drugs. So I spent about the most hideous twelve hours of my life not getting drugs before they realized my complaint was actually real.

"They operated on me the next day—the surgeon was really good," he goes on. "Afterward, he explained to me that I have this raging infection in my hip. They cut out a lot of stuff in there when I had the cancer, so there's all this space for infections to kind of fester and grow. The surgeon actually had to scrub out the hip socket from all the pus and infection. I'm not really sure how exactly he actually did it, but I've got this image of him just industriously scrubbing away with a toothbrush, getting the gunk out. After the operation he asked me where I could have possibly picked this up." Steve gives me a knowing chuckle. "I couldn't stop laughing when he asked that."

"Uh, I've been all the same places you have," I say, thinking of strange bacteria hiding in the crevices of my joints and tendons, just biding their time before they're ready to eat away at my bones.

"Nah, you're good," Steve replies. "I actually asked the doctors about this, and they said if you were going to get anything, you definitely would have gotten it by now."

I temporarily consider abandoning my upbringing as a staunch atheist before deciding instead to give the credit to my peasant ancestors and their hardy immune systems that have been passed on to their lazy and undeserving progeny in America. Because I've got no time for doctors. I'm on a flight to Brazil in three hours.

EIGHTEEN

São Paulo, February 2007

He's a well-dressed fellow, tall, with thinning hair. He speaks fluent English with a clipped Portuguese accent. He pretty much resembles the successful Brazilian businessman that he is, running an import-export shop. What he doesn't look like is the type of guy who spends his spare time bribing security guards and making his way through shantytowns in order to explore abandoned buildings in São Paulo.

Still, this is what Jorge does with much of his spare time. It's what we are planning to do the night I arrive in São Paulo. But an hour after I arrive, the rain starts, and this being Brazil, it does not let up. The abandoned mansion we were planning on going to has recently been condemned due to water damage, so it's not safe at all in this kind of weather. We'll have to wait. Jorge tells me the mansion used to belong to a coffee baron a century ago, when this now run-down part of central São Paulo was the ritzy area, one of the first wealthy neighborhoods built for the coffee barons who controlled southern Brazil during the post-colonial era. In fact, the neighborhood's official name is Campos Elíseos—Portuguese for "Champs-Élysées." Today, though, is a very different story; in fact, a couple blocks south of where we're going is a neighborhood colloquially known as Cracolândia—or, in English, "Crackland."

I had met Jorge in New York the previous year, and he had invited me to call him up for an exploration if I was ever in São Paulo. A few hours ago, when we were at a posh function at a museum downtown, he introduced me to a couple other people, Gabriel and José Rodolfo, who belong to the NGO Jorge had formed, the Associação Preserva São Paulo—Preserva SP for short. I loved the juxtaposition of being at a fancy event, knowing that later we were supposed to be exploring old dilapidated buildings. Jorge's group is mainly an architectural and preservation organization, but I soon discovered that Jorge, Gabriel, and José Rodolfo were always up for a conversation or exploration on anything that has to do with cities. On meeting them for the first time, I felt an immediate professional kinship.

A lot of people I've traipsed around cities with—explorers as well as more standard urbanists and tourists—have a certain inability to see or respect anything beyond their particular interests. Hard-core explorer types don't see the point in wandering the streets; indeed, some have a rather disdainful view of anything that doesn't involve trespassing. In contrast, more highbrow urbanists can take the attitude that the guts of what actually make a city run are unimportant next to architectural detailing and landscaped parks. Many people interested in how a city is structured aren't interested in actually having a conversation with the individuals who live there, and others who are interested in the communities and social aspects of a city don't understand that its physical structure plays a large role in dic-

tating how these develop. What frustrates me the most are
people who think that the only areas in an entire city worth
visiting are populated—or about to be populated—by people
like themselves. And many of these people don't really grasp
that any other kind of place even exists—that there are dozens
of neighborhoods and millions of people for whom their life is
completely irrelevant. Not everyone is able or willing to walk
for hours in unfamiliar areas, or climb bridges in the middle of
the night, or strike up a random conversation with the guy next
to them at the lunch counter. But I've always found it hard to
respect people who don't even show an interest in the parts of
the city that are outside their zone of familiarity or, even worse,
think that they have a complete knowledge of the entire city
based on the narrow part they do know well. This shared philosophy was why I got on so well with the people I met in São
Paulo. We spent several days conversing, exploring, and debat-
ing pretty much all aspects of their town, from the sidewalk
tiling, to the layout of the street markets, to what should be
done with the distinctive antennae on the roofs of the skyscrapers that line Avenida Paulista. After the rain finally lets
up a few days later, we head to the mansion.

M any, many urban explorers start off in this hobby because
they find beauty and intrigue in abandoned buildings,
factories, and hospitals. There are countless websites with
heavy use of phrases like "the majesty of decay" and "tenderness
in rust" to document these kinds of places. I've always thought
the places interesting myself, and have certainly never turned
away from an open door to an old abandoned building. Many

times abandonments are noteworthy because they're some of the very few places where the past hasn't been painted over or bricked up, offering an unmediated glimpse into history. Exploring them, you often find clues to how people lived and worked twenty, or fifty, or sometimes over a hundred years ago, the experience falling somewhere in the crack between sociology and archaeology.

In addition, many urbanists and explorers look at the city like doctors look at a human body. Abandonment and urban decay is part of the life cycle of many cities the same way death and decomposition is part of the life cycle of the human body. In medical school they offer classes on geriatrics as well as obstetrics, and both are important in understanding and caring for people.

But there is a big difference between being a doctor and being a mortician. Some urban explorers' interest in urban decay can become fetishistic, almost ghoulish in a way, leading to what many people have dubbed "ruin porn." Especially in cities that are facing challenges of disinvestment and depopulation, an attitude of fascination toward this decay—even if meant appreciatively—can be construed as akin to visiting an oncology ward to observe the aesthetics of the patients.

Abandonment is vastly different in different cities. In economically strong cities like New York, abandonment is usually a transitional phase: it's usually only a matter of time before the building is either restored or torn down to make way for something new, with the few that aren't usually having a unique, case-by-case reason for stagnation. In cities that have shakier economies but a general sense of optimism, abandonment is an investment. Old buildings are secured until it's profitable to restore or replace them. In cities with bad economies and de-clining populations, abandonment is simply part of the urban landscape.

Exploring abandonments in these three types of cities is different too. In the first kind, where abandonment is actually fairly active, you're generally looking for a friendly worker to let you in or some kind of easy unsecured entrance during inactive times. The second type of abandonment is the toughest: an inactive site leads to none of the many possibilities of entry that become available when a site is continually being entered and structurally changed. However, the fact that it is also perceived as having potential value often results in its being heavily se-cured and sealed, at least by abandoned-building standards. Fencing is added and topped with barbed wire, entrances are cinder-blocked up, occasionally security guards are even sta-tioned there. These are the ones that take a little work. In the third type of city, exploring is generally as easy as walking down the street and going through a hole in the wall.

B ut these three types of abandonment really apply only to the cities of North America and Western Europe. Most cities in South America and other more recently heavily urban-ized parts of the world follow a very different pattern. Even in cities with depressed or only mildly vibrant economies, there is still enormous population growth and a huge housing crunch. This leads to a different type of abandonment, one in which the buildings aren't really abandoned but populated informally by various squatter communities. This is the case with the abandoned coffee baron's mansion that we are going to visit in

São Paulo—as well as pretty much every other abandoned building of significance.

S quatting was also common in the New York of yesteryear, at least by American standards. New York never experienced the heavy depopulation of other large northeastern and midwestern cities. At its worst, in the late 1970s, New York's population was off only about 10 percent from its peak. Compare this to Pittsburgh, Buffalo, Cleveland, and numerous other cities that have lost 50 percent or more of their population. St. Louis today is home to a little over a third of its peak population. As a result, there is simply not much of a housing crunch in these cities. Sure, you might run into some empty buildings populated by squatters, but not very often. The reason is simple: there are a lot more empty buildings than there is need for them. In New York, even at its worst, this was never the case. In addition to less depopulation, abandoned (or sometimes occupied) buildings were likely to be actively destroyed—torched by the landlords for the insurance money, by the tenants to gain preference for homeless housing, or just accidentally, victims of disinvestment and a failure to follow the fire code—rendering them uninhabitable, even to the homeless.

The abandoned coffee baron's mansion we're at now is also in this condition. Water damage has led to the city declaring an emergency evacuation of the squatters. The result is an abandoned building, and a thriving shantytown behind the gates in the yard.

The folks in Preserva SP have been there before and know some of the inhabitants. They call off the barking dogs, which

ABANDONED MANSION.

they have in place to keep out druggies and not curious urbanists, and let us in. We bring some presents and chat for a bit with the residents before entering the actual building. I end up talking mostly with a friendly, middle-aged woman named Neiva.

You would think a shantytown in the concrete yard of a half-decomposed building would be a residence of last resort. But it turns out it's not. I learn from Neiva that the government has offered the residents new housing virtually for free. The problem: it's situated over three hours away. Most residents have opted to stay instead, because many people have jobs and connections downtown that they have to be close to. This demonstrates the enduring problem of the South American megalopolis.

Many people in New York complain about the poor getting

forced out of neighborhoods with convenient access to the city center—in our case Manhattan. While this is true, it is nothing on the level of the amoeba-like urban sprawl of the poorer parts of the globe. A lack of comprehensive public transport (São Paulo has three full subway lines and a six-station stub line, unconnected to the main network, for twenty million people) and heavy traffic all conspire to make getting from point A to point B a lengthy and wholly unpredictable task. It's not even an option—a best-case scenario of six hours a day in traffic commuting, and a worst-case scenario of working late and having to grab your few hours of sleep on the sidewalk? The folks would rather stay in a shantytown than endure it. It's a good bit of perspective for those people in New York who complain about being forced to move two subway stops farther out into Brooklyn.

After conversing with the residents, we head into the mansion. It's a beautiful old building. My companions are mainly interested in the colonial architecture, pointing out old detailing and brickwork. But for me the most interesting things are the murals. The mansion is covered with them—some whimsical, like a painting of a Garfield-style obese cat, others serious and sad, commemorating the expulsion of the residents of the abandoned building. There are some examples of *pixação*, the harsh and angular graffiti style native to São Paulo.

I notice some writing by one of the murals, partly in English and partly in Portuguese. It reads "Saudades—Last Day Sadness." *Saudade* is one of those wonderfully untranslatable words that encapsulates a feeling endemic to a particular culture. It's sometime loosely translated as "homesickness."

"Last Day Sadness" mural.
"Saudades" is written above in *Pixação*.

Zezão.

"Longing melancholy nostalgia" is more accurate, but even that is far from perfect. It's a particularly Portuguese word, one that I'll probably never really understand.

There's also a strange design, a snaking pattern of two shades of blue, which I notice on a few walls throughout the building. José Rodolfo tells me he sees this pattern only in places like this—places the people walking down the street normally never see. Later I find out this is by a Paulista artist, a guy named Zezão, who started painting this pattern in the sewers of São Paulo.

This is one of the most rewarding things about going exploring: the ability to see things other people don't. What it happens to be—an old sign on an abandoned observation deck, a message on the subway tunnel walls, a mural painted in an empty building—isn't even all that important. Anyone who says they don't get at least a small kick from the exclusiveness of going places you aren't allowed is lying. I leave happy, saying good-bye to Neiva on the way out.

NINETEEN

When trying to get official access to interesting, generally off-limits places, you're usually looking at one of four different scenarios, depending on how popular and well-known the place is. These scenarios are really not too different from trying to get to any place that you can't just walk right into. Nightclubbers will recognize at least two or three of these stages as well.

In scenario one, the place is so obscure and unknown that the challenge is just finding the guy with the keys, who is usually happy to let you in as long as it isn't dangerous or too much of a hassle. He'll usually talk your ear off too: it's always exciting when people show an interest in something you own or manage, especially when it's a rare occurrence.

In scenario two, the place has become better known and more popular. As this happens, access becomes easier. Since people are interested in the place, an infrastructure is set up. There's someone to handle calls, someone who can open the doors, maybe even official hours. At the very least, when you ask about the place, you don't have to deal with responses like "What? Why do want to go there?" or "Uhhh, I don't really know who would be in charge of that." For the owners, the benefit is social. People like showing off what they own, like the idea that others consider their area of expertise important and interesting.

In scenario three, as interest in the place grows, a tipping point is reached and the process reverses itself. Now it's a hassle to let in everyone who wants to visit. And there's no social benefit to doing so, either, because the place is already popular. The point of giving people access to an interesting place that you happen to be in charge of is pride, social value. If that pride and social value are already there, what's the point? Why bother with the time and hassle anymore? And, worst of all, now exclusivity becomes the way you gain even more social value from the place. A vicious cycle begins: the fewer people you let in, the more exclusive it becomes, the more social value is gained, and the more people want to go.

Finally, in stage four, as interest grows even further, another tipping point is reached. Now people figure out how to make money off the place. The value is no longer social but monetary. If they can make enough money to make the hassle worthwhile, then the place becomes open—but always on a monetized basis. This isn't necessarily a standard admission charge; it could be for special events, for professional photo or film shoots, for high-end fund-raisers, for any number of things. In fact, the most disturbing trend is when this monetization and exclusivity are combined: instead of trying to make a small amount of money off a large number of people (like a standard observation deck), the building tries to leverage its exclusivity in order to make a large amount of money off a small number of people, thereby making money, saving time and hassle, and preserving exclusivity all at once.

This can easily be graphed on something I call the "Access Curve."

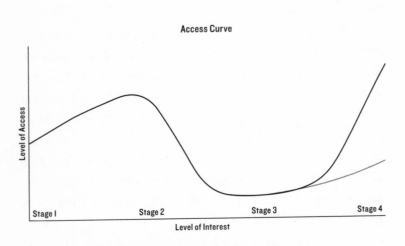

Access Curve

THE UPPER LINE REPRESENTS WHAT HAPPENS WHEN OWNERS ULTIMATELY CHARGE A STANDARD ADMISSION FEE IN STAGE 4. THE LOWER LINE REPRESENTS WHAT HAPPENS WHEN THE OWNER INSTEAD TRIES TO LEVERAGE EXCLUSIVITY AND BECOME A HIGH-END DESTINATION IN STAGE 4.

In New York, all interesting rooftops have long since progressed to stage three or even stage four. For instance, one nice spring day a few years after this trip to Brazil, I'm riding around with the cast and crew of *Off Limits*, a show on the Travel Channel about places normally closed to the public. I've already done some scouting for them and helped host a segment, and on their last day we're looking to get a rooftop shot of the city for the opening credits.

"I use what I call my 'good ol' boy' charm," says the field producer. "You know, just be real friendly, pretend I don't quite know what I'm doing. It usually works pretty well."

I already know we are doomed for failure. New York City is not a place where you can just go where you want with a smile and a nod—even if you are on TV.

Still, we give it a shot. I know several roofs that will provide great views and be easy enough to film on. The producer and I try six or seven. At every one the response is the same: either a flat no or an invitation to try to make an appointment to rent the rooftop (at a hefty rate) through the management.

Luckily, in São Paulo, rooftops—as well as the city itself—are still sitting in stage two. People are excited to show off their city, and they feel that what they have to show far exceeds the interest generally shown in it. São Paulo is the largest city in the southern hemisphere, and arguably the financial, social, and fashion capital of the continent as well as the Lusophone world. Yet it's never mentioned in the same breath as Paris, London, New York, or Tokyo, or even thought of as a vacation destination like nearby Buenos Aires or Rio de Janeiro. I'm not entirely sure why this is, but it probably has something to do with the outside perception of Rio as being music and beaches, and Buenos Aires as beautiful people and tango, while São Paulo is, quite unfairly, just thought of as a kind of generic, third-world megalopolis.

I make it up to half a dozen rooftops when I'm here. Some are your standard tourist observation decks, although almost all are free of charge. Some are open only sporadically or, as is standard in Latin countries, seemingly at the whim of whoever happens to be on duty. Some are private, but it is simply a matter of asking building management to let you up. Most of these decks are in the old downtown, affording only somewhat different views of the city, although I also get up to a rooftop bar in the Avenida Paulista area a few miles south, which has a gorgeous view of the row of rooftop antennae that is a São Paulo skyline landmark.

There's been talk of removing the antennae—which are located on top of the skyscrapers on Avenida Paulista because the avenue is geographically the highest point in São Paulo—and replacing them with one large antenna similar to the CN Tower in Toronto and the Space Needle in Seattle. Personally, I hope this doesn't happen. Even though the antennae are somewhat outdated and not terribly aesthetic, they're an interesting identifying feature of the skyline and a symbol of the city. For a town that doesn't always do a great job marketing itself, some kind of unique identity is always a plus.

On my last day in São Paulo, I decide to head up one more observation deck, the Edificio Itália downtown. The Edificio Itália was erected by the city's Italian community (hence the name) and has both a restaurant and an observation deck at the top. My guidebook tells me I have to patronize the restaurant in order to visit the deck, but I have quickly learned not to believe what I read in guidebooks concerning what's open and allows visitors and what doesn't. Some information is right, some is half right, some is officially, factually correct but not at all relevant to actual reality, and some is dead wrong. It turns out the observation deck of the Edificio Itália is currently perfectly open and free of charge, no restaurant visit needed. I head up

there for the view, and as a
surprise end up encountering
Gabriel from Preserva SP and
his friend Guto.

The Edificio Itália used
to be the tallest building not
just in São Paulo but in all of
Brazil. That honor now belongs to the Mirante do Vale,
a narrow rectangular building
a little ways away. Downtown
São Paulo is hilly, and despite
being the tallest building, the
Mirante do Vale actually ends
up being lower than some
others due to its being con-

VIEW OF THE MIRANTE DO VALE.

structed in a valley ("Mirante do Vale" roughly translates into
"Overlook of the Valley"). We decide to head over and see if
they'll let us up on the roof.

São Paulo is kind of schizophrenic when it comes to residential security. Middle-class people tend to live in high-rises
surrounded by fences, topped with barbed or even electrified
wires, and staffed 24/7 by security guards. You might think
this would make for difficult access to the roofs of residential
buildings. But no, we simply go up to reception and ask, and
five minutes later a janitor is escorting us up. The elevators have
an interesting transport philosophy: they stop halfway between
two floors, with either a half-flight walk up or a half-flight

FIVE FLOORS OF NOTHING.
TOP OF THE MIRANTE DO VALE, SÃO PAULO.

walk down the stairs to get to the floor. This leads to half as many potential stops and, at least theoretically, less transportation time.

We go to the top floor, walk up a half-flight of stairs, and the janitor unlocks a door. But we aren't on the roof yet. It turns out the top five stories don't exist. Not empty floors but nonexistent floors. No floors, no ceilings, no walls. Just five-foot-wide concrete ledges forming huge rectangles surrounding nothing, one for each level. We get up to the top level, the middle third of which is actually covered by a helicopter landing pad. The view is spectacular.

The janitor hangs out while we go traipsing onto the other part, the topmost of the aforementioned five-foot-wide ledges. The ledge is crumbling to the point where there are holes in the concrete you can stare right through. There are no guardrails, no nothing, with a fifty-foot drop on one side and a five-hundred-foot drop on the other. I cannot imagine anywhere in the United States letting us do this—for free no less. We hang out for a while, take some pictures, tip the janitor 10 reais (about $4), and head back down. I am already in love with Brazil. And it's the weekend before Carnival. And the next stop is Rio.

Rio de Janeiro, February 2007

Rio is my chill city. I've decided to take a break from adventuring and just hang out on the beach, listen to great music, and otherwise be a regular tourist for a while. This is greatly helped by knowing my friend Felipe, a native Carioca (as residents of Rio are known) whose family always makes sure to make me feel welcome in their city—although sometimes in unexpected ways.

"Oh, man. I totally forgot to tell you. Tomorrow we have to dress up like women." This is the news from Felipe as we're sitting enjoying the best black beans in Rio after heading back to his house from a street party in Ipanema. The party was terrific. The music was great, the atmosphere fantastic. My only complaint was the complete lack of bathrooms. The default men's room turned out to be a palm tree on the beach. I have no idea where the default women's room may have been—or even if there was one.

But as fun as the Ipanema party was, it was just a warm-up. The next day we wake up, and Felipe presents me with a piece of black negligee that I somehow manage to make fit. He dons a red bra and dress himself and we're off, picking up a few friends en route.

Three days earlier I was ready to skip Rio de Janeiro. I'd

been there before, seen the town. It wasn't on the way to where I was going. I was having problems getting in touch with Felipe. I had a whole host of reasons not to go. What could I have been thinking? In my book, anyone who doesn't want to see Rio every chance they get needs to have their head examined.

Rio de Janeiro is undoubtedly the most strangely beautiful city I've ever visited. From an urban planning perspective, nobody in their right mind would plunk down a city where Rio is: it's literally built around (and sometimes on or through) mountains. Not a few nice little hills like in San Francisco or Rome— mountains. Throw this together with over a dozen beaches and a rain forest, as well as the culture, people, architecture, neighborhoods, and everything else you can expect from a big, diverse city. Add one of the world's most famous landmarks, and then put the whole thing in Brazil. It's not hard to see why they call the place "La Cidade Maravilhosa"—"The Marvelous City."

Like most interesting cities, at least from a geographical perspective, Rio came about because it had a great harbor, which led to early colonial settlement and development. But its surrounding terrain is not exactly conducive to a traditional city structure. When viewed from above, it becomes even more clear how absolutely ridiculous it is to have a city there—and how great it is that there actually is one. And luckily, this isn't too hard to do.

For anyone traveling to Brazil, my advice is this: You'll probably fly into Guarulhos, São Paulo's international airport. Stay awhile in São Paulo, and then fly to Rio. If you fly from abroad directly into Rio, or if you transfer from Guarulhos to Rio, you'll almost certainly end up flying into Galeão Inter-

ASCENT FROM CONGONHAS.

national Airport, north of the city. However, if you book a ticket from Congonhas, São Paulo's domestic airport, into Santos Dumont, Rio's domestic airport, you'll be rewarded with one of the most spectacular flight descents in the world. The ascent from São Paulo isn't bad, either: going up you can see just how vast the world's seventh-largest city really is.

As Congonhas–Santos Dumont is the most traveled flight pattern in the world, with over one thousand flights a week, you don't have to worry too much about reservations. Multiple airlines have planes leaving at least once an hour, and there's even dedicated ticket desks for "buy and fly" purchases.

Now, don't get on the first plane, at least not if you can't get a window. Wait until the one after, where you should pretty much have your pick of seats. Both sides have great views, but I'm partial to the left-hand side just a bit more. Santos Dumont is a little two-runway job right next to downtown. This isn't the difference between flying into LaGuardia instead of JFK: flying into Santos Dumont is the equivalent of flying into the Wall Street Heliport. Not only are the views astounding, but you can grab your stuff and walk right into the middle of Rio. Getting to the subway, which will take you to the touristy parts of town, is only about a fifteen-minute stroll through downtown. Felipe picked me up a couple days ago fresh from this descent.

Our current destination is Felipe's friend Pedro's house in Jacarepaguá ("Alligator Harbor" in Portuguese), a middle-class neighborhood next to the Cidade de Deus, or "City of God," well off the tourist path in the western zone of Rio. In true Carioca fashion, we show up about two hours late. Pedro is none too happy with our tardiness but quickly changes into his outfit (an old woman, complete with cane), and we hit the street.

Now, there is "drag," and there is "guys wearing dresses." This is definitely "guys wearing dresses." No one is bothering to look good. And, if anything, the guys are acting even more boyish and rambunctious than usual. A group of six hairy Playboy Bunnies meets us with various gestures and chants as soon as we get there. The whole thing is a blast, the sheer exuberance and energy nothing like I've ever experienced.

It starts to rain. Everybody cheers. The light tropical sprinkling quickly turns into a driving maelstrom. Nobody leaves. We hear thunder, and huge winds threaten to blow down electrical wires. Everybody climbs onto the roofs of the houses. Then, in unison, everybody starts to chant "Ah! Ah-ha! So de Jacarepaguá!" If your Portuguese isn't up to snuff, that basically translates as "Ah! Ah-ha! I'm from Jacarepaguá!" I don't feel

LOOKING GOOD!

out of place chanting along; Felipe said he was pretty sure I was the only gringo in attendance, and that was enough of an honorary membership for me for the afternoon. After all, I am standing on the street in the torrent, wearing women's underwear right along with everyone else.

By this time, the rain has completely soaked through my negligee. Now, I do have something else on. True to Brazilian form, I have slipped a Speedo on underneath. The problem is that it's Felipe's Speedo. Felipe's got a good forty pounds on me. I take off the negligee and end up in my three-sizes-too-big Speedo, drenched, in the middle of Brazil.

In addition to being a ton of fun, the whole experience is great for another reason: it reminds me of a fundamental truth about cities. While things like climbing bridges and exploring tunnels can provide a great, seldom experienced perspective, ultimately cities are products of their citizens—infrastructure is there only as a means of support. The experiences that most capture the essence and character of a city are almost always social, not structural, encounters.

We finally make it home, where hot showers, not to mention dry men's clothes, are extremely welcome. I've managed to make it back without flashing half of Rio, but just barely. Of course, La Cidade Maravilhosa is pretty much the only city in the world where you can still feel comfortable wearing nothing but a pair of falling-down Speedos while just walking down the street.

TWENTY

Bolivia, March 2007

After Brazil I take some time to do some backpacking, heading through Argentina before crossing the border into Bolivia. One bus ride later and I'm in a town called Tupiza, bargaining with a tour operator over a fairly standard four-day trip through the Altiplano, a beautiful, remote area in the southwest of the country, fifteen thousand feet in the air, with salt flats, pink flamingos, and rock formations that are straight out of a Salvador Dalí painting. It's an amazing, otherworldly landscape, and the remoteness means that it's generally visited by the young, Lonely Planet–bearing backpacker crowd. As a result, tours are still fairly cheap. I get the operator down to $105 U.S. for the ninety-six-hour excursion, they throw me in a 4x4 with five other tourists, and away we go.

Fifteen-thousand-foot altitude can do weird things. One of the weird things it can do is wreak havoc on your digestive tract. For three days I eat a pretty normal diet, consisting mostly of hearty helpings of rice, beans, and vegetables, and have absolutely no urge to move my bowels. And now those last three days have suddenly hit me all at once. I have to take the worst shit of my life. And I can't.

The problem is that I'm currently riding in the 4x4, on the way out to our last stop. And the five other tourists with me are all girls. Sarah, a frizzy-haired Canadian backpacker. Mathilda and Hanna, two Danes on a trip around the world together. Kate, a cute and sassy young Irish lass with a whip-smart sense of humor. And Natalia. Natalia is a lovely creature, a nurse from Barcelona with sad eyes, a beautiful face, and a certain vulnerability to her that makes it hard for me not to hug her each time she talks. She wants to improve her English, which is halting, and I likewise want to improve my Spanish, which is far from fluent, so we've been getting to know each other in a strange bilingual manner: I speak Spanish to her, she speaks English to me. Our lack of proficiency makes for a linguistic directness that precludes the subtleties of flirting. It takes only a couple of stumbles on the constraints of our communication style before it becomes embarrassingly obvious that we have a mutual attraction.

Since getting divorced, I've had dalliances, hookups, and other assorted fun and friendly encounters. But they've all had that feeling of "We're mostly doing this because we're both just kind of bored." I haven't had anything resembling romance. No girlfriends, not even something that could properly be called a "fling." And certainly not a beautiful Catalan woman looking at me with trust and desire in her eyes. The returning feeling is unexpected and wonderful, nostalgic but also still familiar: it's like running into an old friend from high school and remembering how much fun you used to have before life got so complicated. It's only a matter of time before we hook up. But not if I stop the car and take a giant shit on the road right in front of her.

And that's pretty much the sole option. The terrain is currently completely flat and featureless for miles. There is nowhere to hide, no pretending I've just got to pee and ducking behind a hill. And the only other guy in the car is our Bolivian driver, Pedro, who, while a nice enough fellow, I'm fairly sure will not understand the nuances of what is happening. Essentially, I have no wingman. Nobody I can grab and say, "Hey, cover me so I still have a chance with Natalia." I've got two choices: be the disgusting guy who has to stop the car and crap in the desert, or sweat it out.

I never have that moment of decision where I choose to sweat it out. I have to shit so bad I can't really tell if this is even going to be a matter of willpower: there might come a time when my body might betray me against my brain's every command. I reevaluate every minute, every mile, of the trip, resolving to hang on as long as I can. After not too long, it takes even more of a turn for the worse.

When I was a child, my mother would not let me say I was starving. "You're hungry, you're ravenous, you're not starving. Children in Ethiopia are starving." Starving is a completely different thing from simply being very, very hungry—something those of us who have never experienced it can't even imagine. I've heard it described as a maddening gnawing deep in your muscles for nourishment. What I've got is the "Have to take a shit" equivalent of starvation. It's totally alien from anything I've felt before. It goes well beyond the uncomfortable feeling of fullness in my lower abdomen, the piercing desire to relax my gluteus muscles. I can feel it in every inch of my body.

I start to sweat. It feels like I have a bad case of the flu, except somehow I know that as soon as I release my bowels the nausea, cramping, and general feeling of illness will vanish. I'm shifting uncomfortably around in my seat, trying to find the best position. Some are better than others—folding my legs under me and shifting my weight onto my left hip seems to be the best—but the problem is they deal only with the "hungry" part of having to shit. No matter how I shift, what muscles I half relax, the "starving" part stays with me at full throttle, growing steadily worse with each mile.

Still, I manage to hold out. Eventually, I see the town we're heading to, Uyuni, off in the distance. I'm exuberant. A light at the end of the tunnel. I forget we're in the desert. After an hour, the town appears no closer. As we rumble forward, each mile covered bringing no corresponding change in the size of the dots off in the distance, I feel like my spirit is being ever so slowly crushed in a vise. If I had some idea of how long it would be, how much longer I had to endure this, it would be bearable. But I don't. It's a mirage in the distance. I can't tell if we're going to be there in five minutes or five hours. All I can do is somehow manage to not spill the contents of my colon all over the seat every time we hit a bump in the road. *"No sé—no creo que es esto. Espere aquí,"* says Pedro. I almost cry.

After about an hour and a half of agony, the town starts to grow perceptibly larger. Twenty minutes later we roll by the first building. Cities in the Bolivian Altiplano are not large. It shouldn't be too long now.

The problem, as I find out, is that Pedro doesn't know

where we're staying. And I have no idea how to find a public bathroom in Bolivia. We stop for the fourth or fifth time. Each time I'm sure we've made it, only to have Pedro continue on. This time I can't help it. I have to ask if we're almost there.

The entire trip I've been quiet. I'm worried that any diversion of concentration will prove fatal to my efforts at bowel control. I have never concentrated on anything this much. Not while taking my graduate school admission exams, not while walking in a four-track mainline subway tunnel during the middle of rush hour—never. Every ounce of focus is on my anus. I slowly, carefully tear away a tiny corner of my brain and manage to get the question out. I hope the tremble in my voice is noticeable only to me.

Upon hearing his tepid response, and being told to wait in the car, I almost lose it. I can't worry about being conspicuous anymore. I slowly make my way out of the 4x4, hoping Natalia doesn't notice my halting shuffle as I slowly follow Pedro into the hotel.

"*No, no, esto no es el hotel,*" Pedro says, but now I don't care. With Natalia out of sight I can afford to blow my cool a bit.

"*Necesito el baño,*" I reply.

Pedro starts to protest, but after seeing the desperation on my face understandingly points to the back of the place. I drag myself down the hall. I don't care what the bathroom looks like, what it smells like, what diseases might be floating around in there, nothing except that it's somewhere Natalia can't see me. I find the place and hurriedly enter a stall. It's actually not so bad—fairly clean, as far as Bolivia goes.

I can't believe it. I'm actually going to make it. As soon as I let myself believe this, though, my concentration lapses and the strangest thing happens. My anus starts to spasm. It's always remarkable when your body does something you didn't know it could do. Generally this happens under the influence of drugs, or maybe at the chiropractor's office, not as a result of not pooping for four days. But I don't have time to stop and marvel at nature. Already I can tell this spasming is going to end soon, and I don't want my pants on when it does. But it's OK. I'm here. All I have to do is pull down my drawers and this whole horrid nightmare is over.

I unzip and yank on my pants. They stay up. Fuck. I forgot I was wearing a belt. The spasming grows worse. I contemplate surrender for a split second. Maybe I can somehow throw away my soiled pants, get new ones, and explain it as an impromptu fashion choice when I see Natalia. It would all be so easy.

It isn't the implausibility of this plan that keeps me from giving in. It isn't even the thought of the look of horror on Natalia's face when she realizes what happened. It's the fight. It's like getting knocked out in the last round of a boxing match when you're ahead on all the cards. I see flashes of Rocky making it up at the count of ten while Apollo Creed is still down on one knee. I've come this far. I manage to muster up every remaining ounce of mental strength for this last hurdle.

The moment when mind and body truly come together is amazing. An almost Zen-like calm comes over me as I realize I can control the spasming. I am completely in tune with a part of my body; it's like the spasms are in slow motion and I can feel every different muscle fiber expand and contract. I imagine it's the same feeling Tibetan monks get when they realize they can willfully slow their heartbeat. In the moment it seems like I can control it forever, but intellectually I know it won't last.

I'm a novice, and not really even that. Extraordinary circumstances have temporarily gifted me with mental powers it takes a lifetime to develop. I know they'll soon vanish. Still, there's no panic as I unbuckle my belt, slide my pants down, and take a seat. I take one last nanosecond to enjoy the moment of victory and discovery, and then I let it all go.

After I'm done I realize there's no toilet paper, but I don't care—I actually prepared for the contingency by tearing out a few pages from my guidebook while I was still riding in the car. I sit and relax for a while, use "French Guiana" to wipe, thoroughly wash my hands, and head out, a happy man.

Later on, when we're alone and I'm quite confidently in control of my bodily functions once again, I speak with Natalia. Again our language barrier eliminates the option of smooth talking. I tell her, in horrible Spanish, that I want to kiss her. She raises her head and the look in her eyes turns me to jelly.

"I like to Moses," she says in her heavily accented English. "I like to much. But I don't know. I don't know it is good. You are, are . . ." She struggles for the English word. "You are . . ." Frustrated, she reverts back to Spanish. "*Estás cerrado, Moses.*"

Estás cerrado. You are closed.

TWENTY-ONE

I thought Rio would be the prime example of people building a city in a place that God never meant for urbanity. But that was before I made it to La Paz.

There are many cities throughout the world set on hilltops and mountains. It makes sense, as high ground lets the city have a natural defense. But La Paz is one of the only that's essentially the opposite of this—a city set into a giant canyon. On the rim of this canyon is El Alto, a sprawling souk-like neighborhood. Our bus winds down the valley from El Alto for what seems like miles, until depositing us about three-quarters of the way down. There are still hundreds of feet to descend before it picks up again. Usually my instinct is to go up, get to the highest point around me. But I know my destination in this city is going to be different. At the bottom of the canyon, running through the center of La Paz, is the Choqueyapu River, the dirtiest river in the world. And it runs underground. How can I resist it?

I'm not sure if it's actually the "dirtiest" river in the world. Bolivia is a country somewhat given to hyperbole. For instance,

THE "ROAD OF DEATH."

I've just biked the Yungas Road, billed as the "Road of Death." It's a tricky descent down a winding mountain road with no guardrail, with an overall drop in altitude of almost twelve thousand feet. Counterintuitively, the group leader gave us the advice that going faster is safer.

"The reason people die is not because they are going too fast and can't stop," he told us. "What happens is that people get nervous about going too fast and spend the whole time squeezing the brakes. Their hand muscles get exhausted, and then later on in the ride when they need to brake, their hands are too tired to do it hard enough, they can't slow down, and they end up going over the edge."

I kept this advice in mind, and the ride ended up being pretty fun, but nothing that deserved its billing. It actually got the name in 1995 when the road was still regularly used for two-way vehicular travel: most of the deaths would come when buses and trucks would go over the edge while trying to pass each other. They've since built another, safer road, and the Yungas is now used mostly by tourists who want the cheesy "I Biked Death Road" T-shirt with a skull and crossbones that we got upon finishing the ride. It's all a bit silly, reminding me of tour operators trying to convince me that I was somehow going on an "adventure" instead of a tour. Of course, the week after I did the ride I did learn that two people had died biking the road the same week I did. So much for my take on Bolivian hyperbole.

And it turns out "dirtiest" very well might not be hyperbole in the case of the Choqueyapu River, either. Gravity is the ultimate arbiter of this: because the river is at the bottom of the canyon, it's the final destination of the runoff from the city and its environs—a metropolis of about two million people, all of whose sewage, garbage, and pollution are eventually going to make their way downhill. I head down the canyon until I find the top of the tiered concrete tunnel that covers part of the river. I'm on the upriver side of this tunnel. There's no way in, so I decide to try the downriver side. The journey is tricky, and I have to head back up into the canyon a few times before finding a way to slide down a hill to the downriver section, where it exits the concrete tunnel, now several dozen feet lower.

Up close, the first thing I notice about the river is that it's a disgusting shade of brown. The second thing I notice is what I suspect is the source of this—what appears to be a sewage hookup flowing right out into the river, which I can only assume is one of many. Just as in Naples, it looks like the official sewer system is taken as just one of many options for waste disposal. Even if it isn't an illegal sewage hookup, the pipe is,

CHOQUEYAPU RIVER.

at best, for storm runoff—runoff that's made its way down a hill of several hundred thousand people and the accumulated garbage that they've thrown in the streets. I've been ignoring most of the advice the guidebooks have given about eating and drinking, which is heavily geared toward making sure you don't imbibe any liquid that isn't the result of an industrial bottling process: you're supposed to avoid all fresh juices and anything with ice cubes, for instance, as well as anything that may have, at some point, been touched by someone who, at some other point, may have touched a local water source. I've dismissed all this as paranoia, happily quaffing and chowing down on whatever happened to be close by and cheap. But upon seeing the river, I resolve to stick to bottles of Coca-Cola for the remainder of my stay here.

The third thing I notice is what looks like a lady washing her clothes in the river a bit farther upstream, near where it exits the tunnel. This I've got to investigate. I walk along the bank until I come to the tunnel. The lady has left by the time I get there, and I glance into the darkness of the tunnel. I, of course, have forgotten to bring a flashlight, but I can still make out two more pipes outflowing into the river in the small part I can see. The smell of sewage is present but not overwhelming. It's definitely not as bad as a sewer or even a combined system. But then again, you don't wash your clothes in a sewer. I bend down and dip my finger in the water. Great: now I can say I've touched the dirtiest river in the world. I'm glad Steve isn't with me, as I'd probably find myself dragging him up the hill to the nearest hospital, where he'd have to rely on Bolivian medical care to deal with the six different infections he would have picked up on this excursion.

After this, the rest of the trip is relaxing and outdoorsy. I meet up with my brother to walk the Inca Trail and see Machu Picchu, I climb a mountain in southern Peru, I spend a couple days paragliding in Chile. It's nice. I think about crumbling concrete rooftops, drag parties in the rain, and stale-smelling underground rivers the whole time. And I can't wait until I'm back home, running through the subways again.

TWENTY-TWO

U.S.A., 2007

I get to New York in late March, spending my last week of vacation on a stopover in Mexico City with my friend Sara. Sara lived in Toronto, but we had been friends-with-a-mutual-crush for a while, and were both free of other romances when we arranged to meet up in Mexico City. I was still shaken from Natalia's admonishment, wasn't confident about the situation at all. After all, emotional availability isn't usually a prerequisite for a fling halfway around the world from home. How bad must I be, how closed off, that even that situation was beyond her comfort zone? After that day I had started to think about the other kinds of boundaries I had. Flying into Mexico City, I thought about Sara shaking her head and telling me I was closed, and the thought filled me with despair. I don't know what had changed about me in the month between Natalia and Sara, but something must have. Perhaps just the introspection itself was enough to shake some emotional barrier loose. There was no admonishment this time. In fact, Sara and I ended up spending most of our time in Mexico City in bed together.

After I get back to New York, I work nonstop on the tour

buses through the summer, and come within one class of finally finishing my master's degree in urban planning. Sara and I continue to see each other when we can, and in the fall we arrange to take six weeks and go on a road trip across the country.

About halfway through the road trip we're at the Grand Canyon, where I gleefully bypass the guardrails and go clambering out onto the rocks above the cliff. "Is he on drugs?" a nice middle-aged, middle-American lady asks Sara as she takes a picture of me sitting with my legs dangling off the edge of the canyon. I'm feeling pretty proud of myself as I clamber back to the parking lot. Guardrails, "Danger" signs, these things don't exist for me anymore. I've left all that behind.

Walking back to the car, I get a text from Steve.

"Just got down from the Brooklyn Bridge. Beautiful."

Fuck.

It turned out that, once again, the boundaries aren't real. Steve had broken up with Molly for good that summer, and was out boozing and reminiscing with Miru's sister, Seung Jung, about this and other relationships gone by. This night of heavy drinking was taking place only about a five-minute walk from the Brooklyn Bridge, and the combination of the proximity, the alcohol, the melancholy, and a willing partner had given both of them enough impetus to say "Fuck it," walk over to the bridge, and climb the cables up to the top of the stone tower. There were no police, no alarms, no need to swallow a memory card and fake mental illness. There was nothing other than a great view and one more seemingly impossible thing checked off the list.

EDGE OF THE GRAND CANYON.
© *Sara Power*

I've gone on to climb the Brooklyn Bridge half a dozen times since then—the first time solo as a present to myself on my thirty-second birthday, the other times with an array of the international urban adventure crew who've come to town, often just for this purpose.

There's no secret to the climb: you wait until nobody's around, head up the cables, scoot around the security gates, and away you go. Reaching the top is exhilarating, but for me has always been a little anticlimactic. There's a difference between discovering what's possible for yourself and having someone else pull back the curtain for you.

After Steve and Molly break up, Molly heads abroad for a few months before leaving New York for good. This breakup is actually significant for me also. Because after my road trip with Sara, I have another trip planned. To Europe. With a single-for-the-first-time-in-four-years Steve Duncan.

Paris, December 2007

Steve and I start our trip by traveling through Ireland and England, popping manholes, running through the underground, and otherwise having a blast before heading back to Paris after a couple of weeks. One evening we meet up with Eric, my old peeing-in-the-street buddy from the last trip, and a couple of his friends for a night in the Paris Métro tunnels. As usual, there's no need to break in or twist ourselves in knots trying to squeeze through a fissure or scale a barrier. We simply head to a nondescript door, where Eric pulls out a huge key ring and leafs through the keys until he finds the right one. Once again I am baffled by his resourcefulness.

"Jesus—why aren't you a jewel thief?" I ask.

"Why would I be a jewel thief?" he answers. "I have a very good job."

Palling around with Eric, Rosie, and others we know now certainly helps us on the exploration front, but it isn't the whole story. I feel comfortable in Paris, understand the culture much better. I'm not going to be scared off by a dark tunnel or a fence anymore. Maybe it's personal, because it's the first place I've ever adventured outside the U.S., but out of all the places I've been, the artificial boundaries put in place in Paris are the easiest to recognize and the easiest to overcome.

On top of this, Steve is single. And he's using this opportunity abroad to practice his newfound singledom on pretty much everyone. In fact, on our last night in town we find ourselves with a nice young American girl whom we've just met at an Internet café. It's now three in the morning and we're boosting her over a wall into a graveyard.

Steve has started to realize he's charming and handsome. And while his childhood in an all-boys Catholic school has delayed the development of his pickup skills, the combination of this upbringing and his boy-next-door looks has imbued him with such a nonthreatening "You can trust me" vibe that he can somehow convince a complete stranger that she should join him and his friend in an underground crypt for the night. We know of a quarry network, unconnected to the main network, beneath a cemetery in the south of Paris. I haven't been there before. Steve has, but wants to get more pictures: it's one of the last places you can actually find intact skulls. So now we have this girl in tow as we climb over a wall into a cemetery, pop open a manhole, and descend thirty feet on a rusty metal ladder into a bone-filled cave. I consider asking, several times, what the hell her mother would say to her right now, but I don't want to freak her out.

We climb back out as dawn is breaking and put the girl on the Métro before grabbing a few hours of sleep at our hotel. We're feeling pretty happy with ourselves. So happy that instead of heading to Amsterdam, as we had planned, we decide to continue the adventure here for another day. And then Rosie suggests we meet her friend Nico at a bar that night. And three hours after that we're on top of Notre Dame, the sound of the bell I've rung still fresh in my ears, watching policeman after policeman climb up the ladder into our narrow refuge inside the spire.

TWENTY-THREE

It all ends up being very civil. While back in the U.S., I'd be ready for a "Down on the ground, motherfucker!" over in France, law enforcement seems to take a much less antagonistic view of curious urbanists. The whole thing has the vibe of a necessary if slightly unpleasant interaction between two reasonable parties: they take Nico's Leatherman but don't even handcuff us as they lead us out. It's almost as cool as going up: we're in the attic of Notre Dame. They take us down a wooden catwalk and a set of stairs, and I notice the huge roof supports are also made out of wood. I wonder how old they are and if they had to be replaced. It looks pretty much like the attic of a regular old wood-frame house, except on a much grander scale. Nico even tries to snap a picture of us as we're walking through it, but it doesn't come out. The cops don't seem to mind. We're put in a wagon and taken over to the nearest station. It's right across the street. No wonder we got caught.

We sit on a bench as they try to figure out what to do with us. I'm counting on Nico to tell us what's going on, but all he can gather is that they're out making sure we didn't graffiti up the place. It doesn't really feel like we're suspects in a serious criminal investigation—more like we're sixteen and have just been caught shoplifting at the mall. But still, I'm sweating bullets about the lock we removed to get up the staircase. Everything we've learned about France has indicated a prevailing "No harm, no foul" attitude toward recreational trespassing, and if they gather we're just some harmless drunken tourists, I'm optimistic we'll get through this without having to involve the U.S. embassy. But if they discover we've damaged anything—hence the search for graffiti—consequences could be a lot worse. We're in a country where the person in charge of historic preservation is a member of the cabinet. I start thinking that damaging Notre Dame would be like some punk French kids coming to the United States and hocking a loogie on the secretary of defense.

After a little while they have us take a breath test. Despite the amount of time since we've been drinking and the sobering effects of exercise, adrenaline, and police encounters, I still feel pretty drunk. Not tipsy, not buzzed: drunk. I score a 0.14 on the test. Steve scores a 0.32. Nico scores a 0.68. "My parents are Russian," he says, and shrugs. I am sober enough to realize they can't be using the same measurement system as in the States, or (Russian parents or no) Nico would dead.

We sit there anxiously until the chief finally gets there. He's wearing slacks and a casual button-down shirt, and appears not to have shaved for three or four days. First he takes Steve into a room with him. I sit there trying to figure out how I'm going to sublet my place back home from a French jail cell. Roughly ten minutes elapse and the chief comes back for me.

He takes me in the room and we sit down.

"So," he asks in barely accented English, "did you get good pictures?"

I contemplate my answer. I have no idea if this is friendly banter or the beginning of a dastardly interrogation. "I'm not a photographer," I answer.

He takes my name, address, and a few other pieces of information. Then he pulls out a piece of paper.

"OK, so you are tourists, you're taking pictures, you don't know you can't climb the cathedral, you're very sorry, and you won't do it again. The report will stay here, you can go. Sign this."

I can't believe it. I look at the paper, scanning for something that might reference the broken lock. Unfortunately, my French-language education consists of one semester in the eighth grade and some weekend trips to Montreal. In just about every other country on earth you'd have to be crazy to sign a statement some cop puts in front of you that you can't even read. But France is different. I just can't see the chief smirking and leading me off to a cell after I unwittingly confess to vandalizing a national landmark. So I sign. The chief dismisses me, and I sit out in the lobby while he talks to Nico. After another ten minutes, Nico comes out. He's followed by the chief, who says, *"Voilà,"* tosses the pen over his shoulder, and lackadaisically strolls into the other room. It is the most French thing I have ever seen.

Steve is waiting down the street. "They even let me keep

the pictures," he says with amazement. "The chief said he wanted us to have a nice memory of our vacation here." Dawn is breaking, the Métro should be running by now, and I can think of nothing better than a hot shower back at the hotel.

"OK, cool," says Nico. "So there is another church near my house where we can do a climb. You want to go?"

So much for the shower—it looks like we're taking a victory lap first.

About a year later I see an online video about touring Paris. Toward the end there's a short segment on the people who built the underground cinema and repaired the Panthéon clock. It starts with one of the members, a loquacious bald guy, talking to the reporter about the cinema. Again, it turns out that in Paris secrets are hidden in plain sight. After months of operation, the cinema eventually had to be abandoned once it was discovered. Nobody went looking for it—the police just accidentally stumbled across it one day.

"The funniest thing is, they thought our couscous maker was a bomb," he says with a mixture of incredulousness and pity for the authorities' obvious stupidity.

"So they thought you were making a bomb, when all you were doing was making couscous," the reporter replies.

"No, no," the bald guy replies, to the puzzlement of the reporter.

"They didn't think you were making a bomb?"

"No, they did think we were making a bomb. But we were not making couscous. The couscous maker was purely decorative."

And the French wonder why they get made fun of.

The segment goes on to feature shots of the catacombs, and more of the reporter talking with the bald guy, before a final scene shot at night from a Gothic rooftop. I recognize it immediately. They're on the roof of Notre Dame. They have the keys. In Paris, someone always has the keys.

TWENTY-FOUR

Amsterdam, December 2007

Three days after getting arrested on Notre Dame, I'm in Amsterdam Centraal Station, preparing to catch a train to the airport, where we have a flight booked to Stockholm. I am all set to go, having finally gotten a good night's sleep at a friend's place, one of the charming houseboats that line some of Amsterdam's canals.

Steve, on the other hand, has been up for a day and a half and has spent last night going on a four-drug bender with the local pimp. I meet him at the train station at noon after a morning walk by the Amstel River.

Steve has a problem when I meet him at the station. He has too much cocaine. He can't remember how he came by so much cocaine, but he's pretty sure the Dutch pimp and "at least two" trips to the ATM have something to do with it. I conservatively estimate he's been taken for about five hundred bucks by his new buddy.

There are two solutions I can see to this particular problem. Solution number one: cut your losses, throw the cocaine in the garbage, and head to the airport. Solution number two:

keep the cocaine with you on an international flight and hope no drug-sniffing dogs come by. I am praying Steve does not take solution number two. Unfortunately, he informs me he is definitely not going to take solution number one.

Luckily, though, Steve sees two other solutions I haven't thought of. Solution number three is to snort all the coke before we get to the airport. This becomes my backup plan once it becomes apparent that I can't convince him to throw away the drugs. I tell him to go do this in the bathroom of the train we're taking to the airport. However, Steve opts for solution number four.

"I'm sorry, ladies, this is going to sound a little strange, but I have too many drugs. Would you like some?"

Solution number four is to try to give the coke away to the two Dutch college students sitting down the train carriage from us. They decline, so he falls back on solution number three: snort all the coke. He does not go to the bathroom for this, as I suggested, but instead dumps it out on the girls' tray table and, not even bothering to roll up a euro note, pinches a nostril and inhales it in one go. I consider telling him that snorting coke next to strangers on a train at twelve-thirty in the afternoon is not, in fact, acceptable behavior even in Amsterdam, but I'm so terrified he's going to try to take the coke on the plane that I figure I should just keep my mouth shut. It's a good thing Steve looks absolutely cherubic with his blond hair and delicate features, and the drugs actually enhance this look by dilating his pupils so much that his eyes sparkle. The girls tell Steve he's "the most charming creepy guy" they've ever met and give him half of their pink-frosted donut. I cannot imagine what would have happened if I had tried this little trick. I haven't showered, shaved, or changed clothes in three days and currently look like a cross between a hobo and an Albanian mobster.

For a moment I consider just ditching Steve and letting him find his own way to Stockholm after he's done playing Scarface, but it's a bit too late now, as we are already off the train and at the station, where Steve is smoking a joint on the platform. I pray that this chills him out enough to not offer cocaine to random strangers in the airport.

We head up the stairs to the terminal. I'm wondering if he hasn't maybe forgotten about some other drugs he bought from some other Dutch pimp he met, so I send him to the bathroom with instructions to ditch whatever's left and brush his teeth, as he absolutely reeks of whiskey.

"OK, watch my bags for me," he says.

Yeah, right—I can see the scene right away: "Oh, no, those aren't *my* bags, Mr. Customs Officer with the snarling dog. What do you mean, 'Come with us'?" I send Steve into the bathroom complete with his two backpacks and duffel bag. When he comes out I ask if he's gotten rid of all the drugs.

"Well, I'm definitely not throwing out the Ecstasy," is the reply. Great.

Amazingly, check-in goes completely smoothly. Steve can't help flirting a bit too much with the agent, but again his altar-boy looks get him by. He buys two bottles of whiskey at duty-free, we get on the plane, and he promptly falls asleep in his seat, drooling.

We land, and I manage to drag him through the logistics of flying into a new city: off the plane, on the bus, get a map, find the hostel. As soon as we get there he passes out again.

Our Swedish contacts call about an hour later, telling us to meet them by the train station. I wake Steve up and tell him about the meeting.

"Should I come?" he asks groggily.

This is it. I've spent the last five hours schlepping him through two countries on three modes of transportation, all the while doing my level best to keep him out of prison halfway around the world from home. He can get up and drag himself down the block if he wants.

"I have no idea. Do what you want." I head out the door. Even though the whole reason we've come to Stockholm is to meet these guys and explore the city's underground, I put the odds of hearing him moan and get out of bed at about 5 percent. The odds prove correct.

I head off to the train station to meet our contacts. The first guy, Mats, shows up and tells me that his companion, Sven, is going to be late. We hang out and chat until Sven shows up about a half-hour later. He, like Mats, is a young guy. I place them both in their early twenties. We're all set to go, when I glance over and see Steve stagger up to us, looking like death and reeking of booze again.

"It took some willpower and a whole lot of whiskey. Let's go." I am again amazed at what this guy will go through simply to see what's down a hole in the ground.

Stockholm, December 2007

It's a heck of a hole in the ground. Sweden is built on solid granite, and the tunnels underneath the city are blasted through this granite. The feeling is incredibly raw; it's like being in a working cave. The other tunnels we've been in—catacombs, subways, drains—are obviously part of the built urban world. Walls are concrete, cement, brick, reinforced and finished. Even the catacomb tunnels, built two-hundred-plus years ago, still looked human-made, just old. Here you can cut yourself on some of the sharp granite edges that are left from the blasting.

STOCKHOLM GRANITE SUBWAY TUNNEL.
© *Lucinda Grange*

To get to where we're going, Sven first tells us we need to use a connection in the subway tunnels. We haven't taken the subway yet, so I ask him how we get in—meaning do we buy a token or get a pass? Talk to the guy in the booth or use the machine? In response, Sven simply goes to the exit gate, waits for someone to exit, and squeezes through without paying a fare. This doesn't seem to be hugely controversial; the guy exiting actually holds the gate open for him. At first I hesitate, but then remember that the exchange rate is awful and a ride on the metro currently costs the equivalent of about $4. So, when in Rome and all like that.

Sven tells us to wait in the station while he checks something out. He slips around the corner, changes into subway worker clothes, opens the gate at the end of the platform, and heads down onto the tracks. A few minutes later he returns.

"OK, the connection's still good. Come on," he says. We follow him down onto the tracks. Later Sven explains the need for the scouting excursion. "Yeah, we were painting graffiti in this station a few weeks ago. The police vandal squad came just as we were finishing up, so we ran out onto the tracks and through the connection to escape. I was worried maybe they'd seen us, found the connection, and sealed it."

We spend only a short time in the subway tunnel before finding the connection and heading into the tunnels for the telecom network. Upon reaching the first laser alarm, hidden behind a doorway, the Swedes show us what to look out for and how to either climb over or slide under the invisible beam. OK, cool. We navigate a couple more, and then forget to check behind a doorway and trip one. I wonder if I should freak, but the Swedes seem to be OK with it, so on we go. The next thing of note that we reach are empty shell casings. I again wonder if I should freak.

"Oh, yeah—the army does training exercises for urban warfare in here," Mats tells me.

The army has not yet come after us for the tripped alarm, and we make sure to not trip any others, so I don't freak. Steve, in his fatigued state, almost screws up once, noticing the alarm just in time to stop his stride.

"What happens if we trip another one?" I ask Mats.

"I don't know," he replies. "I've never tripped the first one before."

Finally, the Swedes tell us we've reached the exit, which turns out to be a ten-foot chimney climb up a vent shaft, after which we have to squeeze out a grate into a park. I'm a little worried about Steve, with his combination of fragile hip and four-substance hangover, but he scurries right up. Stockholm is an archipelago, built on a series of islands, and it turns out we crossed underwater four times during the excursion. Altogether a good night. And as it's pretty easy to be a slacker in Sweden—free health care, free housing, and even a cash allowance—our youthful companions are taking full advantage and, as such, don't really have anywhere to be the next day. So we decide the night is yet young.

"We need beer," Steve says. I'm also thinking it's time to hit the bar, but the Swedes don't look very excited at the suggestion.

"Why go to a bar? There's beer right here," Sven says, motioning to a 7-Eleven next to us on the street. "We can drink in the park."

"Yeah, sounds cool," I say, although it's pitch-black and about twenty degrees Fahrenheit out. "And don't worry about the beer: I got it."

Sven laughs at the offer. "No, man, you don't need to do that. Just go ask the clerk behind the counter for directions. Pretend you're French or something and don't speak very good English. We'll come in after."

I know where this is going. I can't believe I'm thirty-two years old and helping steal beer from a 7-Eleven. Despite our best efforts at distraction, the clerk easily catches on to the fact that Mats and Sven are stuffing six-packs into their backpacks.

"Those two were stealing," she tells me and Steve in English as they leave, packs bulging. As she tries to excuse herself to call the police, Steve decides the best course of action in order to distract her and give our companions a head start is to flirt with her in French. Astoundingly, this almost works, until

Steve presses his luck by trying to kiss her hand and the clerk gets fed up and reaches for the phone. We leave, meet up with the other two, and are rewarded with cans of watery Carlsberg 3.5-percent-alcohol beer, which is the strongest you're legally allowed to buy outside of the state-sponsored liquor store. There you can get up to 14-percent-alcohol beer, which tastes like someone decided to ferment ammonia and add it to charred wheat mash.

There's not a whole lot else to do in Sweden in December other than drink and go in tunnels. As we've now seen most of the tunnels, drinking is taking the front seat for the next couple days. I'm pretty happy with this: after weeks of exploring, I'm ready to just chill out, wind down, and get ready to head back to New York. The year has been great: I've ended up making it to eighteen countries; run around subway systems on three continents; explored countless drains, tunnels, abandonments, and bridges; and even gotten to ring the bell of Notre Dame. But these last few days have solidified what I've been suspecting. It's been a great year. But I don't want this to be every year.

And the next year, 2008, is different. I take this year to work on breaking other kinds of mental barriers—not the ones keeping me out, the ones keeping others from coming in. To start it off, I do something harder than forcing myself around the "Do Not Enter or Cross Tracks" sign for the first time, harder than taking the deep breath and crawling down the rabbit hole into catacombs. I call Sara and tell her I love her. It's simple to love when the recipient is something inanimate: adventure, travel, a city. It's only people who can make love a complicated emotion, make it a difficult thing to do.

Still, my love of New York remains full-fledged, doesn't wane, and there are plenty of days spent wandering the streets— and even some nights spent adventuring above and beneath them. But these nights grow much fewer and further between. Life settles down: I finally finish grad school and get my urban planning degree, stop the tour bus hustle, and get a nine-to-five. Sara still lives in Toronto, so most of my weekends are spent either visiting her in Canada or hosting her in New York.

In the spring of 2009, Steve gets accepted into a doctorate program for history in California, with plans to start in the fall. Around the same time I leverage my first nine-to-five job into a better one: I can take some time off in between them, but once I start this new job I'm not going to get a vacation for a while. These two developments mean our available window for another trip is closing fast. If we're going to get out of town for an adventure again, it's got to be now. So we plan one last hur-rah. Russia.

{ PART THREE }

TWENTY-FIVE

Moscow, June 2009

The first job of a parent is to protect your children. At first it's fairly easy: feed them, clothe them, don't drop them. Once the kid starts to walk and comprehend simple sentences, the task becomes tougher. You have to keep them from falling down the stairs, sticking their fingers in the electrical socket, eating whatever they pick up off the side of the road. You soon graduate to teaching simple lessons—things like "Look both ways before you cross the street," "Don't run with scissors," "Don't take candy from strangers." As the child gets older, more advanced lessons—"Use condoms," "Don't drink and drive"—start to be conveyed. Eventually the child becomes an adult and hopefully has internalized all these lessons enough to live a long and fruitful life devoid of venereal disease, DUI citations, and abduction by candy-toting strangers.

Of course, there are some things so obvious, and so lacking in any reason that someone might want to engage in them, that there is really no point in even wasting your breath to warn against them. My mother certainly never sat me down and said, "Moses. Remember. Don't go to prison in Russia." Yet here we

are, sitting next to a huge statue of Karl Marx, staring uncom-
prehendingly at four guys in military uniforms holding machine guns, with this fate looking increasingly likely.

Three hours earlier

We meet Max, a contact we were set up with through Dsankt
and Siologen, on our first day in Moscow. He's a giant, about
six-foot-six, resembles a bouncer at a mid-1980s biker bar, and
is one of those people who you can immediately tell forms
loyalties quickly and unbreakably. I instantly like him.

He opens his mouth. "So, guys, my English, it is fucking
very, very bad," he says. "I take a class in school, but I stop
because teacher, she is a fucking bitch. I know my English
because I listen to a lot of rock-and-roll music."

I actually think Max's English is pretty good—especially
for someone whose main instructor seems to have been a
combination of Led Zeppelin albums and Andrew Dice Clay
routines.

Unfortunately we've missed the golden age of Russian exploration by about fifteen years. Post-Soviet, pre-Putin-era
Russia was both an economic and an urban exploration free-
for-all.

"Oh, yeah," says Max. "Nobody would go anywhere under
the Soviets. But then with Yeltsin, there is, like, one old lady
guarding the entrance to the basement of the Kremlin. And if
she is not asleep, you can just bribe her."

But those days are long gone. Tales of getting into Metro-2,
Stalin's secret subway system that links the Kremlin to an air-
field and bunkers outside the city, have intrigued us to no end.
In the 1990s, it was simply a difficult challenge: Steve once met

a guy on a bus who claimed to have been there after a twenty-four-hour jaunt walking in the subway system. Now, with security back to Soviet-era levels under Putin, it would be like breaking into the Pentagon.

Luckily, our goal for the evening is a bit more doable, and no less historic. We're going to travel the length of the Neglinka River, where the original city of Moscow was formed. Today the Neglinka has been put entirely underground, doubling, as do most underground rivers, as part of the storm drain system. We meet a few other local Russian explorers and head to the entrance point just inside the city's innermost ring road around dusk.

Max gives us semi-official-looking vests to wear as we approach the manhole. This is OK?

"Oh, yeah. Nobody will mind. Only the special government police. And they are only around the Kremlin."

We pop the manhole and head down into Moscow's original river. The Neglinka runs through a lovely tunnel, changing its structure every few thousand feet or so. Storm drains are generally thought of as simply functional, something built so that the water has somewhere to go and the city doesn't flood when it rains. But there is a real beauty to many of them. Buildings may be just a place to live, subway stations just a place to stop the train. But that doesn't keep the people who build them from trying to make them something more than this, something that contributes to the city in an aesthetic, not just a functional, way. And this aesthetic sometimes extends to places you would hardly think would be considered—places like the one we're in now.

I quickly notice that we aren't passing many manholes on

our journey. They're much fewer and farther between here than in the storm drains back home. I'm becoming a bit worried about how to get out in an emergency.

Moscow is gigantic. It's 386 square miles, larger than the five boroughs of New York City. There is about half a square mile patrolled by the special police force Max warned us about. So of course we have chosen to walk right underneath their beat. The Neglinka River originally served as the Kremlin's moat. Today a small brook in Manezhnaya Square, just north of the Kremlin, claims to spring from the Neglinka. Tourists dip their toes in it every day. We're about ten feet deeper in the real thing. We're basically walking right under Red Square.

After an hour or so of trekking underground, we reach the junction with the Moscow River. Through the gate we can see the south bank of the river and the reflection of the buildings shining off the water. The reflection, however, is a strangely oscillating one. It takes me a bit before I realize it's because the small ripples outward are caused by the falling raindrops hitting it every so often.

The first, last, and only commandment of exploring storm drains is: "When it rains, no drains." Well, there are other ones, but generally speaking breaking them won't get you killed. It doesn't matter if it's just drizzling. Everything that hits concrete will eventually flow into a gutter and down a drain, where the water will funnel into small tubes. These small tubes will combine into larger and larger ones, until the combined volume of the rainfall is all flowing into one large drain that leads out to a body of water—a drain like the one we're in now. If you're in such a drain when the rain hits, your best-case scenario is that it stays a trickle, leading to a slowly rising water level that you can slog through quickly enough to get to a manhole where you can either get out (hopefully avoiding oncoming traffic) or, if the rain gets worse, at least climb up the ladder and pray the water level doesn't eventually reach the ceiling. Your worst-case scenario is a real downpour, which will create a tsunami-like current that will immediately sweep you off your feet and carry you down the drain until you're drowned, washed over a retaining wall, knocked unconscious by debris, or dashed against the floodgate or bars to the entrance. Being in a storm drain when this happens isn't an absolute recipe for death—people have survived this scenario—but your chances of survival wouldn't be described as "good" by any means. A large collector drain, like the one we're occupying, is the ultimate destination of the storm runoff for an area that's miles wide. Since we're currently right at the end of the drain, looking through a metal gate, if a legitimate rainstorm starts, our fate is easy to ascertain: we'll face a wall of onrushing water that will crush us against the metal bars until we drown. So when I recognize the plitter-platter of rain against the river, I don't panic, but this not panicking takes a conscious act of will. I point the rain out to Max.

"Fuck. This is fucking very fucking bad. Let's fucking go right fucking now. Fuck."

Running through a storm drain against the flow is very tiring, very slippery, and very nerve-racking. Imagine trying to run upriver on a bed of glass while being chased by Godzilla. Finally, after what seemed like hours but is probably closer to ten minutes, we come to the last manhole we passed.

Max stops us. "OK, guys. This is a fucking bad way to go out. We are up and out very quickly and hope we don't be seen by fucking cops. If we do, do not be speaking English. Do not be speaking fucking English."

We pop the manhole and scurry out. Nobody is around. The plan seems to have gone off without a hitch.

We head over to a nearby park. The Russians have kept a few odd statues of Communist heroes around for nostalgic purposes, one of which is a statue of Marx that we plop down by. I try to snap a few shots of us changing as we're laughing and generally being pretty happy with ourselves. The moment is survived, the adrenaline fades, the tension released and replaced with that happy stomach-full-of-sunshine feeling.

"Guys, guys, shhh, shhh," I hear Max say, and my stomach-full-of-sunshine drops straight to the ground. Thoughts of incurable tuberculosis strains I have read about existing in Russian prisons fill my head as I turn to see four guys in uniforms armed with machine guns come marching over to us. I remember the warning my mother never spoke.

My worst realization is that I cannot remember if I have my passport with me. On a separate trip into the metro system, Max had dropped his passport and not noticed he'd done so until we were off the tracks and heading back up through the vent shaft we'd used to infiltrate the system. Now, losing your passport certainly sucks, but if you're in your own country and you don't plan on traveling anytime soon, it's not that big a deal. It's certainly not something you'd consider going poking around for in between the cross ties of active subway tracks you illegally infiltrated ten minutes earlier. Yet Max freaked out in a way usually reserved for people who've lost a finger, not a passport.

"Oh, no, guys. You fucking don't understand. If we are seen by police coming out, I fucking need my passport. In Russia, if you have no paper, no passport, you are nothing. You are no person. If the police stop you with no paper, they do not know fucking what to do with you. No passport, and no money for bribe, you maybe just disappear."

Now, sitting beneath the gaze of Karl Marx, I'm focusing on "money for bribe," desperately hoping that the legendary corruption of the Russian police will trump any terrorism suspicions. Getting out of this with light pockets seems to be a great solution right now. As they jabber at me in Russian, I remember Max's admonition and stare blankly. The police motion for my camera. I give it to Max. Max shows the cop a few blurry photos of us changing. Luckily, they lose interest before they get to the pictures of the tunnel. The bad news is that the reason they lose interest in my small handheld digital is that everyone else is outfitted like they've been hired by *National Geographic*: backpacks full of photography gear, fancy cameras, huge tripods, the works.

There are four other cameras to go. Luckily, while they were busy with me and Max, the other Russians have figured out what was going on. They pass inspection one by one. Steve is the last one. He takes Max's advice about not speaking English to mean he should talk in French to the police. I'm sweating bullets as he pulls out the camera while mumbling something about *"Vous voulez voir cet appareil?"* But somehow Steve has managed to palm the memory card and insert a new

SCENE OF THE CRIME, DAYTIME.

© *Elizabeth Demitriou*

one. The police are rewarded with pictures of a bar mitzvah in Short Hills, New Jersey. When they walk away, not even trying to shake us down for a quick payoff, the astonishment soon gives way to relief. I am, by nature, insatiably curious for almost any of life's experiences. "Almost any," however, does not include getting beaten up by convicts in a Russian gulag.

> Max explains later: "When we got stopped, the cops asked us questions about what we are doing here, why we have waders, why is the place around us wet. When I showed them Moses's camera, the cop said, 'This is only one small amateur camera, but you've got tripods. Did you take pictures on that shitty cam using a tripod? Show me *all* cameras!' So one Russian guy told him that

he's got a film camera, not a digital, ha-ha, another one
that his batteries died, and blah-blah-blah. After a few
questions they fucked off. Steve trying to speak French
was fucking funny!"

When I was a child, one of the things my mother would
regularly tell me—along with "Look both ways before you
cross the street" and "Don't drink and drive"—was not to eat
wild mushrooms. It wasn't until I was an adult that I learned
that this was not part of the standard litany of parental life
lessons—that this constant refrain came instead from one
afternoon during the Summer of Love when my nineteen-year-
old mother had to get her stomach pumped after trying to
impress her hippie friends by eating some mushrooms growing in her backyard. I wonder how long it will be until my
children realize their dad is the only dad who regularly sits
them down and tells them, "Kids. Remember. Don't go to
prison in Russia."

TWENTY-SIX

Szczecin, Poland, January 2007

I belong to a strange generation. We have no direct experience with the Holocaust, like my grandparents' generation. We don't even have the experience of living with people who have, like my parents' generation. But it has not yet faded into history, known only in academic and philosophical ways, like it inevitably will for our children's generation. We still know what it is like to see a person you love turn back into a terrified nine-year-old girl in front of your eyes when she apologizes for not picking you up at the airport.

"I'm sorry, Mose," my grandmother's cousin Maria says to me after I arrive at her flat in Poland "You know I don't so much like to go to Germany."

My great-great-grandparents had twelve children. Six died in childhood. Five more immigrated to the United States between the wars. One stayed in Poland, in the small town she had grown up in, called Krasnystaw. She and her husband had three children. The only daughter, Maria, was sent to hide with a Catholic family during the war. Her father, mother, and two brothers were shot on the streets of Krasnystaw in 1942.

. . .

Some time after the war, with no way to find any family outside of Poland, Maria married Janek, one of the children of the Catholic family, and had a child named Stanislaus, Stashek for short. Shortly after his birth they moved across the country to the port city of Szczecin, where Janek worked in the shipyards. In the late 1950s my great-grandfather finally learned she had survived.

MARIA AND HER FAMILY BEFORE THE WAR.

Szczecin is within spitting distance of the German border. In fact, until the Potsdam Conference at the end of World War II, it was a German town named Stettin, and Berlin's main seaport. Today, you can take a direct flight from the United States into Berlin-Schönefeld Airport and catch a van that will have you in downtown Szczecin in two hours. But my older relatives have never gone that way. To this day, my grandmother, bad hip and all, will fly to London, change planes for Warsaw, and then take a train six hours back to Szczecin to visit Maria. She has been to every country in Europe except Albania—and Germany.

I had taken a couple of days to visit Maria as part of an earlier trip Steve and I were on, the one where he ended up in the Lord Wigram Ward of the Chelsea and Westminster Hospital. Between Italy and England we took a week to travel through Central Europe, making our way from Naples to Venice, Prague, Vienna, and Berlin. It was my first time in Central Europe, and my first time in a place where I have roots, that I could call "the old country."

Talk to most ethnic groups in New York and you'll find at least a little nostalgia for the lands of their forebears, even if it's more manufactured than genuine. Caribbean immigrants dream of their lost island paradise, Italians talk about taking a vacation to visit the little town in Sicily or Calabria or Campania where their grandparents used to live, you can see flags from a dozen Latin American countries flying from houses or storefronts during a ten-minute walk through the streets of Jackson Heights or Sunset Park. The one stark exception to this nostalgia is that you will never hear a Jew pining away for the memory of Central or Eastern Europe. With good reason.

I had been to Italy and France, countries that had been occupied by the Nazis, but not to the extent that the entire Jewish population was destroyed. I had left Rome the previous week, a city that has the oldest continuously active Jewish community in Europe, one that is still fairly active today despite its not being allowed to live outside the confines of the four-block-square ghetto until 1870.

I had also been to the Iberian countries, former centers of a Jewish culture that had been eradicated, and which are virtually devoid of any Jewish community today. Portugal, a country that was once about 20 percent Jewish, today has a few thousand Jews. But half a millennium of time has insulated that period of history to a large degree. Not so with Central Europe.

Being Jewish in Central Europe, even today, even as a young person, is eerie and extremely unnerving. What you know to be alive is said to you to be dead. A culture you are used to experiencing in sounds, smells, and feelings is relegated to museums, memorials, and tourist shops. And, of course, a heavy dose of security cameras and police officers, as a reminder that despite a near-complete extermination, there are still plenty of people willing to come back to try to destroy what pathetic little there is left.

You feel like a living ghost—that who you are shouldn't exist. That you have been told in the most brutal way possible that this is no longer your home, that you are no longer welcome here. Despite the changes in Central Europe over the last sixty years, the fact remains that these changes occurred only after the vision of the old ideology had been fulfilled to a horrific extent—an extent almost beyond capacity for imagining in a world populated by people you actually know, rather than one of history books or science fiction shows set in alternate universes. Politically, the Central Europe of today might not resemble Hitler's dreams of the future, but in terms of the "Jewish question," the undisputed fact is that it does—a fact that I could feel in my bones from Austria to Poland.

Ironically, of the Central European cities I visited, by far I felt the most comfortable in Berlin. One has to remember, during the Weimar era, Berlin was the most anti-Nazi city in the German-speaking world, and one of the most liberal and cosmopolitan in all of Europe. And today, Berlin is well along the road of returning to these noble roots. Immigrants from all over the world walk its streets, multitudes of languages are heard in its cafés, gays and lesbians live openly and freely. There is even a small but growing Jewish community. It makes me smile. I can think of no better historical repudiation of the Nazis' ideals than for their imagined racially pure capital of a totalitarian Third Reich to, in fact, become a multinational, liberal, cosmopolitan city—complete with a Jewish presence and culture—embracing the very values that the Nazis abhorred. I use this argument to try to get my grandmother to visit Maria the easy way, but it falls on deaf ears. I don't agree, but I understand: how much more difficult it is to ask people to forgive their prejudices when they are acquired firsthand, not passed down through the generations.

It was my first time in Berlin. Although I spent only about a day and a half there, it was enough to get a certain feel for the city. It reminded me a lot of New York, as much as any other city I've been to except perhaps São Paulo. The kicker was the subway: it's one of the largest systems in the world and, while not quite 24/7 like the New York City subway, comes closer than pretty much any other system. And the train pulled something straight out of New York City Transit's book: changing lines due to construction in the middle of the trip.

When Berlin was divided, the subway would run through several ghost stations in the eastern section before returning to the West. These came complete with armed guards, and the general "Shoot on sight" directive for potential defectors. When the wall came down in 1989 they were time capsules, unaltered since they had last been used, almost three decades previous.

Within a few years the subway system had returned almost completely to its prewar state. And today you can hardly notice that Berlin was ever divided at all. This isn't very surprising. The idea of completely cutting a city in half—and not even along a natural boundary, such as a river—is unrealistic. Something as complicated as a world city, with subways, sewers, electric grids, and water pipes—not to mention the natural economic and social flows of its citizens—can be cut in half and stitched up on either side only with crippling results. While I never got to see Berlin heal itself after the wall came down in 1989, I imagine it was quick, painless, and completely natural. Even after twenty-eight years of separation, a city will fall into its natural state seamlessly, the way the body heals itself after a wound.

M aria lives alone, without a blood relative sharing the same continent. Janek had died a few years ago, and their son Stashek had died as a young man in an auto accident. I talked with Maria well into the night, and the next day she showed me some of the sights of the city, including the docks where Janek had worked until shortly before the fall of communism. That night we went to visit Janek's family and I got to meet some of Maria's in-laws, the family that had hidden her during the war.

Family is a strange thing. This was my grandmother's cousin's husband's sister's husband's house. I wasn't related genetically to anyone I met in the room. I didn't share a nationality, religion, or even a language with these people. I had never met any of them before in my life; in fact, I wasn't even aware that most of them existed. Still, from the moment I stepped in the door, I immediately felt at home. Part of it might have been because of Polish hospitality, part of it definitely was because of all the whiskey they were plying me with (apparently in the

FAMILY IN POLAND.

Polish cultural consciousness, Americans are supposed to drink whiskey). But most of it was because I knew we were family, and so did they.

Traveling, and especially traveling alone, is one of my favorite things to do: the freedom, the complete responsibility for yourself and complete lack of it for anyone else, the ability to see and do and learn things you thought you would only ever read about. But there's a downside to everything, and for as many interesting people as I meet and converse with on the road, there's still a sort of melancholy loneliness that lingers with me. It's not a totally unpleasant feeling, and there are even times when I quite enjoy it. But the breaks from that feeling are always appreciated while on the road, and there is no better break than being around family. Maria had once told me that the best day of her life was when her family in the United States found her. In some very, very small way, that night I think I may have caught a fleeting sideways glimpse of how she must have felt.

I think of all of this—of family, Berlin, the war, the Prague Jewish Museum with its security cameras and ancient cemetery, the Great Synagogue of Vienna with its gates and armed guards, the stories from Maria about hiding from soldiers and how she still hates hearing German—all of this as I'm in an abandoned limestone quarry under Odessa, staring at a swastika carved into the wall.

TWENTY-SEVEN

The Ukraine, June 2009

After Moscow, Steve and I take a train to the Ukraine—the Muscovites introduced us to explorers from Kiev. Our first day, after walking for over an hour through a Soviet-era water tunnel, we find out the exit is a seven-story climb up and out a shaft. It doesn't seem so hard: there's a staircase, rusty but serviceable. Steve and the two Ukrainians we're with are off trying to leverage an old rail cart onto some tracks to create a sort of roller coaster. I get bored and decide to try to jump-start the end of the trip by starting the climb out. On my second step up the rusty staircase, most of the first flight of stairs collapses.

The others hear the racket and rush over, laughing at my stupidity. Neither of them speaks much English, so instead they show me what we're expected to do. As it turns out, we're not supposed to use the staircase at all. Instead, they scale the rusted insides of the tube—which have a waffle-like pattern affording handholds and footholds—for about fifteen feet, hauling themselves up onto a rusted-through metal landing supported by some crossbeams. They make sure to keep their body weight over the cross-beams and keep hanging on to the wall at the same time. We follow them up, repeat seven times, and pop out a manhole into a grassy field, the shining sun more than welcome.

OOPS. SOVIET-ERA WATER TUNNEL. KIEV, UKRAINE.

We spend a few more class days exploring drainage tunnels; climbing my first-ever cable-stayed bridge, the Moscow Bridge over the Dnieper River, in the middle of the day; and exploring an under-construction metro tunnel.

This last one doesn't go so well. After walking for more than a mile through the tube, one of the Ukrainians and I end up getting seen while checking out the tunnel-boring machine, and we have to book it out through an uncompleted station past a pack of barking guard dogs. Steve, who in addition to being sick is having one of his bad-hip days, has dragged himself for over a mile through the tunnel and has just finished setting up his first shot and is about to hit the shutter when we come running like hell back toward him. "I was about ready to kill myself just to get a rest," he told me later. "When I saw you running I was so pissed, but I knew we just had to cut our loses and get the fuck out of there. I was seriously at my limit: no matter how scared I was, I couldn't go any faster. I just had a

TOP OF THE MOSCOW BRIDGE. KIEV, UKRAINE.

feeling of 'Well, why bother being scared. Whatever happens happens.'"

The Kiev crew, in turn, introduces us to explorers from Odessa. We meet two of them, Anastasia (Ani for short) and her boyfriend, Sasha, the day we arrive.

We stay at Sasha's apartment, where he lives with his mother and siblings, and where we're treated to typical Ukrainian hospitality—meaning Sasha and his family cannot go more than a few hours without making sure we're fed. Steve's innocent charm ends up extending well past the language barrier. Sasha and his mother argue, the way grown children living with their parents will, and during one particularly heated exchange Sasha's mother looks at Sasha, shakes her fist disapprovingly, and then immediately goes over to Steve and pinches his cheeks.

Odessa, as a city, reminds me of no place more than New Orleans. It's not the geography or architecture, it's the similarity of character and of their place in the greater pantheon of the cities of their respective regions of the world. Like New Orleans, Odessa isn't a capital—isn't even one of the larger cities in the country. Its citizens are by and large poor, its economy not the greatest. Its best days are obviously about 150 years behind it. Yet it's still full of character, can still hold its own on a cultural level with towns that far outpace its population and economy. "Oh, yes—everyone knows that the funniest comedians/baddest gangsters/best writers are from Odessa," was a constant refrain.

And of course, among these superlatives can be included "longest tunnels." The city lies in a region with no natural forests. Because of this, the limestone of the surrounding area is the main building material and has been continually quarried for about two hundred years. The result is a sprawling, mostly unmapped series of tunnels spreading out from the center of Odessa. The network is gigantic: well over one thousand miles of abandoned stone quarries that, as in Paris, have taken on the colloquial name of "the catacombs."

Our trip is a blast. The tone is set when, after meeting up with a few other Ukrainian explorers, we go to get provisions for our initial excursion. I ask Ani and Sasha if we should get bottled water or if it's OK to fill up from the tap. In return, they inform us that we're not getting water at all. Instead they show us several two-liter plastic bottles of beer that we're taking instead. This is for hydration. For celebration, we have

CATA PARTY. ODESSA, UKRAINE.

three bottles of vodka. This is when I learn Ukrainians drink beer like water and vodka like beer.

Supplies in tow, we drive out to one of the small towns that surround Odessa. It's the middle of the day, and there's no need to be clandestine about where we're going. Exploring the quarries outside Odessa is perfectly legal. In fact, the people we're with are who the police call if they get reports of someone lost in the catacombs.

And people do get lost. These aren't the nice, stabilized tunnels of Paris, with their detailed maps, underground street signs, and generations of patrolling by cataphiles and the IGC. This network is raw, and incredibly labyrinthine; I remember missing out on seeing the similarly uncatalogued one in Naples, and am glad I've come all this way. We do three or four trips to various sections, some new, some old. One time we even drive through one of the newer quarries, which has large, rectangular

tunnels big enough for a small
auto to navigate.

Our trip is mostly social:
a couple hours spent wandering the tunnels underground,
followed by a few more in
a large cavern eating, drinking, drinking some more, and
learning how to swear in
Russian. The network isn't
like the Parisian tunnels, with
something noteworthy around
every bend, but the history we
do run into is haunting.

First we come to a cavern
with several names written in
Cyrillic on the wall, which

ROLL CALL.

Ani and Sasha explain are the names of a group of partisans
who hid in the quarries while fighting the fascist occupation:
Odessa was under occupation by the Axis powers from October of 1941 to April of 1944. During this occupation, the catacombs were used as a base for several groups of these fighters,
who numbered about three hundred overall. There's an official
museum in part of the catacombs that's dedicated to this history (in true Soviet fashion, it's called the Museum of Partisan
Glory) in the village of Nerubayskoye—not too far away from
where we are—but, like the official catacombs museum in
Paris, it's a tiny part of the overall network.

Continuing on, we see plenty of other remnants of this
time: old weapons, bullets, bottles, graffiti, and, most heart-

breakingly, a cavern where one of the walls is painted to represent a bedroom, with windows, furniture, and a plant growing in a pot on the windowsill. And then we turn a corner and see, carved into the limestone wall, a circle about a foot in diameter with a swastika carved into it.

My first thought is that this isn't real, wasn't actually carved by actual Nazis, was instead inscribed later by some punk. This is reinforced by my remembrance that Odessa was occupied mainly by the Romanians during World War II, with Nazi Germany being involved only sporadically after the initial victory. And it's further reinforced by something else I've run into, which is the unbelievable amount of neo-Nazi graffiti in Eastern Europe. And it wasn't just on the street: I found it in the underground, too, in hillside drainage tunnels in Kiev and a utility network in Moscow.

On all my travels, everywhere, I've held open the possibility that I'll run into, as we American Semites put it, fellow "members of the tribe." My favorite thing about being Jewish is the internationalism, the sense that you're part of some vague worldwide crew. It's difficult to even put that on paper, as it brings up images of old anti-Semitic canards of secret cabals and quests for global domination. But there is something to the bond that's shared simply by being Jewish, even if you don't otherwise share a country, language, ethnicity, or really even a religion. Jews are the most internationalistic people in the history of humanity, which is the primary reason they have always been among the first targets of nationalist movements, turning to nationalism themselves only in a last-ditch attempt at survival after almost two thousand years of rejecting it.

It's not just the fact that there have been settled Jewish communities in almost every nation on earth, although history, and the twentieth century in particular, has seen the extinction of dozens of them. During my travels, expatriates I've run into—or even random backpackers—have all seemed to be disproportionally Jewish. It seems like my people are just comfortable being on the road, rarely averse to rolling into new and unfamiliar locales. I have always wondered how much of my wanderlust is in the blood, part of the tradition passed down ever since my eponymous predecessor led his forty-year migration.

Compounding this possibility, Odessa is one of the most Jewish cities in Eastern Europe, despite the community being decimated during the Holocaust and most of the surviving community immigrating to the United States after the fall of communism. And many urban explorers, as a rule, have much of that same wanderlust, that same curiosity, that I've noticed in my brethren. I always half expect there to be this overlap when I meet new explorers abroad. For instance, I was pretty sure Eric, my jolly companion from France, was Jewish, although it never came up as an overt topic of conversation. As such, I would not have been surprised at all to hear a few Yiddishisms escape from the mouths of any of the people we were with.

But here there's also a strange inversion to this possibility. In my time in Eastern Europe, I gathered that being a neo-Nazi might be something that's extreme, sure, not in the mainstream, yet not so entirely beyond the pale that it's a social death sentence, something that you just aren't allowed to espouse in public. My best analogy is that being a neo-Nazi in Eastern

Europe is akin to something along the lines of being a member of the Westboro Baptist Church in America, the ones who hold up the "God Hates Fags" signs. Someone whose views are taken as extreme, out of the mainstream political consensus, but who isn't afraid of being seen on camera espousing these views (and is definitely not averse to writing them on the wall of an abandoned limestone quarry). One Russian explorer whose tagline read "We must secure the existence of our people and a future for the white race" even tried to friend me on Facebook.

As a result, I've been a little wary about the people I've met. Not suspicious exactly, but just as "Maybe the people we meet will turn out to be Jewish" has been put into the category of "within the realm of possibility" in my head, "Maybe the people we meet will turn out to be neo-Nazis" has been transferred there from its previous home of "something that would make a bad episode of *Seinfeld*" as well.

Already I had run into this issue with Max, whose handle was "Moscowhite" on LiveJournal. When I broached the subject of this online moniker, he responded, "Oh. I know what it is you are thinking. You are thinking I am fucking racist. I want the name 'Moscovite' for LiveJournal. You know, like someone from Moscow. But somebody already has 'Moscovite.' So I take 'Moscowhite' because it sounds like 'Moscovite.' I am not thinking like white people, black people, like that. Later I learn that everyone that is speaking English is thinking I am fucking racist. I am not fucking racist! But now everyone on LiveJournal knows me by fucking 'Moscowhite,' so it is too late."

I look at the carving on the wall for a while, and my companions catch me staring. I relay my skepticism about the authenticity of the carving, suggesting that it was probably neo-Nazi locals who carved it. But my companions insist otherwise.

"No, that is from the war," they tell me. "There are other ones in here. They all look the same."

More than any other modern regime, Nazi Germany has been thoroughly discredited, its historical imprint wiped from current existence. In Italy you can still run across buildings whose keystone reads "built during the XIVth year of the Fascist regime." In the United States there's a Tennessee state park named for the first grand wizard of the Ku Klux Klan. But there is no place in the entirety of Europe where the government would allow a Nazi relic to be displayed openly, at least outside the confines of a museum with a very good explanation for it.

This carving is one of the rarest things a person could find. Even in the German bunker in the Paris catacombs there was nothing past a few generic words of German on the walls. Much of the purpose, the excitement, in urban exploration is finding this kind of thing, a historical remnant preserved because of the remoteness and inaccessibility of the location. I've gotten to see something incredibly rare. My emotions are telling me differently, but my head says I should leave it as is, leave it for others to experience, to have their own thoughts and feelings upon its discovery. After all, ideologically the Nazis have been universally debunked and destroyed. There is nothing left to fight, the victory long since complete.

And if I were someone different, had a different family with a different history, I would have likely heeded this thought and left it alone. And if another, different person had made this choice, I would have understood, made no judgments.

But I'm not a different person. To me, these people aren't a vague historical ideology, just a symbol and an epithet now. All I can think of when I look at the carving in the stone is that whoever put it there wanted to murder my whole family.

I pick up a piece of glass, dig it into the soft limestone, and start to hack away. I don't stop to think how it will be thought of by the others. After a few moments one of the Ukrainians, a gruff black-haired man who doesn't speak English, gets up, takes out his pocketknife, and joins me in my erasure.

Our last trip is a group one, with Ani, Sasha, and a few other people I haven't met yet. This time we're not in the surrounding towns—we're underneath the city itself, exploring the old Cold War–era bunkers. Unlike visiting the suburban quarries, what we're doing now is not legal, so we have to wait until nightfall before heading in. The bunkers aren't stand-alone, instead being connected by the remnants of the oldest of the quarries, the ones that are below the city proper. Steve and I are scheduled to leave the next day, and this feels like a last hurrah, the end of an era.

After a couple hours of exploration we pop a hatch and climb up onto the street, happy with ourselves. There's some grumbling among the others, though: Ani tells me it's about the area we're in right now, which is not a very good one, and

BEFORE.

AFTER.

it's now late at night. Still, I'm not worried. There are seven of us. We walk down the street, chatting and laughing, and I hear footsteps behind us. I turn around and see a man half jogging, half walking up to us. The man is a giant. A very, very drunk giant. And a very, very drunk giant who does not seem happy with us. As he babbles at the others, swaying slightly back and forth as he does so, I make out the word *angliski*. This word is said in a tone that indicates he does not like *angliski* at all, and I determine it's time to keep my mouth shut at all costs. I can't tell if he's looking for a fight or not, but even though there are seven of us, I'm really hoping it's "not." Now, if he actually does take a swing at us, I put the chances at about 90 percent that he'll miss wildly, lose his balance, fall over, and immediately start snoring. But I don't want to see what happens with that other 10 percent.

The others attempt to pacify the giant until finally his companions usher him away and we get a move on back to the car. There are only five seats in the car, and no hope of squeezing in any more because of all the photo gear people have with them, which leaves two of us to find another way home. Since I like nothing more than to stroll through unfamiliar city streets, I volunteer for pedestrian duty. Sasha, who as host feels duty-bound to protect me, insists on being the other person to walk.

Sasha is still a bit shaken from the earlier encounter. "Moe. Listen. If what happens with that man happens again, we are running," he tells me. "You are not speaking English and we are running." But as it happens, we make it back to Sasha's without incident, and the next day Steve and I leave the Ukraine.

. . .

When I was in high school, the Ku Klux Klan used to rally at City Hall every year, which was a few blocks from my school. We'd cut class, the teachers all but encouraging us to do so, and head over to yell, throw stuff, and otherwise think we were fighting them and what they represented. It wasn't until I was an adult that I realized that the reason the Klan chose my very liberal college town for this rally was precisely because they hoped to provoke a fight. But I still didn't understand why this would be a bad thing.

Later on it came together for me. In one New York neighborhood, Greenpoint, a local kid started an anti-fascist organization when there was an uptick in Nazi graffiti in the mid-2000s. I read their Facebook page, and it finally made sense. The page starts:

> For the fascist, violence is a happy condition and fits with their view of the world, where war and military struggle are understood as part of the human condition. For anti-fascists, violence is not part of their world view, they do not seek to create a society where violence is natural or common-place, violence is not something the antifascist can glorify.

A few years later, I read an interview with the guy who started the anti-fascist group, Joey Olszewski. A quote from that article stayed with me as well:

> If you're familiar at all with any other anti-fascist move-ments in the United States, if you're going to stay non-

violent . . . I'm not a fighter. I want to be a history
teacher. I can't get assault charges and things like that.
That wouldn't be good for me at all. You kill a Nazi with
exposure.

"You kill a Nazi with exposure." I am ever thankful to live
in a place where this is true.

TWENTY-EIGHT

Paris, 2009

I am the best boyfriend in the world. Instead of a fancy dinner or tickets to the opera, I have surprised my girlfriend Sara with a trip to Paris for the weekend. It's her first time there.

Of course, most boyfriends during a surprise trip to Paris would probably plan their first day along the lines of, say, a couple of museum excursions, and then a nice dinner followed by a nightcap in a charming hotel room overlooking the Seine. I, on the other hand, have planned a different day. First, I take Sara down a muddy embankment and into an abandoned train tunnel, where a couple of Australian friends of mine are shooting off fireworks. One shoots between us, missing us by about six inches, and we laugh hysterically. After we're done with this particular nonsense, our plan is to walk for four miles and then sleep in the train station. But of course, if we have enough time, I'll first take her down the rabbit hole nearby and into the network of abandoned limestone quarries that I spent my first trip in Paris exploring.

Most girlfriends would probably not like this plan too

much. But Sara is having a blast. Because I don't have most girlfriends. I have a girlfriend who's had sex on a bridge.

I don't remember when I first got it in my head that I wanted to have sex on a bridge. I think it was around my second or third bridge climbed. It seemed so logical: climbing bridges is fun, sex is fun, so sex on a bridge must be really fun. I even had the perfect candidate: the Williamsburg Bridge.

The Williamsburg is, by far, the easiest bridge to climb in New York. People have put sculptures on top of it, had dinner parties in the maintenance rooms that crown its tower, even done aerial shows hanging from its beams. The logistics, though, are still strictly for the able-bodied: there are a couple barriers to get over and a couple hundred feet of stairs to climb.

Now, having sex is a two-person operation. And finding someone to have sex with on top of a bridge is tougher than you might think. The sex part wasn't tough, the heights part wasn't tough, but as soon as I mentioned, "Listen, there's a small but realistic chance we might get arrested," the conversation usually ended there. I suppose I could have just stayed away from the topic altogether, but I wanted everything to be totally up front.

So where do you turn when nobody in real life will suffice? Craigslist, of course. I put an ad in M4W, Casual Encounters, and Miscellaneous Romance, titled "Need a 'best place you've ever done it' story?" It got two responses. The first was this:

> *Hey. 41 yo female 6'2" rock climber, liberal radical, ready*
> *for some Civil Disobedience. Would love to assist in your*

endeavor, as well as hang a sign that says Make Love Not
War sometime on our entanglement on the bridge. Cur-
rently fighting a rap upstate, so maybe have to wait til it
is resolved, have biners, and slings, harness, but no rope.
Willing to purchase to belay you and you set up a TR at
the top. Enclosing pic. Peace my brother.

This one I didn't write back. The second response was pretty
normal (considering the circumstances). We met up and resolved
to do it in short order, but each time we made plans for it, she
always ended up backing out at the last minute. Other dalliances came and went, but it never ended up happening. Then
came Sara.

I mentioned having sex on a bridge shortly after we met
in Mexico City, the spring before we went on our road trip.
At first I was a little worried about mentioning it, as Sara
was Canadian and I didn't want her to get deported—in which
case I wouldn't be able to see her again without leaving the
country—but eventually I brought it up. She was a little hesi-
tant initially but quickly warmed up to the idea.

"I sometimes get vertigo, but I think it'll be OK. Plus my
cousins have been talking all this shit about how I'll never do
it. Fuck that noise, I'm totally going to show them."

What a trouper. So late one night we hopped the fence, I
boosted her over a wooden barricade, and we headed up the
dozen or so flights of stairs to the top. This was it: time to do
the deed.

As it turns out, I'm very glad I went with Sara instead of a
random Craigslister. Because even on a beautiful spring night,
it's still cold as hell when you're naked on top of the Williams-

burg Bridge. It ultimately ended up being a great time—but it certainly would have made for an awkward moment or two on a first date.

Sara says:

Once we got to the top we looked out for a bit. Then Moe took me to this other part that is like a large utility room with windows. We put down all our stuff and said hooray! I was a little nervous and felt awkward about starting anything physical. But Moses just started kissing me and everything felt normal after that.

I had found out that there was more to the plan than the room. Moe's plan was to start things up in this room and then we would have to climb again *up these beams and out the window to the actual top of the bridge. That part felt crazy, but fun. To be climbing around this thing all serious and scared about falling while in my underwear. It felt so ridiculous, but I also felt like the coolest gal at the same time.*

So we got up to the top and there were some cold winds a-blowin'. We both got undressed. But we couldn't really continue fooling around. We took a minute to soak in the view and headed back for the utility room. It was so nice to see the city and the water and feel the wind (in my face—not like being naked in the wind; that felt awful and cold) and see it all totally uninterrupted. No glass windows or wire gates, and you could turn around full circle and see everything. It was sooo beautiful.

We went into the utility room and were totally happy

with ourselves. We warmed up and started fooling around again, and so we tried the top again and it was a success!

So that was it . . . Surprisingly the sex itself wasn't awkward, which is a testament to us since we were in a very awkward situation. It was actually a really great time, and at first I thought I was doing it for him and that the part for me would be that I got an amazing view and kind of conquered a fear . . . but it turns out that everything was really awesome, climbing and sex included.

TWENTY-NINE

New York City, 2010

The reason New York will never get rid of graffiti is that everyone writes graffiti in New York. Everyone. One of the biggest misconceptions about graffiti in this city is that it's done by one specific culture or demographic. Ask your average person in America, "Who writes graffiti in New York?" and they'll probably think of a teenager from the projects.

Now, teenagers from the projects certainly write graffiti—but so does everyone else. I've seen everyone from nine-year-old kids to college professors throw their name up somewhere. The Bangladeshi immigrants who lived next door to me in a middle-class neighborhood in Brooklyn off the F train wrote graffiti. A Hasidic Jewish guy I knew who would lower his gaze when a woman in a short skirt walked by wrote graffiti. There are cops who write graffiti. There are people who've been in Hollywood blockbusters who not only write but are some of the biggest graffiti names in the world. Some of the most prolific writers are completely indistinguishable from your average middle-aged midtown office worker. Others are indistinguishable from your average Barnard coed. Put it this way: If you're a New Yorker—any New Yorker—I won't be surprised if you tell me you write. If I were walking around town with Woody Allen and saw him pull out a marker and tag up WOOD1 in a doorway, my reaction would be, "Huh, didn't know you wrote, man."

In short, graffiti writers are individuals. And the ones I know on an individual level I like and get along fine with for the most part. Graffiti culture, however, is a different story. Every subculture or social circle (and urban exploration is certainly no exception) has its petty jealousies and rivalries, and being involved in it can sometimes feel like you're an extra in the movie *Mean Girls*. But in the graffiti world, it's like the girls are also at a prom where the punch bowl's been spiked with PCP. In addition to the constant gossip and drama, everyone is also always "beefing": fighting, painting over one another's work, and talking shit (mostly talking shit). Compounding this, everyone also views themselves as kind of a modern-day Billy the Kid: part underground outlaw, part minor celebrity. It's the most ridiculous, drama-filled, paranoid subculture I have ever encountered, and it seems like if you get two graffiti writers within ten feet of each other, you get issues. Every graffiti writer will also tell you this themselves, although each one will blame the drama on everyone else and claim it's stupid and that all they want to do is paint.

Now, the paranoid attitude is not entirely unwarranted: the authorities often treat graffiti writers as criminal masterminds on par with Professor Moriarty, devoting an amazing amount of police time and prosecutorial energy to going after people engaged in a crime on the level of yelling in church or reading *Juggs* magazine on the N train. (Literally. Making graffiti; disruption or disturbance of religious service; and public display of offensive sexual material are all class A misdemeanors in New York.) Because of this persecution, discretion is something that's ingrained: talking with graffiti writers, even ones where there's a mutual trust and friendship, can feel like talking to a member of the mob—you just don't ask certain things.

Politicians, police, and the establishment in general all hate graffiti with an unbridled passion because it's a constant visual reminder of the limits of their control. In the battlefield for public space, graffiti writers are the front-line shock troops for the rebellion, the faction that fights back against this push for ever greater control of every inch of the urban landscape. Maybe it would be different if I had experienced the New York of thirty or forty years ago, the one in which a lack of control of public space was a genuine problem. But in our city's current incarnation, the one in which the pendulum has swung so severely the other way, I'm always heartened when I see this challenge shouted in any way, shape, or form, from the tunnels, to the streets, to the rooftops. The authorities hate graffiti way more than exploring. If you're caught somewhere you shouldn't be, it's a good bet the difference between a gruff warning and an impromptu vacation at Rikers Island is going to be the Sharpie in your front pocket.

So when I find out there's a secret art gallery under way in an abandoned subway station, I know the name of the game is now going to be "Don't let the cat meow too loud, much less make it out of the fucking bag alive." I also know it will eventually lead to drama, as it's the magic combination of a secret, something that'll get a ton of press, and graffiti. What I don't know is that it would lead to my first arrest in New York.

The merits and appropriateness of graffiti are a constant discussion among urban explorers, among whom the prevailing attitude can be summed up as "I don't like graffiti, except for the graffiti I like." It's part of the blanket discussion of the "ethics" of what we do. Some people try to make a code of ethics, mostly along the lines of the naturalist "Take only photos, leave only footprints" variety; others rip it apart; still others say how silly ethics are in general and then illustrate their own attitude, which they expect everyone to follow. The whole thing is an exercise in futility, almost a paradox. You are, by definition, dealing with people who will ignore rules that they think are stupid. Why do you think whatever you come up with is going to be treated any differently from the legal code?

The gallery isn't really a graffiti thing, though. It's the work of the street art crowd. The difference between "street art" and "graffiti" doesn't really have a lot to do with the end product or even with the people who do it. There are people from all different walks of life in both scenes. There's plenty of stuff that looks like graffiti that's done by street artists, and plenty of stuff that looks like street art that's done by the hard-core, old-school graffiti writers. And there's plenty of overlap between the two worlds; in fact, some of the biggest graffiti writers out there have pieces in this secret art gallery. The difference is cultural, tribal. When you think about it, it's not like there's a whole lot of difference between the Serbians and the Croatians, or the Northern Irish Protestants and the Northern Irish Catholics. But they're two groups of people fighting over the same little slice of land, each wanting their own small differences in the unspoken rules, each wanting respect.

And where the project is taking place isn't actually an

"abandoned" station at all, which would imply that it was at one time in use. Instead, it was built almost eight decades ago but never put into service. It's a small glimpse into a kind of parallel dimension, a New York City that came close to happening but never did.

New York City is successful in large part because of foresight. Many of the key components of the city—the street grid, the subway system—weren't built for the city that existed at the time; they were built for the city that was due to exist in the future. The street grid was surveyed and planned out 142 blocks beyond the northernmost actual street at the time. The subway system was built miles and miles into farmland and wilderness, on the premise that development would follow its path. Many cities are organic, the people determining how it develops by speaking with their feet, with infrastructure built as a reaction. Not so with much of New York.

This foresight sometimes takes unexpected twists. Central Park—planned and developed decades before apartment buildings lined Fifth Avenue and Central Park West—was put where it was in part because it was regarded as one of the least valuable places in Manhattan. At the time, as throughout the vast majority of its history, New York's economy was based on maritime activity. The closer to the waterfront, the more valuable the land, which is why the avenues near the East and Hudson rivers are closer together than those in the middle of the island—more valuable street frontage in the most valuable part of the island. The land that would become Central Park, a good three-quarters of a mile to the nearest river, was seen as almost expendable. Today, Central Park is the most valuable undeveloped 843 acres of land in the country, perhaps even the world. In 2005, the property appraisal firm Miller Samuel estimated its worth at a smidge under 529 billion dollars.

But not all of this foresight has worked out every time, either as planned or as a fortunate accident of history. In addition to the successes, there have also been failures—parts of the city developed for a future use that never came to be. The subway tunnels are filled with these forgotten failures: beginnings of route extensions that never happened, extra tracks that have ended up being useless, blocks' worth of tunnels dug for lines that were never installed. One of these failures is a giant concrete shell, the unfinished remains of a station meant to be a transfer point for two separate lines, neither of which was ever built. This is where the art gallery is currently being created.

This is the easiest of these hidden places to get to in the whole system. It's at the unused end of one of the least-used stations on one of the least-used lines. You don't even have to walk any tracks: just slip around the red sign and you're there. It's our go-to place for friends who want to see something interesting in the subway but don't have the willingness to actually get in the tunnels and dodge the trains. But as a result of the need for secrecy concerning the project, this is no longer our chill place to bring friends. Steve and I had taken a couple of journalists there a few years ago, not thinking much of it at the time. As the project is going on, consumed in "Don't say a fucking word to a fucking soul," there's a detailed account of exactly how to get there online in *GOOD* magazine.

While the organizers had a plan not to mention the exact location of the gallery until they were done with the project and the story hit the papers, I knew this was an exercise in futility: subway enthusiasts, not to mention the MTA (the Metropolitan Transit Authority, the agency in charge of the subway system), would easily be able to figure it out from the description and photos, and the place would almost certainly become known and sealed. For the organizers, this would simply be collateral damage, but for us it would be a bit of a heartbreaker. And it's a shame that while the project is going on we have to take a step backward, not mentioning that the place even exists to anyone who doesn't already know. But I accept it, an inevitable consequence of circumstance. The organizers just have an idea—a good one—and are trying to bring it to life. It's not their fault that municipal authorities are so uptight about this kind of thing.

Sometimes there's no choice—sometimes greater knowledge of a place leads to less access, not more. The more people learn of a place, or how to get entry to a place, the greater chance there is that someone will bring its unsanctioned use to the attention of the authorities somehow. Someone will get caught entering it, or someone will trash it, or (as most often happens) someone will simply put a story about it on the Internet that'll get seen by the wrong person. I wasn't worried that perhaps an odd subway worker or two knew what was going on in there. After all, there had been graffiti in the abandoned station for years, before the project had even started; workers had to know that people hung out there from time to time. What I was worried about was the publicity. There were big names and big concepts involved in this, and it would be a big story if it came out. And there's a big difference between knowing that some people like to hang out, or even write graffiti, in a place where you happen to work and having your boss come up to you, slam down the newspaper, and go, "What the fuck

is this shit?" when this fact is plastered all over the front page.
We had learned this lesson a while ago with one of our favorite
places, the Old Croton Aqueduct. In 2006, Steve took a *New
York Times* reporter there. The week after the story hit the
paper, all of the entrances were sealed with cement. And with
a project like this art gallery, sealing it with cement would almost be a best-case scenario. A worst-case scenario would involve arrests, restitutions, and grand juries. All we can do is to
try to keep it quiet until the project runs its course and the
story hits the papers in an orderly fashion as planned.

Still, it's a little hard to swallow. I have always been attracted to the idea of spaces like this one as uncontrolled, outside the everyday rules of the city. I like that people can do
what they want with them: put art in them, write graffiti, hang
out, set up a home, even. I love the general concept of the art
gallery, the idea that people are creating something from
scratch in this place not for a show, not to try to sell the works,
but just because it's a cool thing to do. But the end vision is a
different case. For the organizers, the gallery—constructed off
the grid for an audience of next to nobody—is at least partially
meant to be a statement about fighting the commercialization
of street art, with the space just a vehicle for a larger point to
be made.

Jasper Rees, writing for the website The Arts Desk after
the project was completed, quotes one of the organizers:

> *For the last few years urban art was getting ridiculous.
> You could go out with some cute little character that you
> drew, or some quirky saying, and put it up everywhere for
> a few months, then do a gallery show and cash in on the*

sudden interest in urban art. It really was that easy for a while. Banksy pieces that were selling for $600 one year were suddenly selling for $100,000 a few years later. It was nuts. People were going out and literally sawing walls in half to steal Banksy pieces. Electrical panels were being ripped off leaving live wires exposed that had Shepard Fairey stencils on them. It was commercialism at its worst. This atmosphere starts to fuck things up. Early in the street-art years, I relished the ability to feel like I was my own island. [This] was our way of feeling like we were an island again. We finally had a space in the world that collectors couldn't contaminate. A space that couldn't be bought.

But I have a different point of view. I love the place for itself; the art is just decoration to me. No matter how good it is, how skillfully done, it still isn't the ultimate point, doesn't overtake the place itself. And it's always bothered me when people try to control or claim ownership of these spaces, whether that's the city closing them off, or hipsters throwing a super-secret party with a cool-kids-only guest list, or artists doing their best to enforce a need-to-know-basis-only policy on a place that never had one before. I like the idea of these places being accessible to anyone with the interest to get to them, which is always why I appreciate the people who put art in them, creating an unexpected treat for anyone who happens to find it.

This line between use and control is a fine one, one that I'll freely admit really lies in my own head; after all, I never resent it when people stake the ultimate claim of ownership and control to these spaces, which is to live in them. But the

artists have benefited enor-
mously from both the space's
obscurity and its ease of access. After the gallery hits the
papers, both these benefits
will be gone.

RED HOOK GRAIN TERMINAL.
© *Nathan Kensinger*

But still, losing this station is far from losing
everything. There are other
great off-the-grid places in
the city where it's pretty easy
to relax and hang out. One of
these is the Red Hook Grain
Terminal, a beautiful old industrial building, cathedral-
like on the ground floor, with
a roof that provides an up-close, unobstructed view of New York
Harbor: you almost feel like you can take a running leap off the
building and land on the Statue of Liberty's torch. I've loved
hanging out there since the first time I went, accompanied by a
Montreal explorer named Nel who was in town for the day. Nel's
a soft-spoken flamenco dancer in her fifties who, on the side,
travels the world to explore abandonments, drains, subways, and
anything else that strikes her fancy.

The organizers of the art gallery are making a documentary about the project and ask me to do an interview for it. So
when the filmmaker wants an "explorey" place to film my
interview, the grain terminal is my first suggestion. She's

already been there with me, Shane, and another friend of ours, Eric, to do some action shots of us rappelling into the abandoned concrete silos that used to store the grain, and it went off without a hitch.

I had met Eric last year at Steve's going-away party. I was boozed and up for something, so I put out a blanket suggestion of a bridge climb. Eric, Sara, and I, and a fourth friend, headed over to the Manhattan Bridge, Sara staying on the pedestrian path as the rest of us quickly made our way up. We got to the top just in time to take pictures of the flash thunderstorm that had surrounded us. The other two really, really wanted a picture from the top of the bridge with a bolt of lightning in the background. Since we were currently on top of the tallest metal structure for hundreds of feet around, this did not really seem like the smartest plan. I guessed we weren't in any real danger—after all, plenty of people cross the bridge during thunderstorms—but I certainly wasn't enthused about testing this theory. Luckily, they quickly got their shot and we made our way back down, absolutely drenched, somehow managing not to slip and fall on the descent. When we dropped off the structure and back onto the path, Sara was huddled with a random old man, who was somehow not surprised when her three companions basically fell out of the sky.

"He asked me what I was doing here in the rain and I said I was waiting for some friends," Sara told us. "Then he asked me if I wanted him to wait with me until they got there. I said sure. After a few minutes I felt bad—the guy was so nice. So I came clean about where my friends were."

I meet the filmmaker in a park by the grain terminal. This time she's got two girls with her, her interns, who look barely old enough to vote. They turn out to be college students, one from New Jersey, the other from California. They're excited about this excursion. While they've been interning on the film for weeks, they haven't actually gotten to see the space where the gallery is being created. This is the next-best thing.

The interview goes great. We head in, navigate the tricky walk to get to the rusty staircase, and set up on the roof, complete with boom mic and sun shield. After a couple hours it's starting to get dark, and we wrap it up, heading down the stairs, out the building, and back through the courtyard. As we're about to hop the fence to exit, we see a van circle around. A police van. By myself I'd make a run for it, bailing over a wall on the other side of the courtyard, but I've got three ladies and about fifty pounds of film equipment in tow. Shit—well, maybe they didn't see us.

"OK, we might have to deal with the cops," I tell the other three. "Don't say anything. Just act like we're hanging out by the water."

Even if they saw us, this shouldn't be a big deal. We'll probably get a warning, a summons at worst, which will be annoying but far from anything that'll ruin our night. And I can't imagine it'll even go that far: I'm with three nondescript grown-ups, not shady-looking teenagers or graffiti writers with backpacks full of aerosol spray cans.

"Could you step over here, please?" The cops have indeed spotted us. Damn. OK, time to deal. We step over the fence.

"You know that's private property?"

We start the cop game: be exceedingly polite, say as little as possible, and deny everything. Unfortunately, when you're caught red-handed, there's not a whole lot to deny, so we just stick with the first two. Apparently being three feet on the wrong side of a waist-high fence warrants five different officers, three men and two women. They're nice enough, but why shouldn't they be? We're an easy collar.

The guy who's doing most of the talking is young, maybe twenty-five or so, a big guy with a build that falls just short of chubby. He seems inclined to cut us a break.

"OK, hang on a minute," he tells us. "This will probably just be a warning. I just got to check one thing." He talks on his radio for a few minutes and then starts conversing with the fellow officers.

"OK, so it turns out we can't just give you a warning," he says.

"So we're getting a summons?" I ask.

"Well, uh, unfortunately it's going to be a little bit bigger deal than that," he says to us. "We're going to have to take you in."

I can't believe it. I've been up a dozen bridges, done countless trips into the subway, trespassed on national landmarks and World Heritage sites. One time Steve and I had to deal with cops after we'd been messing around on the underside of the highway bridge that leads to the approach to the George Washington Bridge. The cops hadn't caught us in the act, couldn't prove anything, but knew we were the ones they were looking for. We, of course, kept our mouths shut, and their exact words before letting us go were, "Word to the wise: You're out here fucking around on the approach to one of the biggest terrorist targets on the East Coast. You don't think maybe that's not such a great idea?" All of this, and the first time I end up in handcuffs is with two college film interns and a woman who has just gotten done telling me about how much she loves double Dutch jump rope.

After they tell us the bad news, they cuff us and drive us down to the precinct. I'm in a van with the big guy and another nebbishy officer—short, balding, and with an accent like Joe Pesci. We get to the precinct and they take us inside.

"What're they here for?" the desk sergeant asks.

"Trespassing," the big guy replies.

The desk sergeant is not happy with this answer. "So give them a summons," he says.

"It's criminal trespass," the officer replies, with a "Hey, I don't want to do this either, but what can we do?" kind of look. For a moment I think we might get out of this.

"OK, put 'em through," the desk sergeant says with a shrug. Later I learn that the owner of the building has gotten tired of the neighborhood kids messing around in there and asked the precinct to arrest everyone they caught.

They take everything out of my pockets for vouchering, the short guy going through my wallet and removing and examining every card stuffed in its nooks and crannies. I know what he's looking for: a Patrolmen's Benevolent Association card or something else that will let him have an excuse to let us go. He's not going to find one. I try to look on the bright side. I want to see everything in New York—I've never seen the inside of a jail cell.

We're the first ones of the night. There are two cells next to each other, each with bars facing a common processing room; you can hear the people in the next cell over, but not see them. I go in the one on the left, the ladies go in the one on the right.

"OK, so you're gonna to wait here. We'll try to get you out on a DAT," the cops tell us. That's a desk appearance ticket. If you've got no warrants and otherwise seem like a good citizen, it means you get let go that night instead of having to go through Central Booking.

The next two arrestees of the night join me a few minutes later. They seem nice enough: a father-and-son team. They've come in with a daughter who got picked up also, and who gets put in with the filmmaker and interns next door. They don't say a whole lot, their vocalizing limited to answering questions from the police and occasionally muttering to each other in Spanish, and I certainly don't ask any questions. The father doesn't speak much English, but he seems to know what he's doing. I'd be pretty surprised if they haven't been in here before. My processing officer is a young, soft-spoken woman who says they'll get us out of there in a few hours. I marvel that in the days of instant credit check it still takes this long to figure out I don't have a warrant out for my arrest.

The next arrival, about a half-hour after the father and son, is a skinny, nervous black guy. He's one of those people for whom silence is like a vacuum that can be resisted for only so long before it has to be filled. I don't talk. The father and son don't talk. So he talks. A lot. I quickly learn he got picked up in the Red Hook houses, a public housing project a few blocks away from where we got arrested. He was leaving his girl's apartment, was drinking from an open container, got stopped, got frisked, had a joint on him, and voilà.

"What you in for?" he asks the father-son team.

Wisely, they don't answer directly. Instead the son tells the story of how they got arrested.

"I hear a knock on the door so I open the door, right? And there's, like, a million cops. So I say, 'Hey, what's going on?' and they're just like, 'Come with us.' So here we are."

He makes a few other generic statements when Skinny's never-ending verbal assault takes the form of direct questions. My guess is that they've been dealing drugs out of the house. The fact that they know not to say anything solidifies my suspicion that this is not their first time here.

Next to enter the cell is an extremely stoned fellow with dreadlocks that reach down to his lower back. He sits down, eyes bloodshot.

"What you in for?" Skinny asks.

He ends up having much the same story as Skinny, except this time the weed came first and the open container second. He's also from the Red Hook houses; it turns out he actually knows Skinny. He's too stoned to say much, so Skinny continues to fill the aural void solo.

Unlike the father and son, Skinny does not know what he's doing. He has the worst curse of the lawbreaker: the need to confess. At one point he even confides in me, completely unprompted and not even in a whisper, "I'm dirty as fuck right now," meaning he has drugs on him. This is in a police station, with cameras pointed right at the cell, and officers directly on the other side of the bars. I determine Skinny is the absolute last guy I would ever hire to deal my drugs.

About two hours after we get there, the last arrival is brought in. This guy is huge. He looks like Fat Joe the rapper: bald, beady eyes, caramel complexion, and, well, fat. While he's wearing glasses that make him look kind of bookish, it quickly becomes clear that he's the closest thing to a real criminal we've had so far. He starts trouble right away. He doesn't like the cops and the cops don't like him. Fingerprinting becomes a drama. Removing his shoelaces becomes a drama. Asking to make a call becomes a drama. Skinny finally has a partner in his battle against the silence. A loud partner.

Everyone in the cell wants a desk appearance ticket, although the father-and-son team seem resigned to spending the night in jail and put their energy into trying to get the daughter in the women's cell out. If you don't get a DAT and you end up getting put through the system, you're usually looking at at least twenty-four hours before you can see a judge and get out. Now, while I've been told Central Booking sucks and the food is pretty bad, the most important thing getting a DAT will do for you is avoid screwing up your next day: there's no need to give your boss an excuse for why you missed work, no angry girlfriends to deal with, no skipped appointments.

The problem is you have to be a hundred percent squeaky clean to get out on a DAT. First comes the bad news for the guy in dreads. He has an outstanding summons. The summons is for riding his bike on the sidewalk, but it's enough to ruin his next day.

"Shit," Dreads goes. He doesn't look that surprised. It doesn't seem like he remembered the bike summons specifically. It's more like he was just counting on the fact that something or other would end up screwing him over.

Next comes the bad news for Skinny. Skinny comes back a Blood. As in, a gang member. I barely manage to keep in my guffaw when the officer breaks the news. Skinny is no more a Blood than I am. He would make the worst gangster ever known. Even the cop seems to accept this diagnosis as faulty.

"Look, I'm not saying you're a Blood. That's what the computer says. Maybe you are, maybe you were just hanging out with the wrong guys, I don't know. But I can't get you out on a desk appearance. Sorry."

It seems Skinny, at some point, must have been standing too close to someone wearing red. This is somehow constitutionally sound grounds for a night in jail.

Then comes the bad news for Fat Joe. Fat Joe has an outstanding warrant. It's from 2001, for an open container. Fat Joe is livid at this news.

"I was in prison in 2001!" he screams. "I got put in for eight years for assault! How can I have a warrant? Look it up, look it up! I am a violent felony offender! You should know me! Eight years, it's in there!"

I am in a ten-by-seven cell with a three-hundred-pound self-described violent felony offender. I'm actually not too stressed about it, never feel like I'm in any danger. My biggest worry is that the cops will decide to impound the film footage, find out about the art gallery, bust it before it finishes, and I'll be the idiot who fucked it all up.

And it would have been my fault, not fairly chalked up to bad luck. A couple weeks previously, Shane and Eric were hanging out on the roof of the Red Hook Grain Terminal when security spotted them. They played a cat-and-mouse game until dark, at which time they managed to sneak out the back. Shortly afterward I read an article in the local paper about how the owner was complaining about all the trespassing that was taking place ever since the city made him replace a ten-foot solid metal fence with a shorter see-through one on the grounds that the old fence obstructed the view of the water. I should have known the consequences of being caught would be more than a stern lecture, and definitely should have paid more attention and not been so cavalier about our exit. I didn't even wait the few minutes it would have taken for it to get dark enough that the cops might not have seen us. Once again, I'm reminded that injury and arrest are almost always the result of complacency, laziness, and otherwise getting too happy with yourself.

Fat Joe continues his harangue, insisting the warrant is a screwup. But even if it is, I can't imagine the cops are going to let a convicted felon who's done nothing but cause trouble since he got in not make the trip down to Central Booking. After ten minutes or so of this tantrum the cops let me and the girls out of the cells and start typing up our desk appearance tickets. It turns out one of the interns' moms was supposed to meet her at Grand Central two hours ago and has called her in as missing. I feel like the worst person in the world.

As we're waiting to get our tickets, the cops lead the others out in handcuffs to be transferred over to Central Booking. There's something different in all of their demeanors, something that says they know they've fought, lost, and don't have a rematch. Fat Joe wants his cell phone so he can call his boss and tell him he won't be in the next day, but he's not yelling for it anymore, more like pleading for it.

"Please, man, this is going to fuck up my job. I can't fuck up this job, man, you know that!" It turns out Fat Joe got the open-container summons in 2001 and then got arrested for assault before his court date. Nine years later that can of beer is still on his record, probably costing him his job, his parole, and any semblance of any kind of a second chance he'd gotten.

. . .

The gallery—which the organizers dub "The Underbelly Project"—finishes up, although the documentary never ends up getting completed. It hits the papers with a big feature article in *The New York Times* a few months later. It takes five minutes for the subway aficionados to figure out where it is, slightly longer than that for it to be posted on the Internet, and about twenty-four hours for the cops to start patrolling it. For a couple weeks they station officers in the space to collar who-ever's dumb enough to try to visit.

Surprisingly, the MTA says they won't paint it over. This might seem to make sense, as the art in the station would be fairly valued well into the six figures, but to the MTA it's less than worthless: it's graffiti. The MTA hates graffiti, which first started as a large-scale endeavor on the subway trains, probably more than any other municipal agency in New York. They have a blanket policy of never running a train with graf-fiti on it, no matter how much it might be needed. If you so much as mention the word "graffiti" to them when you're try-ing to get their permission to film or do an interview, even in a completely historical context, they'll stop talking to you im-mediately. Officially, for the MTA, graffiti is subject to a sort of Orwellian denial: it certainly doesn't go on now, and as much as possible, they'd like to pretend that it never even ex-isted in the first place.

But on an unofficial level, I wonder if the project has fans among the higher-ups. On an official tour of a tunnel con-struction project I once took, one of the people from the MTA said that whenever the higher-ups came down in the tunnels and saw some of the old graffiti, they'd ask her about it, and that she wanted to do some research and write a paper on it.

"They'll let you publish that?" I asked.

"Oh, no," she replied. "It would just be an internal thing."

And I wouldn't be in the least surprised if the art gallery became an "internal thing" as well. I can easily imagine kids like the two interns I got arrested with asking their MTA-executive dads to take them there some weekend afternoon. It would hardly be unprecedented: public servants often have a bad habit of treating the structures and systems they're charged with overseeing as their own personal playgrounds. For instance, right before he quit, MTA chairman Jay Walder arranged for an exclusive tour to the top of the Verrazano-Narrows Bridge for himself, his wife, his son, and two friends. Fine for him—but the structure doesn't actually belong to him. It belongs to the public: built with our taxes, operated with our (considerable) tolls. Instead of considering a tour of the bridge as a job perk he could arrange for friends and family, as might be justified in a private building, I would have hoped that Walder would have seen it more his duty to find a way to offer the tour to the people who paid his salary. It's not like it would even have to be free, like it was for him. Maybe the revenue from giving tours up the bridge could even go toward offsetting the $13 charge we have to pay to cross it.

Our court date's a few months after the arrest. I end up being the only one who actually gets charged with anything; everyone else's tickets seem to have somehow disappeared. The filmmaker hires a lawyer for the four of us, although the parents of one of the interns have, from California, hired their own lawyer. I get two days of community service, which I spend at a church in Brooklyn handing out bags of food, the case is dismissed, and my arrest record is supposedly sealed. I'm not surprised. I assumed this outcome, or something similarly benign. I remember how Dreads, arrested on an equivalent class B misdemeanor charge, had assumed a different kind of outcome.

The project ends in some mild graffiti-world drama, with local graffiti writers going over a lot of the pieces. This is something I, the organizers, and pretty much everyone else with any knowledge of the project assumed would eventually happen in some way, shape, or form. I still can't quite make head or tail of the specifics, but the graffiti world resembles the end of the movie *Chinatown* at times, and I've given up trying to figure out who's on whose side, who told who else what and when. For my part, I'm happy to get out of the whole thing with two days of community service and a resolution to finally stop doing stuff that might lead to any kind of more in-depth knowledge of New York's criminal justice system.

THIRTY

D ude, come on, you've got to join the club." This is Shane talking to Steve, who's back in town for the summer after finishing his first year of grad school in California. We're hanging out, relaxing after finishing up a few hours at the climbing gym, and Shane is grinning at the fact that he has recently become one-half of the third couple to join the Sex on Bridges club, after me and Sara and a random Estonian couple whose photo I found on the Internet having sex on an arch bridge in Tallinn.

I started the club as a lark, paying ten dollars to register SexonBridges.com and setting up a basic website one insomniatic night. Anyone can join the club by having sex on a bridge, although I decided that charter membership would be reserved for the first people to christen any one particular bridge. Sara and I have snagged the Williamsburg, and now Shane's picture of him and his girlfriend coupling on top of the Manhattan Bridge is in full view on the "Hall of Fame" page of the site. Steve's is still missing.

Steve is actually a little upset about this, although he's try-

SHANE JOINS THE CLUB. TOP OF THE MANHATTAN BRIDGE.

© *Shane Perez*

ing to hide it. He's always been the one to push the envelope, using the prospect of other people beating him to places as motivation to overcome laziness and other obstacles and maintain his status as the trailblazer. This has meshed well with my method of motivation, which is to plan out a new adventure and then talk a lot of shit, knowing that this will make Steve come along and provide the final push when I inevitably want to bottle out. We've developed a sort of mutual cooperation society disguised as a false competition, one in which we're happy to each play our roles. But this trend has always ended with Steve being first, or at least an equal member of the accomplishment. He doesn't like the fact that I, and now Shane, have gotten out in front of him on anything, even something so silly as this.

The issue, though, isn't that Steve hasn't been able to get a girl to go up a bridge with him. In contrast, ever since I first came up with the whole idea of having sex on a bridge, date night on these structures has become one of the most popular ways he, Shane, and some other friends of mine have come up with to impress girls. The first time Steve told me he had taken someone up the Williamsburg Bridge on a first date, I was amazed—but then thought back to Chi, the Australian in Rome who'd climbed the obelisk with us, and the American in Paris we'd taken down a hole in a graveyard, and remembered that it's incredible what someone (or at least Steve) can get relative strangers to do with a smile and a confident attitude. After using the stairs to go up the bridge, Steve decided to descend via the suspension cables, not realizing that, unlike the Brooklyn Bridge, the Williamsburg has suicide guards covered with chicken wire, making them significantly harder to navigate. He ended up almost killing the poor girl, a complete bridge-climbing novice, whom he had gotten to go up there with him.

"I'm assuming there was no second date," I said to Steve upon hearing this.

"Yeah," he replied. "But I don't think that's because of the getting-stuck-on-the-cable thing. I think I might have spent too much time talking about how hot her friend was."

No, the issue is that on this, and every other bridge date night I've heard of, there has not been actual sex on the actual top of the bridge. And so Sara and I and the Estonian couple have stayed the only members until Shane and his girlfriend's tryst on top of the Manhattan.

And I am being absolutely adamant about the criteria for inclusion being fully fulfilled. My problem isn't the "sex" part: in an effort to make the club inclusive and queer-friendly, the definition of "sex" is simply "If all parties could, in good conscience, say they had gotten laid last night if it had happened in the bedroom, then it counts." No, it's the "top" part. There's hundreds of ways to have sex. But there's only one definition of "top." The catwalk under the maintenance room of the Williamsburg Bridge, with its see-through floor 250 feet above the East River? No. A romantic night in the lift room of the Broadway Bridge (not during pigeon season, obviously)? Not a chance. On top of the castle-like towers of the Hell Gate Bridge, accessible only by a rusty spiral staircase? Oh hell no— not only are they not structurally part of the bridge, they're also shorter than the top of the arch. Tenzing Norgay and Sir Edmund Hillary didn't reach a nice promontory a few feet lower than the summit of Everest, snap a couple photos, and call it a day. The top is the top is the top is the top. The only caveat I make is that the sex has to take place "where it is possible to have sex relatively safely." After all, I don't want anyone killing themselves pursuing membership. There's no need to climb up one of the twenty-five-foot turrets of the Queensboro Bridge to the dinner platter–size platforms housing a blinking red airline light on top in order to do the deed, for instance.

This obstinacy over "the top" has caused no shortage of arguments with Steve, Shane, and my other bridge-climbing friends. "What do you mean, 'That doesn't count'? Whatever, fuck your stupid club, Moses," I've heared more than once. But as I have the password to the website, and in our day and age the Internet is the ultimate arbiter of truth, I hold the keys to the Sex on Bridges club and I am unlocking membership only for the worthy. And despite "Fuck your stupid club," the applications keep coming. Shane's is the first one that passes muster.

Steve is against Shane's inclusion in the club. "You guys didn't do it on top of the globes," he tells Shane. "That's the top."

I remind Steve about the safety clause. Shane's grin widens.

"Oh, you're so full of shit, Moe," Steve replies. "You're completely just making this stuff up as you go along."

I am not making this stuff up as I go along. The criteria for membership are sacrosanct. It's not my fault if Steve hasn't fulfilled them correctly and Shane has. Steve and I start to argue.

Shane interrupts after not too long. "Wait. So, Moe, if I have a threesome on the Williamsburg Bridge, does that mean I'm a charter member even if you already did it up there? I mean, it's still the first threesome, right?" Count on Shane to ask a question like this.

"Shane, you're already a charter member, remember? You got the Manhattan first."

"Right, yeah, I know. It's just that it'd kind of be awesome to have a threesome on a bridge. And then I'd be, like, a double charter member, right?"

"Jesus Christ, Shane, there's no 'double charter' membership, okay?" Somehow this discussion has turned almost Talmudic. "That's not the point at all."

But taking a step back, I think that having discussions like this one certainly isn't the point, either, although I also take a minute to marvel at the exchange: it doesn't seem like that long ago that I was petrified to scoot around a sign at the end of a subway platform; now I'm arguing about having threesomes on top of suspension bridges. But as I compare Sara's and my happy afterglow from our night on the Williamsburg Bridge to this inane competition, I feel like I've created a monster with my silly little website. It's true that Tenzing Norgay and Sir Edmund Hillary didn't reach a nice promontory a few feet lower than the summit of Everest, snap a couple photos, and call it a day. But I'm also pretty sure they didn't reach the peak and think, "Wow—wait until the Royal Geographic Society learns we totally boned up here!" Somehow, instead of just being happy with the best and most exclusive date night in New York City, we've turned this into the world's dumbest pissing contest.

This competitive edge among us serves its purpose; I don't think we would have gotten to half the places we did without it. But the disadvantage of having this edge is that it can leak out in wholly inappropriate times. Maybe it's tough to shake off a cocaine hangover and get out of a warm bed to go in a freezing granite tunnel, or plan a trip to go trespassing in Russia, or scale Notre Dame in the rain, without that sense of competition to fuel you. But for some things—like sex, how and wherever it might take place—enjoying them for their own sake should be motivation enough.

THIRTY-ONE

I first met QX when he came to New York City for a weekend with Marshall, another Australian living in France. Our first night we found ourselves climbing up the Brooklyn Bridge. Relaxing later, we traded the regular stories about arrests, injuries, and close calls.

"One time I was up on a wall, right?" QX says. "Just a regular abandonment, nothing special, but we're really high up. All of a sudden, a bit of it crumbles and I lose my footing and start to fall. And I just remember thinking, 'Well, there you go, mate. Had a good run of it. Guess you're done now,' before the guy I was with caught me by the back of my shirt."

QX goes on. "To tell you the truth, though, that's not really how I'm worried about dying. I'm more worried about getting held up somewhere. If someone was pointing a gun at me, I just know I couldn't keep my bloody mouth shut. I'd end up taking the piss out of him and probably get shot."

Trading these kinds of stories is a staple of meeting new explorers. Usually these initial encounters end up with more than a bit of dick swinging. I've heard plenty like this, where the person telling them tries to project a sort of roguish, devil-may-care attitude toward life and limb, and I usually just roll my eyes a bit internally and chalk it up to the ubiquitous human tendency to present the person they want to be, not the person they actually are. But with QX, I never question the veracity of such stories for a second. I have not a shadow of a doubt that if he were facing down the demon reincarnation of the Praetorian Guard armed with antitank missiles and laser guns, he'd meet them with a wink and wisecrack. This is the guy I'm planning to climb the Great Pyramid of Cheops with in December of 2010, a month before the country explodes.

I never really meant to try it. It's been some months since I got arrested at the Red Hook Grain Terminal, over a year since my last trip with Steve to Eastern Europe. It's been three years since we were arrested on top of Notre Dame, and over five years since we first met and went out the window of the Williamsburg Savings Bank Tower onto the abandoned observation deck. I was originally going to take this trip with Sara, but we had broken up a couple months earlier, the different countries and constant travel too much. But still, even solo, I'm not thinking of doing anything too off the beaten path. I've been happy to settle into a new job, concentrate on my career, leave running through subway tunnels and such for the very occasional foray. I've checked off almost all of the places I've wanted to see in New York, with the remaining ones easier to get to through official channels. And I never thought I'd do the traveling that I have, go to the places around the world I've been. So in my three weeks of vacation coming up, I'm thinking of a calm trip, one spent backpacking and relaxing, not trying to climb the only remaining ancient wonder of the world. I have friends in Sicily, which seems like a good destination. I figure Tunisia's just a ferry ride away, and the cheapest way to get from Tunis back home is Air Egypt, which has a stopover in Cairo. A three-hour or three-day stopover is the same price, so I jump at the chance to take in a new city. Then, once again, my mind turns to borders, to what might be possible versus what people say is possible. I get to thinking: "What's there to do in Cairo?" My first thought is of the pyramids. The Great Pyramid of Cheops was the tallest human-made structure in the world for almost four thousand years. I'm always trying to get to the top. And this would be much more than getting to the highest point in a city. This would be getting to the highest point of an entire era of civilization. I start to wonder if I can climb it. And, to my complete surprise, it turns out that I probably can.

Actually, until fairly recently, anyone could. In fact, they were encouraged to; as Mark Twain famously recollects in *The Innocents Abroad*, when he visited the pyramids he was "besieged by a rabble of muscular Egyptians and Arabs who wanted the contract of dragging us to the top—all tourists are." The possibility continued to be there for the fit and adventurous who found themselves in Cairo, until the growing number of tourists started leading to concerns over safety and preservation, and Egypt began putting up the now ubiquitous "Do Not Climb" signs in the mid-1980s. I'm reminded again of how different traveling used to be, how more and more people leads to more and more control, less and less access. Now the pyramids have ropes, fences, guards, and all the other staples of twenty-first-century mass tourism. But that hasn't stopped some tourists—mostly of the young, male, Japanese, or Euro-

pean variety—from sneaking in and making nocturnal attempts at the ascent.

Now, I don't think I'm actually going to do it. I'm mostly
just poking around, researching, finding a couple of accounts
of recent successes on the Internet. One guy is nice enough to
send over a sort of how-to guide when I ask him for pointers. I
still don't think this is going to be relevant to me, but I decide
that this is valuable information, so I send it around to the
people I know who might be up for this sort of thing. Then I
get the following from QX:

> Hey mate.
>
> I was just wanting to follow up on El Pirámide—I'd love to do it with
> you.

Oh, no. I've been called out. And I realize I've subcon-
sciously done what I've always done: put myself in a position
where I can't, in good conscious, say no. I get a feeling. The
same feeling I had right before climbing the Manhattan Bridge
years ago. The feeling that says this isn't me casually bullshitting myself, that this is actually something that's going to
happen. I'm excited. I'm also filled with dread. After some
hemming and hawing, I accept my fate. I write QX.

"Fuck it. Let's do it."

I get back the following:

> Ding ding ding. Let me know the dates, I'm a-comin' down. I have a
> French girl that's willing to come up and get caught with us, if that
> works for you as well. She might work as a diversion for the guards.
> Thoughts?

"Who's the French chick? Will she be OK?" I reply.

The French chick, I think she'll be fine. She just came and did a climb with me, and then slept in a squat afterwards. So I guess it'd be fine.

"I guess it'd be fine" is not what I really want to hear for our plans to illegally infiltrate and summit the most famous landmark on a continent. But I let it go.

Rome, November 2010

I get my brother, Micah, to come along for the Italian and Tunisian legs of this trip. We plan to start by flying into Rome. From there we'll make our way down through Italy and then across to Tunisia. Then Micah will head home and I'll fly to Cairo.

We spend our one night in Rome at the Roma Sotterranea society with two of its members, Luca and Adriano. They had e-mailed Steve after finding his online photos of the strange offshoot in the sewer system that we had found during our trip in search of the Cloaca Maxima. They wanted to talk with us further.

"So we didn't know about this area at all," Adriano tells me. "We haven't been there, the archaeologists haven't been there. Just the sewer workers."

He continues: "What happened was, in the nineteenth century, the tunnel where you were, called the Basso Sinistro, was constructed parallel to the Tiber River as an interceptor drain. It ended up cutting through a lot of the old sewers and other tunnels underneath the city. It also cut off the Cloaca Maxima. You actually passed right above it, the Cloaca intersects at the bottom of the Basso, below the water level. What you found was another one of the spaces cut off by the Basso."

"Well, what do you think it is?" I ask. "And when do you think it was built?"

"Oh, what you found is definitely from ancient Rome," Adriano replies.

I'm a little stunned. But I really shouldn't be. In antiquity, Rome was a city of almost a million people. But after its decline, it didn't come close to approaching this population again until the early twentieth century. As a result, almost nothing new was built in the city in the intervening period, so any ruins are almost certainly going to be at least 1,500 years old. In fact, much of what was constructed during the Renaissance, when the city started to grow again, was recycled from the materials of the old imperial capital. Rome, at its low point during the Middle Ages, had about 5 percent of its peak population from the imperial era. Rome was the Detroit of the Middle Ages— but even that's inaccurate. It was Detroit cubed. In order to be as abandoned as Rome was at its nadir, Detroit would have to experience, proportionally, another population decline equal to the one it's already experienced—and then another one after that. Still, this doesn't stop me from feeling a bit like Indiana Jones. We've legitimately discovered part of ancient Rome. How many people can say that?

Luca has been silent most of the time. He doesn't speak much English, occasionally commenting in Italian, which Adriano translates. As we're leaving, though, he addresses me directly.

"You know, is not safe to do sewer," he says with a heavy accent. "We go with suits and . . ." He struggles to find the words. "You know just go, just go like this"—he motions to me, indicating my street clothes and lack of any protective gear— "just go like this in sewer is not safe, is . . ." He struggles again, mutters something in Italian, and gives up. "Next time, next time you go with us."

I think about this as we say our good-byes. The last time we were in town we were looking at a 500 euro charge to tag along—a charge I suspect was plucked out of the air to provide an easy way to say no without having to say no. But now that we had demonstrated our worth, things were different. It justified everywhere illegal I'd ever gone, every time I'd ignored the fence, or the sign, or the storm drain retaining wall. The best way to be taken seriously at something is to just do it. To ignore the hoops—legal, social, financial, or otherwise—that you're told you're supposed to jump through to someday maybe get a foot in the door. The key is never negotiating these endless hoops, trying to work your way up a ladder to nowhere. It's finding the person who can say yes—the person who can tell everyone who's been leading you in circles about liability insurance and permission from municipal agencies to just make it happen—and approaching this person as a peer. And it's a lot easier to be accepted as a peer if you've done something to break the chicken-or-egg "How do you get a job without experience? How do you get experience without a job?" cycle—something like, in this particular case, jacking open a floodgate, making your way down a sewer channel, and seeing what's there. There wouldn't be a "next time with us" if there hadn't been a first time without them. I remember the old adage: "It's easier to ask forgiveness than permission." As it turns out, a lot of times you don't have to ask for either one.

THIRTY-TWO

Tunis, November 2010

From Rome, Micah and I head down through Naples to Sicily, and from there prepare to take the ferry to Tunisia. With a couple hours left until our departure, I check into an Internet café and find the following from QX:

> Hey mate.
> Am in Nepal—will write more when I get back. Will probably be coming alone, or not at all if my soon-to-be-ex doesn't take the news well . . .

This makes me nervous. My entire process is predicated on putting myself in the right place at the right time with the right people—people who I know will get me over the final barrier in a timely manner. When the moment comes, I know I don't have to go through the torturous process of gathering my nerve and pushing myself beyond my mental limits, like I did that first time I grabbed my right leg and shoved it past the red metal sign at the end of the subway platform. Instead, I can just relax and go with the flow I've created.

I can control two of the three variables, right time and right place, with a degree of certainty, more or less. But the third one, right people, is tougher. If QX bails on me, it'll mess everything up. I write back. "Actually, I might change my plans around a bit (and will definitely bottle out of the climb) if you're not coming, so try to let me know the plan in a few days if you can." I send this with equal doses of regret and relief. Right away, I get the following back:

> Hey mate.
>
> I am definitely coming—no worries about that. The part about me not
> was more a joke if the French chick kills me. I'll be there with bells on.

I immediately get up and take the opportunity to discharge my bowels before getting on the boat.

The first thing I notice upon arriving in Tunisia is the huge visage of the President for Life, Zine el-Abidine Ben Ali, staring at me. It stares at me pretty much everywhere I go. It stares at me when I arrive at the airport, it stares at me as the cab drives us into town, it stares at me in the Internet café next to the *"IL EST STRICTEMENT INTERDIT DE CON-SULTER LES SITES PROHIBES"* sign. (Flickr and YouTube are banned. Google and Facebook make the cut.)

I'm a tourist, don't speak the language (Arabic), don't even speak the second language (French), so I get only glimpses of what this Orwellian world actually means to regular people. Toward the end of the trip, after a couple weeks on the standard tourist circuit, we return to Tunis. I head to the medina, the

oldest part of the city, where
most of the souks are, to shop
for a soccer jersey. There
are two main soccer teams in
Tunis, Espérance Sportive
de Tunis and Club Africain.

Sports loyalties in many
places abroad differ from
sports loyalties in the United
States, where team prefer-
ences are almost always
formed on the simple basis of
geography: you live in Detroit, you're a Tigers fan; you
live in St. Louis, you're a Car-
dinals fan; you live in Brooklyn, you pine away for the
Dodgers and make do with

PRESIDENT BEN ALI.

the Mets. In Europe and South America you have middle-class
and working-class loyalties, teams with nationalist or even fascist bents and ones with communist sympathies. I imagine the
same might be true of Tunisia, so I want to make sure I'm not
mistakenly getting the jersey of a team supported by the local
phalange.

"So which kind of people like which team?" I ask the vendor, who speaks OK English.

"In Tunis, here, we like both teams," he answers.

I try to get clarification. "No, I mean, do people in one part
of the city like one team, and people in another part of the city
like the other team? Or do rich people like one team, and poor

people the other? Or is there a team with left-wing politics and a team with right-wing politics? Like that?"

The vendor's expression changes immediately, the routine false smile growing wider and even more forced. "Oh, no, no, no, no, no, no. You do not understand. There is not left-wing politics or right-wing politics in Tunisia. There is only just Tunisia," he says, clearly sketched out that I would even ask such a thing.

I pick the Espérance Sportive de Tunis jersey and start the bargaining. We negotiate back and forth for a few minutes before we get to the endgame. I offer twelve dinar.

"Take my hand," the vendor says.

I take.

"We are shaking."

We are.

"Sold for fifteen dinar."

I start to open my mouth but let it go. Fine. I will take my bipartisan democracy over three Tunisian dinar.

Shortly after this exchange I meet Farthi, a middle-aged perfume dealer, in the middle of the Tunis medina while I'm sightseeing with a Canadian I met at our hostel. I'm initially suspicious when he starts chatting with us in English, thinking it's some kind of sale attempt or scam, but something about his demeanor leads me to relax my guard after a few minutes and follow him into a nearby building he suggests we go see. I still think this is some sort of sale attempt, but it seems like it'll be a pleasant and worthwhile one. He leads us up two flights of stairs and out onto the roof of the city.

The Tunis medina is an amazing place. Without context, if you were dropped there at night you would think it was one of the scariest, most dangerous places on earth. The streets, which can barely be called "streets," being better described as paths or alleyways, twist and turn, with anything possible around the next bend. These dark passageways are made even darker by the fact that many of them are partially or even completely covered over. There is no hard-and-fast line between indoor and outdoor or even between public and private space. The streets and arcades flow together with courtyards, souks,

MEDINA ALLEYWAY AT NIGHT.

and alleyways. A door or passageway might lead to a factory, garden, yard, alley, street, staircase, or right into someone's home. I have never been anywhere else like this, somewhere so different from the modern planned city of streets, sidewalks, and storefronts. And on top of this, within the square mile of the medina are almost seven hundred historic monuments, reflecting Tunis's history as one of the wealthiest cities of the ancient Arab world.

And this is just one level. After we ascend to the roof, Farthi shows us the other level of the medina. Because of the narrowness and crowdedness of the streets, and the fact that many of them are partially or fully covered over, I haven't experienced anything you could call a "view" in the medina. Sight

ON THE ROOFTOPS WITH FARTHI.

lines are limited to what's right in front of you, the entire experience taking place in a sort of tunnel vision. This is the first
time I've seen a vista, gotten a lay of the land. Because of this
tunnel vision, despite the numerous mosques in the medina,
until now I've never been able to look up and actually see a
minaret. Our view now unimpaired, Farthi points out several,
explaining the difference between the square minarets of the
Arabs and the octagonal ones of the Ottoman Turks. The Al-
Zaytuna Mosque, for a millennium one of the preeminent centers of Islamic learning in North Africa, and one of the oldest
mosques in the world, is only a few roofs over. I wonder if I can
get there without going back down to the street. I consider trying this for a split second before remembering that if it's insult-
ing to walk in a mosque with shoes, it's probably even worse to
walk on one.

Still, this gets me thinking. One of my favorite experiences

is traversing a city on a different level from the one that 99.99
percent of the population traverses: the street level. But I have
only ever done it on the level below—journeying through the
catacombs of Paris or the subways of New York. The level
above has always been a point, not a path—something to be
climbed up to, enjoyed, and then climbed down from. There
are many places in New York where you can walk across a city
block on the rooftops, and even a few where you can cross a
street via the level above and make it across two blocks. I know
of one place where you can manage a three-block walk without
hitting the ground. But here in the medina it looks like you can
walk across the roofs forever. It seems like taking a canopy
tour of the rain forest, except on an urban level. I ask Farthi if
it's possible to walk across the entire medina on this upper
level.

"Oh, yes," he replies.

I ask if he's ever done it.

"Well, we tried," he says. "When I was a child we used to
race. But we never finished. Somebody would always fall and
get hurt."

He goes on to explain that within the medina are some of
the oldest and most valuable jewelry stores in the Middle East.
Even if you could avoid falling and walk on top of the numerous mosques, guard dogs prowl the roofs of many of the shops.
Not said is the fact that in addition to the numerous shops in
the medina, there are several government buildings such as the
Palais de Justice—the main courthouse. The pyramids, even if
we get caught, seem like they'd be a laugh. We'd be far from
the first Westerners to try it, and surely won't be the last. It
may not be smiled upon, but it's easily explained. Getting

caught on top of the Al-Zaytuna Mosque or the Palais de Jus-tice is not easily explained. And from the moment I arrived in Tunisia, I have been sold on the idea that this is not the kind of country where you want to have to deal with questions from the authorities that are not easily explained. Geographically, France is only a two-hour flight, closer to Tunis than New York is to my hometown in Michigan, but mentally Paris has never seemed farther away.

Later, after the Canadian leaves, Farthi leads me into a few more nooks and crannies around the medina, taking me inside the ancient library and a working fabric shop still using pedal-operated looms. I can tell it's not the first time he's guided a random American around, and when I ask him how often he does this, and why, he answers that he enjoys showing people his city and does it whenever he's feeling like practicing his English. I know that's not the entire answer, that there's a sale to be made, but still, it's not an insignificant part of the answer. The boundary between friendliness and business, salesmanship and socializing, is not hard-and-fast, not even a boundary, really. It all flows together, same as the streets and shops, alleys and courtyards, of the medina. After this impromptu tour, I go to his perfume shop and buy what I think I'm supposed to buy. I don't know what the polite thing to do is, the social norms of this particular interaction. Luckily, Farthi, who has told me he's visited the States and has relatives there, doesn't seem like he expects me to have the least bit of familiarity with them, so the process of ending up with a small vial of massage oil and another one of jasmine-scented perfume isn't too awkward. I want to ask Farthi about life, politics, the universal visage that gazes at me, but I remember the vendor's reaction and don't bring it up. Three weeks after we leave, a young man named Mohamed Bouazizi lights himself on fire, the city erupts, and I think of Farthi.

U pon returning to our hotel I get an e-mail from QX:

Hey mate.

Hope all is well.

OK, here's the low down: Still coming, but one or two notes:

I. I need to go to Turkey tomorrow to get some shit sorted. All going to plan, I will still be arriving in Egypt as planned. All not going to plan, I'll call you.

2. French [ex] gf took the breakup amazingly well (we'd only been together a few weeks)—and still wants to come to climb shit. So even if I'm not there, you'll have French climbing partner.

At first read, I'm heartened. The guy I'm doing this climb with flits between France, Nepal, Turkey, and Egypt at a moment's notice in order to "get some shit sorted." It's a bit more James Bond than Indiana Jones, but pretty cool nonetheless. However, this is quickly outweighed by a sneaking suspicion that this is a slow setup for backing out of the climb.

I type my reply. "Oh, no. I'm not hearing 'even if I'm not there.' I fall into a certain pattern with these things. As part of this, I need a certain kind of person there—namely a bad-ass ninja motherfucker. It's too late to switch patterns now, and a random French girl won't cut it."

Shortly afterward I get the following response:

> There's no bailing out of anything. This fucking pyramid is getting
> climbed. By all of us.
> I'll be there whatever happens. From Turkey, from France, whatever.

Despite the tone, I'm still worried that everything is falling apart. My brother headed back home a couple days ago, and I go to the airport solo to fly to Cairo. I land in Egypt. As I fear, three hours after landing, I get the following text from QX.

> Sorry mate. Actually ends up I'm not going to make it. Feel bad about
> it. Julie (French Girl) is still coming though.

And this is how I end up in Egypt not with a daredevil Australian adventurer but with his French ex-girlfriend.

Cairo, December 2010

Everything in my head is scattered, my carefully laid path to the top of the Great Pyramid completely thrown off course. I marvel that my gut feeling has failed me. It's the first time.

I meet Julie at the hotel. She's lovely company, and speaks enough English for us to communicate passably if not fluently. But I'm not in much mood for company or communication. I've already put the pyramids behind me after my loss of QX, accepted that it's not going to happen like an artist who's dropped his brush down a drain accepts he isn't going to paint a picture that day. I'm inclined to just wander the streets, walking off my disappointment alone, but Julie feels bad about the situation, wants to see the town together and maybe even still give the pyramids a shot. In my frustration, I don't stop to think what this must be like for her—to be a French woman in Egypt, ditched at the last minute by your traveling partner, with the only person you know your ex-fling's American friend, who doesn't even speak your language.

She asks what our plan was, wants to see if we can still make it work. I don't have the inclination or the mutual language fluency to try to explain my process, how it's just not going to happen now, so I just tersely answer her questions. Our plan was first to try to hide inside after the complex closes. If that didn't work, jump the wall. Either way, head up the pyramid at about two a.m., stay on top long enough to take a couple photos, and then head down and bail back out over the wall. And if we run into anybody, do what everyone whom I've talked to online who has pulled off the climb has told me to do: bribe early and often.

Bribing cultures are annoying as all hell. It was summed up to me once by the following explanation: "You bribe someone to do their job, not to not do their job." Bribes aren't there so that you can do all this great stuff you're not allowed to simply by discreetly slipping a guy a ten-spot. They're there to clean out your pockets.

For instance, the following is a scenario encountered fairly often in Egypt: there is a rope a few feet away from something—the edge of an observation platform, the pyramids, whatever. The guard will then motion for you that it's perfectly OK to cross the rope and take pictures. Then you're supposed to give the guard—or whoever it might be—money. They could, of course, just not put the rope there, but then there would be no bribe. This is how bribing cultures work. The word for this in Egypt, "baksheesh," isn't even actually translated as "bribe"; it really means more like "tip." It's so ingrained in the culture they even mention it in the official guidebook they give you on the airplane.

This has been going on at least since Twain's time. As part of his climb he's "harried and be-deviled for bucksheesh from the foundation clear to the summit." Of course, this is not in order to actually climb the pyramids, an excursion he's already contracted and fully paid for. Instead it's because the escorts "had a way of asking sweetly and flatteringly for bucksheesh, which was seductive, and of looking fierce and threatening to throw us down the precipice, which was persuasive and convincing."

The next day we have some small successes going the baksheesh route. Twenty pounds to the squatters gets us into a beautiful abandoned mansion next to the Dutch embassy. And that evening we find ourselves alone on one of the minarets of the Bab Zuweila gate, the oldest remaining gate of the medieval Islamic city. I don't know if the man we talked to works there or not. But he has the keys, takes our bribe, opens the door, and leaves us alone to climb the narrow spiral staircase and squeeze out onto the small deck high above the old city of Cairo.

We still want to go see the pyramids, of course. And our small successes with baksheesh have Julie thinking that maybe it will work for the pyramids. I'm skeptical, but I know Julie feels bad about this, so I figure I'll give it enough of an attempt with her that at least she'll feel like we tried.

We hail a cab and tell the driver we're going to the pyra-

MINARET, CAIRO.

mids. About two-thirds of the way there, a man standing on the side of the road flags down the cab and the cab pulls over. The man exchanges a few words with the driver and then gets in the front seat. At first I think he's simply hitching a ride, but then he starts to talk to us in English, asking our names and where we're from. After a couple pleasantries, the sale begins.

"You are going to the pyramids? Don't go the tourist way, my friends. You can go the Egyptian way. I have a company. You come with me. You don't go the tourist way. You can do everything, it is cheaper. Just come . . ."

I'm a tour guide. I know something about hustling tourists. And in my two days in Egypt, I have discovered most Egyptians who speak English know something about this also. I am not going for this sale at all.

"Thank you, but we'll just go the tourist way," I tell him.

The man takes great offense at this, like he's just offered us the deal of the century and in return we've spat in his face. I realize we bantered a bit too long with him during the niceties at the beginning, indicated just enough interest for him to think he'd be able to hook us.

"OK, OK. Look into my eyes. Look. You think I am lying?"

I don't think I've indicated any distrust in the guy, but he seems to believe this is the main obstacle in his path to a sale. "OK, OK. Look into my eyes" continues to be his go-to line.

For a little while I fall into the trap, trying to reassure him that I don't think he's lying, just that we don't want to buy whatever it is he's selling. Quickly, however, I accept that there's no way out without mortally offending him, and realize the best course of action is just to continue to repeat "Thank you, but we'll just go the tourist way." I have to repeat this at least ten times before the cab pulls over and the man gets out of the car. He tries one last attempt at the sale.

"Thank you, but we'll just go the tourist way," I say again, and motion to the driver to start going already.

"OK, OK. Fuck you," I hear as we drive off.

We buy our tickets and enter the complex. The pyramids are exactly what I expected: majestic, swarming with tourists, and with various cynical sales attempts (the most popular being a ride on a sad-looking camel) being constantly hawked by the touts. I think about whether I'd trade the niceties of the trip in the twenty-first century for the freedom of the trip in the nineteenth, when the cynical sales attempts and tourist hustling at least involved climbing the pyramids instead of bumping along on a dromedary. My answer is a resounding "Yes," until I remember that the next day I'm due to take a flying metal cylinder 5,600 miles across the ocean back to New

York in approximately as much time as it took Twain to boat from his hometown of Hannibal, Missouri, down to St. Louis.

We stay for a while. I waste five Egyptian pounds baksheeshing the guard to let me take a photo of myself next to one of the pyramids. I'm tired, and the one time I lie down and close my eyes, I'm awoken by another guard after ten minutes on the stone bench. The complex closes and the tourists begin to get ushered out.

If we want to try to baksheesh someone into letting us stay and climb, now's the time. Julie looks around for the people who seem to be in charge. Finding one with a uniform, she asks if we can stay here, inside the complex, while I stand next to her, semi-discreetly holding money in my palm with the corner sticking out, like I've been taught. The man doesn't speak any English and, confused, points us to another man. This one has a different uniform. We try the same trick. He speaks better English and seems to understand what we're looking for. He directs us to a third person, this one in street clothes. This must be the guy in charge. "Wait a minute, this actually might be going somewhere," I think to myself. We talk to the man, Julie giving the spiel again while I make sure the money in my hand is noticed. He listens intently, nodding along and glancing at my hand. Then he speaks.

"I don't understand what you are asking. But tell me where you need to go. The car is right here, I can take you anywhere." We have just tried to baksheesh a taxi driver into letting us climb the pyramids.

As I fly home the next day, I can't tell if I'm even disappointed.

THIRTY-THREE

New York City, December 2010

W ho dropped that? WHO DROPPED THAT? Was it you, Stevie?" The woman cocks her head, narrows her eyes, and glares suspiciously at Steve, who is sitting a few feet away.

"No, wasn't me," Steve says innocently. Immediately the woman's face softens. Once again Steve's angelic looks have allowed him to get away with a bald-faced lie.

The woman turns to me. I don't get the benefit of a suspicious glare. I get one in which the suspicion has already been confirmed as guilt.

"You! You dropped it! I told you I like to keep it clean in here!" Right now we're in a graffiti-covered emergency exit in a train tunnel under Riverside Park.

Before I have time to protest that I was not the one who dropped the empty bottle of Jack Daniel's down the staircase, causing it to shatter, I feel rough rubber press hard against my cheek. This is what I'm choosing to do a few weeks past my thirty-fifth year on the planet: have a homeless woman kick me in the face in a train tunnel at two in the morning.

THE PARTY LOCATION.

We're at a birthday party. It's for Brooklyn—not the borough, the lady who's just put her sneaker imprint next to my
ear. She claims to have lived in this tunnel for the last twenty-
nine years. The party has so far been going pretty well, and has
consisted mostly of everyone drinking copious amounts of
whiskey and singing. Steve keeps trying to get her to sing
Johnny Cash, but Brooklyn is partial to the Jay-Z and Alicia
Keys song "Empire State of Mind." She's also a pretty good
beatboxer, and I've managed a throwback to my high school
days rhyming in the playground to kick a fairly decent freestyle
over it. (Think very 1991. Sample lyric: "Well, I'm on mic, and
Brooklyn's on the beatbox; it's her birthday, so you know she
don't stop.") The gang was pretty impressed with me, Brooklyn
included. This wasn't the first time I had talked to Brooklyn,
and I had, incorrectly, thought that this shared performance
had now cemented our friendship—or at least established the

PARTYING WITH BROOKLYN.
© *Erling Kagge*

kind of bond that precludes a boot to the face as a means of expressing displeasure.

Before the bottle incident, the biggest snag had been when Brooklyn's boyfriend, B.K., arrived. B.K. was none too happy to come home to a *New York Times* reporter, a Norwegian polar explorer, and half a dozen assorted hipsters partying with his girlfriend. In addition, the whole thing is being filmed. For the past year an energetic NYU cinema student named Andrew has been recording Steve's adventures with the intention of making a short film or TV show about him.

"This kid is great," Steve told me after meeting him. "Not only does he think I'm awesome, he'll go with me in sewers and not complain." A willingness to go in sewers and general ego stroking are two easy ways to get Steve to like you.

Anyway, there's something to be said for "A man's home is

his castle," no matter where that castle happens to be, and a good half-hour was spent in a shouting match between the couple before B.K. begrudgingly ambled off into a distant nook to go to sleep for the night.

"I told him it's my party tonight," said Brooklyn. "This is my house, anyway." Brooklyn has, essentially, a duplex suite. On the other side of the concrete wall from the train tracks there are several small "rooms" in a row that are separated by pillars. This area is accessed by going one flight up the emergency exit staircase. You can also duck under the back wall in a couple of places and slide down a pile of dirt to the lower level. Move this setup a few hundred feet east and about fifty feet straight up, pour some concrete floors, and slap on a coat of paint, and the "raw, loft-like space" would probably go for $5,000 a month.

The main tunnel itself is gigantic: two and a half miles long, perhaps twenty feet high, and about three times as wide as it is tall. Two sets of railroad tracks run down the middle, on which Amtrak trains, swift and surprisingly silent, will barrel down every hour or two. There are also grates in the ceiling spaced a few dozen feet apart. These grates let in diagonal beams of light, which give the impression you're inside a huge cathedral. They also provide a link to the outside world, making the space less like a tunnel and more like the basement of the park above. They let in sound—you can have a normal conversation with someone in Riverside Park above without raising your voice at all—and they let in light, rain, snow, and air. This leads the tunnel to have a diurnal and seasonal cycle similar to the outside world. Most tunnels are continually dark and have a consistent temperature and humidity, leading to an entirely disassociated relationship with the natural cycles of the day and year. The Riverside Park Tunnel is different. When it's light outside, there's light in the tunnel. When it's raining, it's wet; when it's winter, it's cold. Burrowing into the hole in the side of the hill in Riverside Park and sliding down into the tunnel doesn't really lead you to feel like you've entered a different world, gone down Alice's rabbit hole or through a closet into Narnia. It feels more like you've found a secret compartment or passageway in your own house—something hidden from the world at large but close enough to home that you can still hear your mother calling you for dinner.

In fact, the Riverside Park Tunnel isn't technically a tunnel at all. In the mid-1840s, the Hudson River Railroad constructed a rail line down the west side of Manhattan. It ran at grade next to the Hudson River, and then turned onto city streets when it reached 60th Street. Having a train barrel down the crowded avenues of Hell's Kitchen wasn't exactly a bell-wether of public safety, so the city came up with a novel solution: they passed an ordinance requiring trains on streets to be preceded by a person on horseback carrying a red flag. These riders quickly gained the nickname "West Side Cowboys." Unfortunately, this was not a good enough arrangement to keep Eleventh Avenue—where the train ran from 34th to 60th streets—from acquiring a nickname also: "Death Avenue." Pedestrians, carriage riders, and later automobile passengers were regularly hit and killed by these trains until the 1930s, when a permanent solution was found. The rail line was taken completely off the street, with various sections either put onto elevated tracks or depressed below street level. The section from 123rd Street to 72nd Street next to the Hudson River didn't actually change grade at all. Instead the rail line was covered over with an extension of Riverside Park. In 1980, this entire West Side freight route was abandoned. The elevated section from 34th to a few blocks down past 14th became today's High Line, a former urban wilderness and one of my favorite haunts in my early exploring years, which has since been transformed into a public promenade complete with a full espresso bar and several signs with a list of the thirteen things that "park rules prohibit," which range from drinking, to throwing a Frisbee, to feeding the squirrels. The section under the Riverside Park extension, where we are now, had a less glorious but no less interesting fate. It became the largest underground homeless encampment in New York City.

In the 1990s, Amtrak acquired the abandoned tunnel and began running passenger trains through to Penn Station. Most of the homeless encampments were dismantled, the people evicted, and today the tunnel is mostly a derelict place frequented by graffiti writers, a handful of remaining residents, and more than a few curious urbanists. It has become one of those places, like the catacombs, that is only just barely out of the realm of official space. This means that it's exempt from the rules and regulations of polite society but still accessible enough that members of polite society—well, relatively polite society—can visit. And visit they do. This is the most famous, and most traveled, "off-limits" space in New York City.

The role the tunnel has played among graffiti artists over the years is legendary. In the tunnel, the artists have three things lacking in most places topside: light, space, and time.

Because of the grates, there's natural light. Because of the height and length of the tunnel, there's enough wall space to do huge murals. And because of the relative seclusion and lack of police, there's enough time to complete these huge murals, which can take days of painting.

The most well-known of these murals are the "Freedom" murals, done by Chris Pape, aka Freedom, from the early 1980s until the mid-1990s. These are mostly in black and silver, about eight or nine feet tall. Many are interpretive portraits: the *Mona Lisa*, Ted Williams, and the artist himself, sporting a spray paint can for a head, are all represented.

About halfway through the tunnel is a color mural, painted by Freedom and Smith, another writer. It's a replica of *The Third of May 1808*, Francisco Goya's masterpiece showing the execution of Spaniards who rebelled against the rule of Napoleon. The mural is gigantic, about fifteen feet high by thirty feet long. This is over four times the area of the original painting, which itself, at over eleven feet long, dominates the wall it hangs on in the Prado, its home in Madrid. The sheer scale of the Riverside Park Tunnel itself leads to the graffiti and art in it being huge: there's one piece that's almost two hundred feet long. But because of this scale, the paintings and tags don't seem particularly large upon first gaze. It's only when you're standing next to them, craning your head up, that you realize just how enormous they are.

These murals have become part of the identity of the tunnel itself, to the point that the tunnel is sometimes referred to as the "Freedom Tunnel," although Chris Pape later told me that the name is just a fluke. "Smith had painted 'Freedom

SELF-PORTRAIT BY FREEDOM.

Tunnel' outside the entrance and it just caught on," he said over a cup of soda with me one day. "It was around the same time subway graffiti was dying and kids needed a different place to paint, so they were like, 'Hey, let's go to the Freedom Tunnel.'"

Still, Chris didn't consider it an unwelcome name. "It's such a completely unexpected ego boost," he went on. "It's bizarre. There're so many other great graffiti writers who painted in there. I grew up in a very history-minded household, especially New York history, and so to become just a little piece of that huge jigsaw puzzle of history is great."

In fact, while much of the graffiti has been painted over by other artists, the rare parts of the Freedom murals that have been painted over have been marked by others with phrases such as "Respect Freedom" and "Where's your respect, Toy?" Like the catacombs, the tunnel and its art have become a destination for a different kind of tourist: ones who are willing to get their fingernails slightly dirty for the chance to see something organic, to interact with it on their own terms, to be part of something—if only in a small, temporary way—that's uncontrolled.

I first met Brooklyn around my fifth or sixth trip into the tunnel. One Sunday afternoon I was taking a few friends from out of town through it. Immediately upon entry we ran into a gang of high school kids. They called themselves "Urban Odyssey" and had a certain endearing quality to them—a curiosity that reminded me of being young and following intrigue and mystery for adventure. They asked me what urban exploration destinations I'd been to, and things like if the rumors of there being dozens of levels under Grand Central Terminal were true. We headed north through the tunnel for an hour or so, chatting and taking photos, until we came to the emergency exit staircase that, a few years later, Steve would drop an empty bottle of Jack Daniel's down.

The kids went poking around up on the second level, heading deeper and deeper into the nooks and crannies. After a few minutes they all came running out looking like they'd just seen something out of *The Blair Witch Project*. Brooklyn was behind them, shouting and shooing them off.

I tried to smooth things over with her, and it wasn't too tough. After some more shouting she calmed down and introduced herself.

"Listen, there's some people back here you don't want to be running into. I'm just trying to help. If you ever come through here again, just ask for me. My name's Brooklyn."

Then she said something you really wouldn't expect a woman living in a train tunnel to say.

"You should know me. I've been in mad movies."

But she wasn't making that part up. Brooklyn's been in documentaries shown in the United States, France, Germany, Japan, and probably several other countries. The tunnel and its residents have been quasi-celebrities for almost two decades now. *Dark Days*, a film by Marc Singer about the people living in the tunnel, won three awards at the Sundance Film Festival in 2000. *The Mole People* by Jennifer Toth, largely set in the tunnel, was published in 1993 and is still selling briskly today. Despite the tens of thousands of homeless men, women, and children in New York City, all with their own stories, it's the few living underground who serve as the media's continuing obsession. In fact, whenever a film crew or journalist from out of town gets in contact with Steve or me to do something on said "Mole People," which is at least once or twice a year, we shove them through the hole, schlep them down the tunnel, and tell them they should give Brooklyn some money for the interview. We've done this for at least a dozen reporters. Brooklyn's always happy to talk.

My third cousin is an A-list Hollywood actor. For a year my ex-wife, Leigh, worked as a waitress at a popular Manhattan restaurant where every few days she'd have a story about a new celebrity she'd served—things like how she couldn't tell if Bill Murray was kidding around with her or not, or that Susan Sarandon still looks incredible in real life. Over the course of my tenure in New York City, I've lived in the same neighborhoods as Norman Mailer, Steve Buscemi, and Spike Lee, and seen them—as well as countless other celebrities—just going about their business around town. But my longest conversation with any of these people was saying "Excuse me" to Sarah Jessica Parker when I accidently bumped into her coming out of Leigh's restaurant. Despite a decade in New York, perhaps the most celebrity-obsessed city on the planet, the most famous people I've ever conversed with live in a dirt tunnel under a park.

The boot to the face turns out to be a temporary hiccup in an otherwise lovely night. The good times start again and continue until Erling Kagge, the Norwegian who's with us, decides it's time for bed. The expedition was his idea. He had contacted Steve with the idea of an extended journey underneath New York City, which has ended up spiraling into a clusterfuck involving journalists from two major media outlets, a professional videographer, and now a birthday party. Erling is easily the most badass of all of us. He once spent seven weeks by himself walking to the South Pole.

"It was not so bad. I listened to my iPod," he tells us.

But despite this, he is also the most considerate: other than Steve with his whiskey, he's the only one who's brought a birthday present. His daughter Nor has made homemade chocolate for Brooklyn. He bids us good night, and beds down in his sleeping bag wearing a red knit sweater with a fuzzy white heart on it. This is a guy who once killed a polar bear that was attacking him—and then ate it. He is Brooklyn's favorite. Despite having a boyfriend, she tries to join him in the sleeping bag later on that night. Erling politely reminds her that he's married.

.   .   .

After a fitful night's sleep, I wake up. I want to wander the tunnel, see what has changed. Something has to be different. Something always is in the tunnel. This is one of the great things about spaces that lie just outside the public realm, places that are remote and unknown enough that you certainly wouldn't find your average citizen in them, yet that also aren't so obscure and inaccessible that various subcultures and enterprising individuals can't find their way there. This combination of being forbidden and yet accessible leads to a hidden but still dynamic area that is not really a part of the everyday city, but is more than just an interesting decaying remnant of history. Somewhere that changes, but solely on its own terms.

I want to explore the tunnel. But I can't. A little ways down the tunnel there's a bright light shining. It's been there since last night. We know what it's from: a work truck. And we know why the truck is there. It's there to destroy the murals.

Amtrak has decided that this is the best use of funds they can come up with. They had started at the south end, around 72nd Street, and are currently proceeding to cover the entire tunnel with a dull grey coat of cheap paint, roughly the same color as the tunnel walls. I've already done a calculation. At two and a half miles long and twenty feet high, there's slightly over half a million square feet to paint.

Later I go back to survey the damage. They've reached the largest mural, the one depicting the residents' eviction from the tunnel in the 1990s. Amtrak has done a completely half-assed job, with much of the scene still leaking through the paint. It's surreal. This mural had been a legend in New York City. It's like going to Paris, heading to the Louvre, and finding it half empty, with the *Mona Lisa* gouged out of its frame, leaving behind a few vaguely recognizable bits of canvas still attached to it. What is the point of this? It's not like graffiti in the outside world, where for every aficionado there are a hundred people who just think it's ugly scrawling on the wall. If you ask anyone who has actually been in the tunnel—explorers, homeless, even Amtrak workers—if they'd rather have grey paint or an art gallery, every one of them would want the murals to stay. It's hard to believe my eyes. After all, even the MTA didn't paint over the Underbelly Project, which would have taken a couple days at most.

But it's not the destruction that leaves the sour feeling in my stomach. Graffiti has never been a permanent medium. Chris Pape himself never thought the murals would last as long as they did, much less achieve this level of notoriety, or mean something to people he'd never met.

Chris Pape says:

> When I found out about the murals getting painted over, I had mixed feelings about it. My work had actually been painted over before. There were over forty pieces that I did. Particularly in the first five years, from 1980 to 1985, the Parks Department would go over my work all the time. They didn't care about me painting, just that someone would see the paintings and think they weren't doing their jobs. There was a nine-panel mural I did that got painted over in 1982.
>
> It's funny, I painted all of these not thinking they'd

ever get seen. I painted them specifically so people wouldn't see them. I wanted to be able to fail. Art is about failing. It's not like I said to myself in 1980: "Hey, for the next 15 years I'll paint in a tunnel specifically so nobody can see it, so that I'll end up in a Los Angeles Museum of Contemporary Art show as one of the pivotal members of the street art movement." It just doesn't make sense. But I'm absolutely thrilled anyone cares enough to go down there and take photos. Back then, nobody painted realistically. So anything I painted realistically, people loved. It didn't matter if the painting had failed in my eyes. And I think some of the paintings are misunderstood . . . but that's fine.

No, it's the encroachment—the assertion of control. For as long as I've known the place, it's been off the grid, one of those wonderful spaces that's exempt from the rules of the outside world. A place where if you want to paint a mural on the wall, you just do it—no hassle, no asking for permission, and no harm to anyone. If you want to live there, you live there—no building codes, no landlords, no electric bills. If you want to have a party, you have a party—no permits needed, no noise complaints, no signs prohibiting throwing a Frisbee or feeding the squirrels. It's ours. This destruction is the government's way of telling us that it's not—that it's theirs, just part of the thousands and thousands of square miles of official, mapped, controlled space. It's saying that this place that was created is illegitimate—that it should be just like everywhere else, subject to the same bland rules as the topside world. It's an insult, a slap in the face. It's the neighborhood bully finding your secret hideout and ripping down all your posters, or the woods you've always walked freely in suddenly sporting "Private Property, No Trespassing" signs.

Gazing at the blank walls down the tunnel, I think about how something so beautiful can be destroyed so easily. I think about whether the murals will leave any legacy, whether the fact that I know they've been here even mattered now. I think about what any of it meant: all the spaces like this one, all the artists and their creations, all the history I've encountered, the adventures I've had. I start to think back to the words I found in the other tunnel a few years ago: "None Of This Matters." And I accept those words. Ultimately all these places I'd been to, these people I'd met, these things I'd seen, weren't there for any larger purpose. There's no grand revelation, no greater meaning, no real point. I had discovered what I loved and I had pursued it. Is there any bigger personal indulgence? My last years had been an exercise in selfishness. And none of it mattered.

But for all my melancholy, I also know this grey paint isn't an ending; it's a new beginning. In fact, I almost laugh out loud at the giant waste of money I know this process will end up being. All the painting is doing is giving a new generation of artists a brand-new canvas thousands of feet long. I know that if I come back for Brooklyn's fifty-first birthday, I'll see other, newer, but probably no less stunning works of art. This generation will build its own hidden legends. Maybe, like the gallery in the abandoned subway station, they'll be part of a larger project, saying something about the state of the art world or the commercialization of creativity. But I imagine they'll probably be created for their own sake and simply left for the curious, for whoever wants to go find them for themselves.

But as I keep walking down the tracks, I start to understand that those people won't be me. I love the tunnel. I'm sad to see a part of it go. I think a lot about what will eventually replace the murals, which artists will be the ones to execute an idea. But something is missing. I'm curious, sure, but I don't have that overwhelming thirst, that drive, to see for myself what's going to be there. After I'd turned thirty, I found myself shivering in an abandoned firehouse across from a power plant. After I'd turned thirty-five, I found myself in a rusting emergency train exit under a park. I don't want to turn forty and find myself hanging out in a steam tunnel, like Lazlo in that movie *Real Genius*. It's time to get going on what's next, time to find a new love, a new pursuit. There's a time and a place for all different points in life—a time to explore and a time to nest. A time to get kicked in the head by a beatboxing homeless lady, and a time to, well, not get kicked in the head by a beatboxing homeless lady.

And besides, even if I wanted to, I couldn't keep up anymore. It seems like every week a new website is popping up with tales and photos of some crazy adventure: climbing the Golden Gate Bridge, sneaking into Michael Jackson's Neverland Ranch, infiltrating active U.S. military bases. But I don't feel pushed by this like I felt pushed by Steve on the adventures we had. I feel like an old man watching the kids at play. And I don't mind this feeling at all. I remember another feeling from five years ago, right after I got divorced and lost my job: the feeling of having tried to grow up and failed. I've allowed myself more than enough years of recovery—maybe it's time to give growing up another shot.

.   .   .

Later I learn the piece I had seen in the subway tunnel wasn't the whole story. It didn't read "None Of This Matters." It read "None Of This Matters . . ." I had missed those three dots at the end, the three dots that indicated it wasn't complete but only the first half of a larger phrase. The second half was written in a separate stretch of tunnel, a stretch I had never visited. The message reads:

"None Of This Matters . . . But Its Very Necessary!"

EPILOGUE

2011

Two thousand eleven was a good year and a bad year for the international urban adventure crew. In the spring the Londoners cracked the last abandoned Tube station they had left to visit: Aldwych. Siologen and three others decided to try a return trip during the week of the royal wedding of Prince William and Princess Kate, getting caught and ending up with a thirty-six-hour stay in solitary, their apartments ransacked, laptops confiscated, and shenanigans firmly on the radar of the authorities all the way up to MI5. Silo decided to leave England, and we threw a raucous good-bye party for him in a storm drain under Hyde Park. Almost fifty people from half a dozen countries on three continents were there. The day before, he had learned that he'd be getting off with a "simple caution."

I had been awake for thirty-six hours and had decided to spend the day walking nineteen miles from Heathrow Airport into the City of London before starting in on a hefty amount of what turned out to be 9 percent alcohol beer (the Wikipedia article referencing the specific brand ends with "This beer is associated with binge drinking amongst vagrants"). I cannot

SILO'S GOING-AWAY PARTY. UNDER LONDON.

© *Lutex*

remember the speech I gave in Silo's honor, but unfortunately it was videotaped by at least half the people in attendance. Later in the summer Silo ended up breaking his pelvis after a nine-foot fall through a subway vent shaft in Philadelphia before going back to Australia.

A couple weeks after Silo got busted, Eric and three of his friends ended up with their pictures in the *New York Post* under the headline "Tunnel-Punk Terror Scares" after they were caught hanging out in a stretch of unused tunnel under Second Avenue. What would normally have been a simple trespassing ticket ended up as an NYPD Emergency Service Unit raid with the four of them getting arrested at gunpoint. The city was already on high alert as a result of the Navy SEAL operation that had just killed Osama bin Laden. Then that night a crazy person jumped off the platform at the World Trade Center PATH train stop, walked under the Hudson River to New

Jersey, and upon arriving told the police that he had left a bomb on the tracks. As a result, the cops weren't taking any chances when a trucker called in a report of four young men opening a hatch in an East Harlem sidewalk. Earlier that night I had been hanging out with them at a bar, celebrating one of the group's twenty-first birthday. They had invited me out with them. "Nah, I'm kind of too old for this stuff," I'd said.

Ten days after that I climbed the Brooklyn Bridge with a college student from Hartlepool, England, named Lucy who was in town for the week. I knew it was my last time. For the first time I could see the under-construction new World Trade Center from the top of the bridge. We were seen coming down by a couple of bicyclists and a group of four middle-aged women, but none of them seemed to care. Lucy finished fourth in her local beauty pageant the next month while wearing a pair of hip waders with her bikini during the swimsuit section.

The same week that Lucy represented for the beauty of draining, two guys from New England got arrested on top of the Williamsburg Bridge after getting spotted by a routine helicopter patrol. Police commissioner Ray Kelly referred to them as "urban explorers," and I didn't know whether to laugh or be worried. A day after that QX and Marshall climbed the Bosphorus Bridge in Turkey on a whim. It's more than 100 feet taller than the Williamsburg and patrolled 24/7 by Turkish police. QX and Marshall got away without a scratch. The bridge climbers back home got charged with felony reckless endangerment. Shortly after that, undeterred by the recent arrests, an aerialist climbed the Williamsburg Bridge in the middle of the day and did a death-defying performance involving hanging from the bridge and twirling around in what looked like a bedsheet. She also got arrested, taken to Rikers Island, and charged with a felony. It ended up getting pleaded down to five free aerial shows for kids.

Anastasia and Sasha celebrated their first anniversary. They had had their wedding in the Odessa catacombs. Ani wore a beautiful white dress. Sasha wore an orange caving suit. The Underbelly Project did a new gallery in an abandoned subway tunnel in Paris, with plans for more around the world. The Williamsburgh Savings Bank Tower got converted into condos, with the penthouse unit housing the old observation decks selling for $1.325 million. *The New York Times* ran a story on the sale, mentioning the appeal of the old signs. They quoted the buyer: "'I was very swayed by the terraces,' she said, which . . . bear plaques retelling the history of the Battle of Brooklyn."

In August, Shane and I managed to tag along on a tour for New York City transportation professionals to the top of the George Washington Bridge. It's the tallest bridge I've ever been up, and the first I have ever been able to relax while on top of. I enjoyed the beautiful day and postcard-perfect view, but somehow it wasn't quite the same.

A couple months later, Shane had sex on top of (as strictly defined by the Sex on Bridges charter) the Brooklyn Bridge.

"Man, that bridge is by far the best fucking experience out of all of them," he texted me after doing the deed. "Solid stone surface instead of steel, unobstructed 360-degree view, and that giant American flag over your head. Makes for epic damn fucking."

Steve and Andrew the videographer produced a half-hour Web video called *Undercity* featuring Steve climbing bridges, running in subways, and talking with the people living in the Riverside Park Tunnel. It went viral, got over a million views, and landed them on the *Today* show, where Steve was called, to my eternal jealousy, "a modern-day Indiana Jones." Myself, I lasted less than a year before I went back for another visit to the Riverside Park Tunnel. I chatted with Brooklyn for a bit; she apologized for kicking me in the face and told me the tunnel had gone back to normal, that Amtrak had stopped coming by. They seemed to have run out of money about halfway through, the thin layer of dull grey paint stopping around 96th Street. There were already dozens of new graffiti pieces.

I want to retire, but I can't. I slow down, but I never really stop. I've taught myself how to recognize the artificial boundaries and how to break them down in my head. But I never learn how to reconstruct them. It all simply becomes part of my new perception, my new reality, and I can't go back even if I wanted to. Imagine that all of a sudden a traffic light's been put at your front door. Would you really wait until it turned green before tying your shoes and heading out to start your day?

My taste for adventure continues to diminish, but it's not even an adventure anymore, just a vacation. I take a few days to climb bridges with Lucy and a few other people in northern England, head to a party in an abandoned mine in Minneapolis, admire the views from the roofs of Chicago skyscrapers. I spend a weekend camping out in the Paris catacombs—I bring a travel hammock, a sleeping bag, a change of shoes, a strong flashlight, some camping provisions, a few liters of water, and a good book. While wandering through some of the

ZEZÃO IN THE PARIS CATACOMBS.

quarries, a snaking blue pattern catches my eye—the same one I saw in the abandoned São Paulo mansion years ago. I smile to myself. I think of how many other people can smile to themselves like that. I think of never smiling like that again.

"Hey, mate," I write QX after the trip. "So when are we giving this pyramids thing another go?"

Acknowledgments

First and foremost, thank you to everyone with whom I have ever shared that wonderful moment of crossing from the everyday comfortable and officially sanctioned world into that strange space beyond it. This numbers, at this point, hundreds of people in dozens of countries, far too many to be named here—and many of whom wouldn't even want to be. A few of these people you've read about in the previous pages, but most you haven't. When one writes a book, some people and stories slot in seamlessly, while others, for whatever reason, do not. Many close friends and favorite memories are left out of this book—please know you're remembered here. BMW, NPT, and all other assorted three-letter acronyms, for life.

Thanks to all who consented to my nagging requests for commentary, photographs, video, fact-checks, blurbs, reviews, translations, and everything else. Huge thanks to Larry Ray, Gilles Thomas, and Gabriel Rostey for review and fact-checking on (respectively) Naples, Paris, and São Paulo; Chris Pape for review and fact-checking on the Riverside Park Tunnel; Jim Alston for review and fact-checking on the Cave Clan and all things storm drain; and Danielle Plamondon for French translation. Thanks to the many who contributed commentary, photos, and video and who took the time to look over the stories of the adventures they were in—if there is ever any contribution to one of your endeavors I can repay you with, you have a written guarantee right here.

Thank you to all the professors and tour guides I learned about New York from during the time the events in this book took place—Joseph Salvo, Stanley Moses, Stan Thomashaw (RIP), Lee Gelber, and many others. You were the counterpoint and complement to the on-the-ground (or in-the-ground) experience I got of the city during this time. A well-rounded education is a very important thing.

Thank you to my wonderful family: parents Judy and David, sister Rivka, brother Micah, cousin Karen, late grandparents John, Mary, and Seymour, and all other members of my extended family up to and including third cousins twice removed.

Thank you to Carolyn, my first eyes on the page, whose support of, and advice on, these pages meant the world to me; Sara, with whom I took much of this journey, and with whom every step was full of joy; and Jennifer, who always encouraged me to be the person I wanted to be and do the things I dreamed of doing.

Thanks to my agent (and fairy godmother), Alyssa Reuben, and editor, Sara Carder, both of whom took a risk on an unknown writer without an online article or Twitter follower to his name. Thanks also to Jason Yarn at Paradigm, and to Brianna Yamashita, Joanna Ng, David Chesanow, Dave Walker, Amanda Dewey, and everyone else at Tarcher/Penguin who worked on this project.

Finally, thanks to the hole in the tunnel wall down the abandoned train tracks of the XIVe arrondissement. Everywhere comes and goes, especially in this hobby, but somehow I thought you'd always be there. You'll be missed by me, and many others.

Notes

ONE

Page 24. **Dozens of average citizens:** A tabulation of employee deaths since 1946 provided to *The New York Times* by the New York Transit Authority indicated approximately 150 deaths from being hit by a train and approximately two dozen deaths from electrocution resulting from contact with the third rail. According to a Columbia University study, there were an estimated 668 subway fatalities in total between 1990 and 2003. Robyn R. M. Gershon et al., "Epidemiology of Subway-Related Fatalities in New York City, 1990–2003." *Journal of Safety Research* 39 (2008), pp. 583–588. In 2011, the last year for which information is available, New York City Transit reported forty-seven total fatalities from being struck by a train.

TWO

Page 26. **My favorite places became a beautiful derelict courthouse:** These are, respectively, the abandoned Bronx Borough Courthouse on 161st Street and Third Avenue in the Bronx; the High Bridge, which was built to carry the Old Croton Aqueduct from the Bronx into Manhattan in 1848 and which crosses the Harlem River at about 174th Street; and the High Line, which runs from Gansevoort Street in the West Village up to 34th Street. The High Line has since been redeveloped into a public park, and the High Bridge and the Bronx Borough Courthouse are in the process of being renovated and reopened as well.

SIX

Page 59. **There are almost no skulls:** Visiting the catacombs, while illegal, is punishable only by a civil fine. But if you get stopped at the airport trying to take home Jean-Pierre's femur, you're going to be in a world of trouble. And regardless, you should really have a little more respect for the dead—although I suppose being taken and put on a tourist's mantelpiece is just as dignified as being thrown down into an old limestone quarry.

Page 61. **But the variety of tunnels is even greater:** These disused cables were removed sometime between 2006 and 2011.

SEVEN

Page 73. **There's plenty written about the catacombs:** There is actually one comprehensive English book on the catacombs, Caroline Archer's wonderful *Paris Underground*, which I didn't learn of until a few years after this trip.

NINE

Page 84. **We have four of the former longest suspension bridges:** These are, respectively, the Brooklyn, the Williamsburg, the George Washington, and the Verrazano-Narrows bridges; the Bayonne and Hell Gate bridges; the Queensboro Bridge; the Marine Parkway Bridge; the Arthur Kill Bridge; the Hell Gate Bridge; the Carroll Street and Borden Street bridges; and, of course, the Brooklyn Bridge.

Page 92. **Before 2001, people bungee jumped:** See Carla Spartos, "Jump: Under Cover of Night, Local Daredevils Bungee off City Bridges," *The Village Voice*, May 26, 1998, http://www.villagevoice.com/1998-05-26/news/jump/.

Page 96. **It's amazing to me that something so ephemeral:** In 2009, the latest year for which information is available, the Manhattan Bridge averaged 71,936 vehicular crossings a day. According to MTA schedules, as of June 2012, there are 136 D and Q trains, 114 N trains, and 103 B trains scheduled to cross the bridge each way on weekdays, for a total of 978.

ELEVEN

Page 113. **You can step off a platform:** This area runs underneath zip codes 10002, 10007, 10012, and 10013. It connects the Chambers Street, Canal Street, Bowery, Delancey–Essex Street, Grand Street, Broadway-Lafayette Street, and Second Avenue stations, and in 2006 was serviced by the Sixth Avenue line (the B, D, F, and V trains), the Broadway line (the N and Q trains), and the Nassau Street line (the J, M, and Z trains). The V train no longer runs, while the M train is now routed through one of the formerly disused tunnels.

EIGHTEEN

Page 173. **At its worst, in the late 1970s, New York's population:** New York City's population peaked at 7,894,862 in 1970, and declined 10.4 percent to 7,071,639 in 1980 before starting to rise again (as of the 2010 census, New York has grown to 8,175,133). By 2010, Pittsburgh, Buffalo, and Cleveland had, respectively, declined 54.8 percent, 54.9 percent, and 56.6 percent from their peak populations. St. Louis had declined 62.7 percent.

Page 175. **São Paulo has three full subway lines:** Since the time of this story, São Paulo has invested heavily in its metro system, with one new line already added and another new line and several extensions under construction.

TWENTY-FOUR

Page 219. **"Pretend you're French":** According to a 2005 European Union language survey, 89 percent of Swedes are conversant in English. Everyone we met spoke perfect, almost accentless English.

TWENTY-FIVE

Page 228. **It's 386 square miles:** The total land area of the five boroughs of New York is 302 square miles.

TWENTY-SEVEN

Page 247. **Our trip . . . how to swear in Russian:** While Odessa has been part of the Ukraine since 1920, the city was founded by the Russian Empire and remains primarily Russophone. All the people we were with spoke Russian exclusively.

Page 251. **In the United States there's a Tennessee state park:** Nathan Bedford Forrest State Park in Benton County, Tennessee.

TWENTY-NINE

Page 266. **The street grid was surveyed and planned out:** In 1811, as part of the "Commissioners Plan," the island of Manhattan was surveyed in the current grid pattern up to 155th Street. The northernmost point of development varied across the island, but the first street to be laid out completely from river to river without interruption was 14th Street, which forms the northern border of the "old" New York City.

Page 267. **As the project is going on . . . *GOOD* magazine:** http://www.good.is/post/urban-cowboys/.

Page 268. **The organizers just have an idea:** I later learned more about how the organizers viewed the project. "The circumstances which originally brought us to the station, introduced us to each other, and formed our subsequent 'working' relationship over the past three years were completely circumstantial," one told me. "The confluence of events which led to the gallery's creation had no grand design, in fact we were unsure if the other person would continue even a few months into the project, let alone follow through over the course of a year and a half. And while we knew we were doing something cool from early on, what that would end up looking like was unknown to us."

The other let me know, "For us, fun was everything. There was no vision. It could be argued that even now we don't have a clear vision. We just wanted to do right by the people who trusted us, and the art they made. We wanted a challenge. The circumstances dictated what that was—not us. We compromised plenty. Our vision morphed, twisted, and changed almost on a daily basis. It still does."

Page 281. **The gallery—which the organizers dub "The Underbelly Project":** Jasper Rees, "Street Art Way Below the Street." *The New York Times*, October 31, 2010, http://www.nytimes.com/2010/11/01/arts/design/01underbelly.html?pagewanted=all.

Page 283. **The project ends in some mild graffiti-world drama:** Interestingly, I later learned that, in a way, we were actually ultimately responsible for the whole thing. One drunken night, Shane had met a stranger in the bathroom of a nearby bar and ended up showing him the station. The guy was one of the people who ended up organizing the gallery. We found out about this connection only after the fact, when I recognized him in one of Shane's photos from that night.

THIRTY-ONE

Page 295. **Rome was the Detroit of the Middle Ages:** Rome peaked at about 1,000,000 people in the imperial era and fell to less than 50,000 during the Middle Ages. Detroit peaked at 1,849,568 million people in 1950 and as of the 2010 Census had 713,777 residents—a population decline of approximately 61.3 percent. Two more population declines of this magnitude would leave it with about 107,351 people, or 5.8 percent of its peak population.

Page 296. **I remember the old adage:** Steve explains further: "Throughout our early trips, Moe and I were both struggling with the conflict in our minds of what we thought was cool and badass and what we thought was respectable and worthwhile. And now I don't think there is a conflict between that. I think you can have an adventure and learn at the same time. I think you can show adventure and teach at the same time. And I think you can have an exciting life and be respectable at the same time. But at the time, what really worked between us was we both had that conflict of: Can you really be a good person and a respectable person if you're also trying to be this crazy, cool guy?"

THIRTY-THREE

Page 321. **Despite the tens of thousands of homeless men:** As this book goes to print, there are 46,773 people staying in the New York City shelter system. This does not include people not formally in the system. The January 30, 2012, Homeless Outreach Population

Estimate (HOPE) survey conducted by the New York City Department of Homeless Services counted 3,262 people living without shelter throughout the five boroughs.

Page 322. **He had contacted Steve with the idea:** This overall expedition ended up as the stories "The Wilderness Below Your Feet" by Alan Feuer, *The New York Times*, December 31, 2010, http://www.nytimes.com/2011/01/02/nyregion/02underground.html?_r=1, and "Into the Tunnels: Exploring the Underside of NYC" by Jacki Lyden, NPR, January 2, 2011, http://www.npr.org/2011/01/02/132482428/into-the-tunnels-exploring-the-underside-of-nyc.

Further Reading

Archer, Carolyn. *Under Paris*. Mark Batty Publisher, 2005.

Dougherty, Peter. *Tracks of the New York City Subway*, 2013 edition. Peter Dougherty, 2012.

Law, John. *The Space Between*. Furnace Press, 2008.

Ninjalicious. *Access All Areas: A User's Guide to the Art of Urban Exploration*. Infilpress, 2005.

Solis, Julia. *New York Underground: The Anatomy of a City*. Routledge, 2004.

Vegezzi, Sean. *I Don't Warna Grow Up*. Fourteen-Nineteen, 2012.

Walsh, Kevin. *Forgotten New York: Views of a Lost Metropolis*. Collins Reference, 2006.

Workhorse and PAC. *We Own the Night: The Art of the Underbelly Project*. Rizzoli, 2012.

If you enjoyed this book, visit

www.tarcherbooks.com

and sign up for Tarcher's e-newsletter to receive
special offers, giveaway promotions, and
information on hot upcoming releases.

TARCHER
PENGUIN

Great Lives Begin with Great Ideas

New at **www.tarcherbooks.com**
and **www.penguin.com/tarchertalks**:

Tarcher Talks, an online video series featuring
interviews with bestselling authors on everything from creativity and prosperity to 2012
and Freemasonry

If you would like to place a bulk order
of this book, call 1-800-847-5515.